Children Achieving

Best Practices in Early Literacy

Susan B. Neuman
Temple University
Philadelphia, Pennsylvania, USA

Kathleen A. Roskos
John Carroll University
University Heights, Ohio, USA

Editors

International Reading Association
800 Barksdale Road, PO Box 8139
Newark, Delaware 19714-8139, USA
www.reading.org

The International Reading Association attempts, through its publications, to provide a forum for a wide spectrum of opinions on reading. This policy permits divergent viewpoints without implying the endorsement of the Association.

Director of Publications Joan M. Irwin
Assistant Director of Publications Jeanette K. Moss
Editor-in-Chief Christian A. Kempers
Senior Editor Matthew W. Baker
Assistant Editor Janet S. Parrack
Assistant Editor Mara P. Gorman
Publications Coordinator Beth Doughty
Association Editor David K. Roberts
Production Department Manager Iona Sauscermen
Art Director Boni Nash
Electronic Publishing Supervisor Wendy A. Mazur
Electronic Publishing Specialist Anette Schütz-Ruff
Electronic Publishing Specialist Cheryl J. Strum
Electronic Publishing Assistant Peggy Mason

Photo Credits Adobe Studios, cover; Kathleen Zimmer, p. 9; Robert Finken, p. 32, 133, 171, Michael Siluk, p. 51, Diane Barone, p. 64, 213; David A. Koppenhaver, p. 83; Skjold Photographs, p. 101; Lesley Mandel Morrow, p. 155, 192; Image Productions, p. 243, 258

Library of Congress Cataloging in Publication Data

Children achieving: Best practices in early literacy/Susan B. Neuman, Kathleen A. Roskos, Editors.

p. cm.

Includes bibliographical references and index.

1. Reading (Early childhood). 2. English language–Composition and exercises–Study and teaching (Early childhood). 3. Literacy. 4. Language arts (Early childhood) 5. Child development. I. Neuman, Susan B. II. Roskos, Kathy. III. International Reading Association.

LB1139.5.R43C55   1998   98-29709
372.6–dc21
ISBN 0-87207-193-6

To the children of Philadelphia

98090

CONTENTS

About the Authors

Editors

Susan B. Neuman is an associate professor of Curriculum, Instruction, and Technology in Education at Temple University, Philadelphia, Pennsylvania, USA. She is Coordinator of the Reading and Language Arts Graduate Program. Her chief interests focus on early literacy and family literacy. She currently is Chair of the Reading/Language in Early Childhood Committee of IRA, and of the Literacy Development in Young Children Special Interest Group.

Kathleen A. Roskos is a professor and Chair of the Department of Education and Allied Studies at John Carroll University, University Heights, Ohio, USA, where she teaches courses in reading diagnosis and early literacy instruction. She is currently an associate editor of *The Reading Teacher.* Her research interests include play, literacy, and teacher education. Recent publications include articles in *Reading Research Quarterly* and *The Teacher Educator.*

Contributors

Gwynne Ellen Ash is a doctoral student in reading education at The University of Georgia, Athens, Georgia, USA. A former middle school reading teacher, she has worked on several projects researching young children's literacy learning. Her primary interests focus on helping struggling readers in the middle grades, content-area reading, and children's literature.

Diane Barone is a professor of Literacy Studies at the University of Nevada, Reno, Nevada, USA. She teaches undergraduate and graduate courses in literacy development of young children and graduate courses in qualitative research. Her research interests center on children who are identified as having difficulty developing as readers and writers. Her current longitudinal study focuses on children's lives in schools deemed to be inadequate. In addition to her teaching and research, she is the editor of *Reading Research Quarterly*.

Renée M. Casbergue is an associate professor in the Department of Curriculum and Instruction at the University of New Orleans, New Orleans, Louisiana, USA, where she teaches courses related to literacy learning and teaching, including a graduate seminar on emergent literacy. Her primary interests are in the areas of early literacy and the instructional use of children's literature. She is Past President of the Literacy Development in Young Children Special Interest Group for IRA, and serves on the IRA Reading/Language in Early Childhood Committee.

Patricia A. Edwards is a professor in the Department of Teacher Education and a senior researcher at the Center for the Improvement of Early Reading Achievement at Michigan State University, East Lansing, Michigan, USA. She is the author of two family literacy programs—*Parents as Partners in Reading: A Family Literacy Training Program* and *Talking Your Way to Literacy: A Program to Help Nonreading Parents Prepare Their Children for Reading*. She was elected to the Board of Directors of the International Reading Association for the term 1998–2001.

Karen A. Erickson is an assistant professor of early childhood education and special education at the University of New Hampshire, Durham, New Hampshire, USA. She teaches graduate and undergraduate courses on assistive and instructional technologies, early literacy, and special education. Her current research focuses on technologies to support early literacy in children with severe and multiple disabilities. She directs the annual Symposium on Literacy and Disabilities in Research Triangle Park, North Carolina, USA.

Linda B. Gambrell is a professor in the Department of Curriculum and Instruction at the University of Maryland, College Park, Maryland, USA, where she teaches graduate and undergraduate courses in reading and language arts. Her primary interests are in the areas of reading comprehension strategy instruction, literacy motivation, and the role of discussion in teaching and learning. Her most recent research has focused on identifying classroom factors related to literacy motivation. She was elected to serve as President of the National Reading Conference in 1999.

Peter Hannon is a professor in the Department of Educational Studies at the University of Sheffield, England. Following doctoral research at the University of Manchester and work as a preschool teacher in a community school, he has carried out a series of studies with colleagues at Sheffield into children's early literacy, the role of parents, and family literacy programs. He has directed research in the Belfield Reading Project, the Sheffield Early Literacy Development Project, and, currently, the Raising Early Achievement in Literacy (REAL) Project.

David A. Koppenhaver is an associate professor of education at Gustavus Adolphus College, St. Peter, Minnesota, USA. He teaches courses in reading and language arts, special education, and classroom technology. His current research focuses on early literacy intervention strategies for girls with Rett Syndrome and development of a reading assessment battery for children with multiple disabilities. He is the past director of the Center for Literacy and Disability Studies.

Linda D. Labbo is an associate professor in the Department of Reading Education in the School of Teacher Education at The University of Georgia, Athens, Georgia, USA. She is interested in young children's computer-related literacy development and their conceptual development of social-studies concepts and informational text. She is currently Chair of the Microcomputers in Reading Special Interest Group of IRA, and she is the Section Editor of the Reviews Section of *Reading Online*, IRA's electronic journal.

Lisa Lenhart is a doctoral candidate in Curriculum and Instruction at Kent State University, Kent, Ohio, USA. She currently teaches in a Title 1 program and also teaches college-level reading courses. She also has taught at several different elementary grade levels and is active in IRA council work.

Lea M. McGee is a professor and Area Head of Teacher Education in the College of Education at the University of Alabama, Tuscaloosa, Alabama, USA. Her research interests focus on young children's interpretations of literature and teachers' knowledge of literature use with children. She is currently a member of the Board of Directors of the National Reading Conference.

Lesley Mandel Morrow is a professor and Coordinator of the early childhood/elementary education graduate programs at Rutger's University's Graduate School of Education, New Brunswick, New Jersey,

USA. Her area of research deals with early literacy development; she carries out her work in schools with diverse populations and focuses on physical and social contexts that motivate reading and writing. She has received the International Reading Association's Outstanding Teacher Educator of Reading Award, and she presently is serving on IRA's Board of Directors for the term 1996–1999.

Heather M. Pleasants is a doctoral candidate in Educational Psychology at Michigan State University, East Lansing, Michigan, USA. Her research is focused on race and class issues in literacy, learning, and development, and on the relationships of parents, teachers, and children within alternative school environments. She is currently completing a dissertation on the decision making and involvement of African American parents in charter schools.

Beth Roberts is Director of the Master of Arts in Teaching Program and Associate Professor of Education at Mary Baldwin College, Staunton, Virginia, USA, where she teaches courses in reading and language arts and works with student teachers. Her current research focuses on the relationships among different language systems used by young children. She was the winner of the 1989 IRA Outstanding Dissertation Award and the 1995 Distinguished Paper Award of the Georgia Educational Research Association.

Terry Salinger is a principal research analyst at the American Institutes for Research in Washington, DC, USA. Her research interests include assessment, early literacy, and teacher professional development. She has been Director of Research at the International Reading Association, a researcher/test developer at Educational Testing Service, a teacher educator in Texas and Ohio, and an early childhood teacher in New York City.

Judith A. Schickedanz is a professor of education at Boston University, Boston, Massachusetts, USA. She teaches courses in the undergraduate and graduate early childhood programs, and serves as the director of the laboratory preschool. She is currently conducting research on the preschool child's ability to learn sequences of various kinds. This basic research project is funded by the National Science Foundation.

Stephanie A. Spadorcia is a doctoral candidate in Special Education and Literacy Studies at the University of North Carolina at Chapel Hill, North Carolina, USA. Currently she is working on a project designed to create a reading assessment measure for students with severe speech and physical impairments. Her research interests include literacy instruction for adolescents with disabilities.

Carol Vukelich is a professor and Interim Director of the Delaware Center for Teacher Education in the College of Human Resources, Education and Public Policy at the University of Delaware, Newark, Delaware, USA. Her chief interests are early literacy, the teaching of writing, and literacy teacher education. She is a past president of the Association for Childhood Education International.

Introduction

Susan B. Neuman and Kathleen A. Roskos

A significant time has passed since Dorothy S. Strickland and Lesley Mandel Morrow's book *Emerging Literacy: Young Children Learn to Read and Write* (1989) was first published by the International Reading Association. This classic, along with William Teale and Elizabeth Sulzby's groundbreaking book, *Emergent Literacy: Writing and Reading* (1989), set the stage for a paradigmatic shift in early literacy development. Challenging the view that reading development precedes learning, these scholars argued for a new perspective–one in which literacy learning precedes development.

This shift offered provocative implications for instruction. It suggested that the wait was over; instruction no longer should be delayed until children showed signs of readiness, until they attained certain prereading skills, or until they reached the critical age of 6.5 years old in grade school. It now was recognized that literacy development begins at birth and is a lifelong process.

These researchers made additional contributions to early literacy research. They highlighted the importance of the active child, the interrelated nature of writing and reading, and the integral ties between the functions of literacy and its forms in children's growing understanding that these communication abilities are part of a much larger system for accomplishing goals. They used the term *emergent* to describe core features that were uniquely suited to educating young children, highlighting the active, evolving nature of children's understandings as they moved toward conventional reading and writing.

The field of early literacy has burgeoned since the publication of these books. There has been much scholarly activity providing further evidence for the importance of these critical early years. Today, many educators recognize that the terms *emergent* and *conventional* may no longer be appropriate to describe the child as literacy learner. In contrast to skills "emerging," it is now fully recognized that there is no beginning point. Even at a young age, young children are legitimate writers and readers. Similarly, there can be no end point, no single boundary denoting conventionalized practices. Rather, literacy development begins early, is ongoing, and is continuous throughout a lifetime. Consequently, the term *early literacy* is used throughout this book, because it better reflects the nature of reading and writing as a developmental continuum rather than a skill that one either acquires or does not.

A developmental perspective of how children grow and learn about literacy, however, does not come without new challenges. Teaching to the wide range of individual variation among young children today has become increasingly complex. How do we provide instruction that meets the diverse needs of children? How can we ensure that children receive the skills they most need? In this book, we have asked contributors well known in the field of early literacy to address these important issues. Each chapter highlights a critical issue in early literacy, examines what we know about it, and describes literacy practices suggested from this existing knowledge base. The focus is on issues of theory and practice appropriate for children ages 2 through 8 in classrooms ranging from prekindergarten settings through third grade. Throughout the book we offer examples of helpful "In Practice" activities for the classroom, which demonstrate connections between theory and practice.

Chapter 1 presents an overall framework for teaching early literacy learners, with guidelines and implications for basic classroom practices. This is followed in Chapter 2 by a provocative discussion of developmentally appropriate practice in early literacy. This chapter focuses specifically on children's understanding of the alphabet, noting the difference between learning letters in meaningful contexts versus learning through rote memorization. Chapter 3 examines the important issue of skill development, targeting skills that are essential for all children to succeed in writing and reading.

The next three chapters focus on key issues of diversity. Chapter 4 highlights the importance of the child's first language in developing proficiency with a new language and shows teachers how they may develop strategies that enable children to maintain their existing language and learn another. Chapter 5 provides a powerful demonstration, through two case studies of children with varying degrees of disabilities, that with appropriate modifications and support, all children in classrooms may benefit from inclusion. Chapter 6 focuses on using an understanding of parents' own stories to create classroom settings that honor diversity and support culturally relevant teaching practices.

Recognizing the importance of the family in these early years, Chapter 7 describes an innovative parent involvement model that provides guidance to both parents and teachers. This chapter highlights some of the subtle messages we may unintentionally give to parents that might discourage their involvement in school activities. As the focus of the book shifts to children themselves, Chapter 8 emphasizes the importance of motivation in learning to read and write. Ideas are shared on preparing classroom environments that support children's independent literacy involvement, highlighting the social, collaborative nature of literacy learning.

Although literature-based teaching is common in many early-childhood classrooms, often it is not used to teach literary language and literary elements. Chapter 9 argues that literature provides children with unique opportunities to learn how to understand stories and provides models of literary language and structures usually not found in daily oral speech. The next two chapters focus on writing development. Chapter 10 describes the importance of integrating computers in early literacy learning, discussing receptive and expressive software that allows children to be creative problem-solvers. Looking at writing from another standpoint, Chapter 11 describes the developmental progression of writing and how teachers can respond to the natural tensions between discovery learning and explicit instruction.

The last two chapters pull together much of what we have learned about children and about ourselves as professionals. Chapter 12 emphasizes the teacher's role as an assessment expert, and explains how assessment adds to teachers' understanding of child development, learning theory, and instructional practice. As assessment experts, teachers grow in their ability to plan and implement instruction that is sensitive both to children's needs and to the accountability needs of the schools and districts in which they teach. Chapter 13 focuses on the ways in which we can continue to grow as professionals, viewing ourselves as continuous literacy learners and thinkers. After all, young writers and readers deserve teachers who possess the knowledge, skill, and personal qualities that make literacy meaningful in their young lives.

The title of this book, *Children Achieving*, comes from an initiative of the same name in Philadelphia, Pennsylvania, reaffirming the goals of literacy achievement for all children. We hope to inspire researchers and practitioners to continue their search for better ways to ensure that all children do achieve, as well as come to discover and experience the joys of learning about literacy.

References

Strickland, D.S., & Morrow, L.M. (Eds.). (1989). *Emerging literacy: Young children learn to read and write*. Newark, DE: International Reading Association.

Teale, W.H., & Sulzby, E. (1986). *Emergent literacy: Writing and reading*. Norwood, NJ: Ablex.

CHAPTER 1

How Can We Enable All Children to Achieve?

Susan B. Neuman

Xavier could read when he just turned 4 years old. He would page quickly through books in his preschool library, such as *Spot Goes to the Farm* (Hill, 1987), *My First Look at Colors* (1990), and *Let's Play* (MacDonald, 1991), pointing to individual words and reading them correctly. The teacher would find Xavier looking with his friends at all sorts of print materials, even English–Spanish books like *What color: Que color?* (Benjamin, 1993). He would try to read Spanish words, like *cielo* (sky), pronouncing it as "kello." Asked who read to him, he replied, "Nobody. I read to myself."

Across the hall in a prekindergarten class, Deon could give a fairly accurate account of the book *When You Go to Kindergarten* (Howe, 1994). He would turn the pages and paraphrase the story. Asked what he liked most about the book, he answered, "I like it because it's about going to school." Having spent a good deal of his afternoons in the local library as he waited for his mother to get off work, Deon seemed to know most of the children's books by heart, chiming refrains to various stories and reciting nursery rhymes.

But for Christopher, we have a different type of data. Slightly above the cut-off date for his grade, Christopher was a 6-year-old kindergartner and a bit of a troublemaker. He could not sit still during class storybook reading—he would hide under the table and climb on the chairs until the teacher became frustrated and stopped reading. His treatment of books in the classroom library was even more alarming; he rode them like skateboards, sometimes tearing them. His teacher said, "He never had books—you can tell, when you're playing with books as if they're a horse, you don't know what a book is."

Since the late 1980s there has been an intense debate about how to teach typical children like Xavier, Deon, and Christopher to read and write. Insights on emergent literacy (Strickland & Morrow, 1989; Teale & Sulzby, 1989) have shown that Xavier and Deon already are demonstrating through their motivation and independent reenactments, key signs of early literacy. However, Christopher's patterns are more troubling, raising a question that requires closer scrutiny. How do we provide appropriate reading instruction to ensure his success and that of others like him? How do we create an environment that enables Christopher and his more informed peers to reach their potential? Questions like these focus on the issue of how to adapt early literacy instruction to meet all children's needs. As many teachers will note, it is clear that what may be appropriate early instruction for Xavier and Deon will not necessarily be appropriate for Christopher.

This chapter examines critical instructional issues for teaching young early literacy learners like Xavier, Deon, and Christopher. I begin by setting out guidelines for literacy teaching that provide a framework for best practice, then I describe their implications for classroom practice. It is my belief that the key to quality early literacy instruction lies in a delicate balance—providing rich, meaningful, engaging content learning within the context of appropriate teaching practices. Teachers should create classroom cultures that motivate children, honor their choices about what they want to learn, and encourage their independence. When teachers do these things, literacy achievement is within all children's reach.

Guidelines for Best Practices in Early Literacy

In many ways we are at a critical crossroads in early literacy education. Great strides have been made toward a richer conceptualization of young children as early literacy learners. Old notions of reading readiness have given way to new theories of young children as active meaning–makers and seekers who are involved in a process of learning about literacy. As a result, literacy learning now is considered a cultural, social, and cognitive achievement, reflecting the mastery of a complex set of attitudes, expectations, behaviors, and skills related to written language.

How can educators translate this sociocultural, developmentalist perspective to instructional practices that benefit all children? Some of the instructional issues that teachers grapple with are indeed mind-boggling. How do we teach in a school where there are 32 different languages spoken? How can we involve parents more integrally in our schools? How can we become culturally responsive to children of many different cultures in a classroom? These are just some of the questions that teachers and caregivers must deal with in classrooms on a daily basis. The following section draws from prevailing research, detailing what we know about literacy learning in these early years. Sound instructional practices may be based on our understanding of basic characteristics of children's development.

• *Diversity is inherent in all aspects of teaching young children.*

Although learning to read and write begins very early in life (McLane & McNamee, 1990; Teale & Sulzby, 1989), there is considerable variation in patterns of early literacy development. In their home and preschool experiences, children encounter many different resources and types and degrees of support for early literacy. Some children may have ready access to a range of writing and reading materials, while others may not; some children observe their parents writing and reading frequently, while others observe this only occasionally; some children receive direct, didactic instruction, while others receive much more casual informal assistance. This means that some children will be better prepared for literacy instruction than others. Consequently, no one method or approach is likely to work for all children. Because children's development varies, so too must our instructional strategies. It is imperative for teachers to be familiar with a wide variety of explicit teaching approaches, materials, and strategies to enrich children's understanding of literacy.

• *Social interaction fosters children's motivation and ability to use literacy in fulfilling and productive ways.*

Especially in these early years, literacy is a profoundly social process that enters young children's lives through their interactions in a variety of activities and relationships with other people. Close observations suggest that children often become interested in writing and reading because it can be useful to them in their social relationships; it can give them power, help them to better understand the world around them, and enable them to express their feelings of friendship or frustration. As they learn about written language and how to use it in contexts and activities that are personally meaningful, children will even seek help from others who are more competent and who can serve as spontaneous apprentices.

The processes that have served children so well in these early years often are discouraged when they begin formal schooling. In many cases children are encouraged to work alone, not to share their answers, and not to talk or work with others, even though these positive social and working relationships have provided the foundation for what they already know. In my studies with Roskos (Neuman & Roskos, 1992; Neuman & Roskos, 1997), we found very young children often engaging in parallel play; for slightly older children, more collaborative activity was observed. In these social contexts, we found children testing their problems and solutions, sharing their expertise, and assisting one another—just like adults tend to do. Although there are times when independence is important, young children often thrive intellectually through social activity.

• *Children need to develop knowledge and skills in literacy.*

Children bring their curiosity and interests in communicating with others to the context of productive activity. They also bring their desire to acquire the knowledge and skills that may be necessary to accomplish these activities. Children feel a sense of power and mastery when they begin to develop the competencies of readers and writers. Even in their play, for example, children strive to be accomplished, like a student who told a friend to "watch me as I write the letter *C*."

Children receive great personal joy and gratification from others when singing an alphabet song or reciting numbers and letter names. These skills represent basic 3R knowledge (reading, 'riting, and 'rithmetic) that has traditionally and strongly predicted reading success (Tizard, Blatchford, Burke, Farquhar, & Plewis, 1988). There is no reason to deny children these technical skills. At the same time, however, we must recognize that real reading and writing skills involve more than just reciting or making letters. Communicating, interpreting information, and reasoning—these skills are developed when children engage in activities for which they can make real decisions and contributions. In fact, when observing young children, it becomes apparent that often there is a reciprocal relation among the more technical skills and these conceptual skills; the more children desire to know and to be able to do, the more skills they want and need to learn.

• *Active participation in writing and reading engages children in practicing not only what written language is for, but how it works.*

In their early years, children find a variety of creative ways to express what they know about literacy. They may combine drawing, talking, and pretend play, mixing many different symbols to communicate meaning (Dyson, 1982). In a recent study (Neuman & Roskos, 1997), we found children in a restaurant-play setting acting as if they were waiters and waitresses, asking customers "whattya want?" They then pretended to write the orders and conveyed this information to the chef by "reading" their scribbles. Through their talk, writings, and actions, children were revealing their procedural knowledge about the functions of reading and writing.

Demonstrations like these suggest that children know a good deal more about literacy than we have previously given them credit. For many, language is not yet well developed; their "I know how" or procedural knowledge may precede their verbal "I know that" or declarative knowledge. Children may express their literacy knowledge through gestures, talking, dancing, singing, and acting out routines. It is especially important in early childhood classrooms to provide time and occasions for children to use what they bring—their multiple literacy capabilities—to independently explore the functional uses of print and its conventions. Letting them actively discover new insights through creative projects and trying on literacy-related roles and routines in playful settings is not just a rehearsal for the real thing; rather, children are involved in the critical, purposeful activities necessary for writing and reading development.

• *Young children's needs are better met in inclusion-based literacy programs.*

Some young children who enter our classrooms will need additional instructional support. They may have special physical or instructional difficulties that require more time and more teaching. Typically we have tended to isolate these young children, sending them off to special resource rooms or individualized programs. Unfortunately, in the course of trying to help, we often have overdiagnosed, and underinstructed these children with special needs.

Further, we wonder what kinds of messages these actions convey about ourselves as teachers as well as the children themselves, by pulling mainstreamed handicapped children out of the classroom dur-

In Practice

DESIGNING A LITERACY-ENRICHED DRAMATIC-PLAY AREA

Children generate ideas for dramatic play from their environment. Set up a post office area with a mailbox, delivery pouch, stationery, and envelopes, for example, and just watch as children engage in post office—like activity. By including literacy objects in housekeeping, book corner, and art areas, children begin to incorporate print in very natural ways in their dramatic-play themes.

Think about the following criteria when selecting literacy props in dramatic-play areas:

■ *Appropriateness*: Can the prop be used naturally and safely by young children?

■ *Authenticity*: Is the prop a real item that children might find naturally in their environment?

■ *Utility*: Does the prop serve a particular function that children may be familiar with in their everyday world?

Guided by these criteria, try designing a "grocery store" with the following props:

kitchen utensils (muffin tins, cooking
    pans, dishes, and plastic spoons)
grocery packages of all types
small-sized kitchen furniture
plastic fruit
paper or note pads
pencils or markers or crayons
cookbooks (preferably children's)
coupons

recipe cards
magazines
calendar
telephone book and telephone
placemats
junk mail
stickers
envelopes

Some General Tips:

1. Arrange the furniture to create an enclosed space for about four or five children.

2. Provide writing supplies and a modest stack of scrap paper for making notes and lists.

3. Ask parents to donate empty grocery packages, recipe books, recipe cards, and unused coupons. Include multicultural sources of environmental print, like food packages and advertisements.

ing the day. There is no doubt that inclusion presents real challenges to teachers' time, energy, and in some cases, instructional expertise. Nevertheless, these programs provide in-class instructional support that enables young special-needs children to learn literacy by engaging in literacy practices within a community. Particularly in the early years, children need a continuity of experiences. It is the classroom that best provides these important connections with adults who children know and trust. (See Chapter 5 for further discussion on providing inclusive early literacy instruction for children with disabilities.)

• *Parent involvement builds continuity and consistency in early literacy teaching.*

Continuity also is enhanced by working in partnership with families and other caregivers. Early literacy learning is embedded in these relationships that shape what children learn and how they come to see the eventual place of literacy in their own lives. Young children stand the best chance of developing a good foundation for writing and reading if their literacy-learning experiences are anchored in their relationships with these people and if they are tied to contexts and activities that have personal meaning and value to them (McLane & McNamee, 1990).

Communication between families and teachers built on mutual respect and the sharing of information creates bonds of continuity, purpose, and consistency in children's early literacy programs. It is not just a one-way street, however, with the teacher sharing his or her knowledge, insights, and resources with family members. On the contrary, families have much to share and to offer teachers as well. They have far more personal knowledge of their children's interests and growing development. They also have the fundamental right and responsibility to share in decisions about their children's care and education. (See Chapter 7 for further discussion on fostering children's early literacy development through parent involvement.)

• *It is the school's responsibility to discover what children already know about writing and reading, and to help them make connections with what we believe they need to know.*

When children leave home to go to school, they encounter new ways to learn about writing and reading. For some students, these activities, though in a different context, will extend the kinds of learning and development that already have been taking place at home. For other children, however, particularly those from low-income or different cultural groups, the activities that take place in the school setting will look very different from their homes and neighborhood cultures. Some have suggested that it is this discontinuity between home and school practices that may seriously influence children's ability to adjust and later succeed in literacy and schooling (Au & Jordan, 1981; Heath, 1983).

There have been many debates about how best to teach children who come from a variety of home environments. Unfortunately, in some cases these discussions have translated into structured academic programs specifically designed for "at-risk" children. The conventional wisdom had been that these children need more controlled instructional programs—more review, drill, and practice. As Polakow (1994) describes, such settings often become "at-risk landscapes" (p. 150) rigidly segregating children by gender, race, and ability, providing the very poorest quality of language and literacy instruction.

Contrary to these practices, the best way to meet the challenge of educating children from various cultural backgrounds is to provide them with the very best quality of instruction, which includes high standards, direct instruction, time, materials, and opportunities for activities that encourage children's self-discovery and exploration. Such programs are likely to benefit all children from all cultures and economic groups to become competent members of the larger community of readers and writers. (See Chapter 6 for further discussion on providing culturally responsive instruction in literacy.)

 • *Assessment of early literacy should be continuous, examined in multiple contexts, and focused on a variety of behaviors.*

Finally, because children's growing knowledge about literacy is moving in so many directions during these years, early literacy cannot simply be measured as a set of narrowly defined skills. Unfortunately, many of our young children are evaluated, screened, and labeled each year using standardized measures that describe what children do against prescribed developmental markers or average norms. In some cases, children are even promoted and retained on the basis of these narrow sets of skills presumed to predict reading achievement and later school success. Particularly during these early years, standardized paper and pencil measures are not effective in measuring what children know and do not know. Because children's knowledge and skills are in constant motion, these tests tend not to be reliable or valid measures of what they can do in typical situations. They are not sensitive to language, culture, or the experiences of young children.

Nevertheless, accurate assessment of children's knowledge, skills, and dispositions can be very useful to teachers, helping us to match instruction with how and what children are learning. A sound assessment, however, must be anchored in real-life writing and reading tasks, and must continuously chronicle a wide range of literacy activities in different situations. Children are complex, multifaceted individuals. Our assessment strategies must reflect these complexities, otherwise they do more harm than good. (See Chapter 12 for further discussion on assessing young children's literacy learning.)

What we know about young children's development suggests that there will be enormous diversity in children's literacy experiences prior to formal schooling. Teaching approaches need to be varied and flexible to account for this range of experiences. Good literacy instruction builds on what children already know and can do and provides knowledge, skills, and dispositions for lifelong literacy learning. Consequently, it is critical that we teach children not only the technical skills of literacy, but also how to use these tools to better their thinking and reasoning.

Child-development principles are embedded in these guidelines for appropriate early literacy instruction. They emphasize the importance of teachers' decision making in the classroom and the importance of what children may bring to these settings as well as what their families may regard as educationally significant in their lives and communities. These principles underlie best practices and suggest the link between what is known about development and what is known about learning to read and write.

Best Practices in Early Literacy

What are the implications for practice in classrooms? These principles are put into action in subsequent chapters, addressing critical issues of practice. Here, however, some activities are described that are likely to be found in all classrooms and are especially supportive of early literacy development.

A Print-Rich Environment

Books, paper, writing tools, and functional signs and symbols have a central place in classrooms that support literacy development. Children are stimulated to use literacy when there are interesting things to write and read about, and when they have access to writing tools to express themselves in symbolic form. Signs that have meaning for children (not mere decoration), books placed everywhere, play centers, a writing table with plenty of supplies, and a bulletin board for leaving written messages to one another, all invite children to use writing and reading in open-ended ways. These learning environments communicate the important message that literacy is an integral part of daily activity.

It is not just enough to develop a literacy-enriched environment, however. Children also need time to use it. During free-activity time in one classroom, for example, the writing table has become a center for sharing and sending messages to friends. Children can write letters to one another and drop them in a covered shoebox made to look like a mailbox, to the absolute delight of their peers. These messages then can be displayed on a bulletin board in the writing center at the children's eye level, so that the whole class can enjoy one another's writings.

Young children also need opportunity for literacy-related play (Neuman & Roskos, 1990), exploring the uses of language and literacy routines associated with authentic everyday activities. A grocery store, restaurant, and doctor's office settings allow children to engage in playful attempts at literacy that are essentially risk-free. In these environments children feel in control and develop a sense of what writers and readers do long before they actually have the necessary skills and knowledge for writing or reading. Such feelings nourish their interest and desires to become literate and provide motivation for working toward learning how to write and read.

Integrated Language Experiences and Explorations

Children are driven to learn language and literacy, not for its own sake, but for its functionality (Strickland & Morrow, 1989). They use their emerging skills to discover and explore their worlds. Engaging children in investigations that are in-depth studies of real topics, environments, and events—activities that are really worth their time and attention—should be a centerpiece of the curriculum. Determining how things work or how to care for a favorite pet is a far cry from curricula that focus on colors, seasons, or community workers. In the course of working on projects, children ask meaningful questions and find ways of representing their findings in multiple symbolic forms through talking, drawing, and writing.

Integrated language activities like these give children opportunities to work with other students having different skills and abilities. Activities may begin as large-group lessons, like "How do we plant our own garden?" However, the real work begins as children work together in small-group investigations. In these situations one child's skill in drawing may complement another's ability to write on the computer, along with another who enjoys talking in front of a group. Such cooperative language and literacy activities provide critical opportunities for children to learn from one another.

Projects are slightly different than traditional theme-based instruction. Though they both emphasize integrated curricula, projects have goals that are established by the classroom community. Creating and maintaining a children's garden, for example, represents a clear and concrete goal for which young children can take credit and feel competent. Developing a Big Book that illustrates the many ancestries and cultures of children in the classroom brings special closure to a project that has involved them in writing letters to family across the world as they explored their multicultural roots. Projects like these actively engage children's minds (Katz & Chard, 1989), and allow them to practice what they know and use literacy for real-life purposes.

Reading and Responding

Listening to stories and discussing them as a group is a vital activity in early childhood classrooms (Neuman, 1997). Children need experiences with a variety of texts: stories, predictable texts, and concept books among others. In many schools children actually prefer books about real things; they are eager to learn about how things work in their environment.

There are many ways to share stories. Some of the teachers I visit like to begin with a song, a finger play, or a brief chant signaling that it is now time for stories. During the reading, the teacher will use her voice to convey meaning. Sometimes she will pause and ask questions, and other times she will simply read the book without stopping, enjoying the language and rhyme of the story. Following the story, the teacher will engage children in responding in a variety of ways. Some like to reenact the story; others like to use participation techniques like student response cards; still others engage in group discussions followed by a retelling of the story using pictures and actual objects. All of these strategies enhance children's understanding and delight in hearing the language of print. And, as many teachers have found, children often want to hear the same story again and again until they have gained a sense of mastery of the story or topic.

It is critical for children not only to hear stories, but to have access to books themselves. After the story time, one preschool teacher put a book in each child's hands and encouraged them to read independently. Another teacher, concerned at first that children would rip pages, involved the group in a page-turning activity, "Over, up, and flip." Once the teacher was confident that the books would not be destroyed, she put some of their favorites in the library corner and watched with fascination how the children carefully turned the pages and pretended to read along with their friends. Library corners need to be in a central part of the room, with comfortable beanbag chairs, library pockets with take-out cards, lots of stuffed animals and pictures, and a repair kit in case a scribble appears on a page.

Skills and Strategies

In literacy-enriched classrooms, reading and writing become a part of the culture—the way in which much information is communicated throughout the day. Skill and strategy teaching occur as children are engaged in meaningful activity. Through their finger plays, songs, and chants, they will begin to hear similarities and differences in language; through listening to stories they will pick up new vocabulary; and after a while, through their writing, many will discover and differentiate print from pictures. However, some children will need explicit, direct instruction in skills and strategies. They will need to see alphabetic letters isolated to better capture their shape, size, and form. Some will need to hear the sounds of letters apart from their context, and some will need to be shown how to write their names and favorite words. Such explicit instruction is an important part of teaching in early childhood classrooms. Learning new skills helps children develop a sense of competence and accomplishment, leading toward greater independence in learning.

Much attention has been drawn to concerns about isolated skill teaching, in which children are drilled on workbook pages at too young an age. Although I agree that these activities are clearly inappropriate for young children, it should not suggest that all direct, skill-based instruction should be abandoned. Sometimes we refer to these skill teachings as "vitamin pill activities," not particularly fun, but brief and necessary. Teaching children a word family by saying the word *at* and asking them to put the letter *p*, then *f*, then *m* before it on a worksheet does not turn them into robots; on the contrary, it is likely to teach them many different words and sounds over time. It is important for us to adjust our teaching strategies to meet the children's needs and not our own. Although Xavier and Deon, described at the beginning of this chapter, might thrive through activities that implicitly use language and literacy in context, Christopher might need explicit instructions on how to behave when visiting a library or hearing a story. It is the wise and child-focused teacher who will adjust his or her teaching to meet this challenge.

These guidelines and suggested practices embrace an attitude of inquiry rather than prescription that results in a broader and more inclusive approach to early literacy instruction. Implicit in this view is the assumption that any approach to early literacy development must begin by asking, Who is this child? What kinds of experiences has he or she had? Guided by a set of basic guidelines of good practice, teachers tailor instructional practices and teaching to their children, creating integral connections between these earliest experiences and long-term literacy development tied to contexts and activities that have personal meaning and value to them. Responding to the challenge of diversity defines both the hard work and the exhilarating rewards of early literacy teaching.

References

Au, K.H., & Jordan, C. (1981). Teaching reading to Hawaiian children: Finding a culturally appropriate solution. In H. Trueba, G.P. Guthrie, & K.H. Au (Eds.), *Culture in the bilingual classroom: Studies in classroom ethnography* (pp. 139–152). Rowley, MA: Newbury House.

Dyson, A.H. (1982). The emergence of visible language: Interrelationships between drawing and early writing. *Visible Language, 16*, 360–381.

Heath, S.B. (1983). *Ways with words: Language, life, and work in communities and classrooms.* New York: Cambridge University Press.

Katz, L., & Chard, C. (1989). *Engaging children's minds.* Norwood, NJ: Ablex.

McLane, J.B., & McNamee, G. (1990). *Early literacy.* Cambridge, MA: Harvard University Press.

Neuman, S.B. (1997). *Getting books in children's hands: The great book flood of '97.* Philadelphia, PA: Final Report to the William Penn Foundation.

Neuman, S.B., & Roskos, K. (1990). Play, print and purpose: Enriching play environments for literacy development. *The Reading Teacher, 44*, 214–221.

Neuman, S.B., & Roskos, K. (1992). Literacy objects as cultural tools: Effects on children's literacy behaviors in play. *Reading Research Quarterly, 27*, 202–225.

Neuman, S.B., & Roskos, K. (1997). Literacy knowledge in practice: Contexts of participation for young writers and readers. *Reading Research Quarterly, 32*, 10–32.

Polakow, V. (1994). *Lives on the edge.* Chicago, IL: University of Chicago Press.

Strickland, D.S., & Morrow, L.M. (Eds.). (1989). *Emerging literacy: Young children learn to read and write.* Newark, DE: International Reading Association.

Teale, W.H., & Sulzby, E. (1989). Emergent literacy: New perspectives. In D.S. Strickland & L.M. Morrow (Eds.), *Emerging literacy: Young children learn to read and write* (pp. 1–15). Newark, DE: International Reading Association.

Tizard, B., Blatchford, P., Burke, J., Farquhar, C., & Plewis, I. (1988). *Young children at school in the inner city.* Hillsdale, NJ: Erlbaum.

Children's Literature References

Benjamin, B. (1992). *What color: Que color?* New York: Simon and Schuster.

Hill, E. (1987). *Spot goes to the farm.* New York: Putnam.

Howe, J. (1994). *When you go to kindergarten.* New York: Morrow Junior Books.

MacDonald, A. (1991). *Let's play.* Cambridge, MA: Candlewick Press.

My first look at colors. New York: Random House.

CHAPTER 2

What Is Developmentally Appropriate Practice in Early Literacy?: Considering the Alphabet

Judith A. Schickedanz

Several kindergartners sat clustered around a teacher. Shouts of "A," "F," "B," and "P" echoed through the room. As each outburst subsided, the teacher spoke: "I think Latisha was first that time. José, you were first on that one." She then handed the card to the appropriate student. When the teacher's stack of flashcards was gone, the children counted to see who had the most.

I imagined this scene while listening to a practicum student respond to the question, "If one of your goals for kindergartners is that they learn about the letters of the alphabet, how might you accomplish this?" The student offering the idea said that she had been concerned after seeing kindergartners study one letter each week. "Studying" involved writing the letter many times on a worksheet ("active" learning, the teacher claimed). The children also colored pictures of items whose names started with the letter being studied, and did related projects (for example, making object displays and picture collages whose names begin with *M*). It seemed to the student that this approach took an inordinate amount of time (26 weeks to cover the alphabet) and yielded relatively little learning.

The game proposed by the practicum student (flashcard recognition) exposes children to all the alphabet letters at once, and it provides a lot of practice in a relatively short period of time. She questioned whether children must write letters in order to learn them. She said that her 3-year-old niece only scribbled when using her crayons and paper, yet she already could name all the letters. She learned them by playing with alphabet puzzles, by listening to someone read alphabet books, and by playing with magnetic letters on the refrigerator door in her kitchen.

Before a second idea could be suggested, another student criticized the first one. She thought the game had no meaning for little children because they were not using the information, except to try to beat other children at a game. She also thought that providing children with many letters at once would confuse them. While volunteering in several classrooms, she had seen both preschoolers and kindergartners confuse letters. She said that young children cannot see small differences. She thought the first student's niece was simply precocious and that standards for most children should not be based on her. She asserted that it was not developmentally appropriate for kindergartners to learn the letters of the alphabet.

A different student also criticized the first student's idea, but not because she considered letters too difficult for preschoolers to learn. Rather, she thought that learning to recognize and name letters was not as important as learning the sounds of letters, which she said the game did not teach. A first-grade teacher in whose classroom she had done an internship complained bitterly because most children were able to fill out worksheets on letter–sound associations, but were unable to spell words. She said this demonstrated how limited letter-name knowledge is, if children could not segment words into phonemes.

What We Say, What We Mean

Asking about ways to achieve the goal of teaching children the alphabet often reveals the criteria teachers use to judge whether a particular content or practice is "developmentally appropriate." When some teachers say their goal is teaching children about the alphabet, they mean only that children will learn to recognize and name letters. But other teachers include learning how to write letters, either because they wish to teach handwriting or because they think writing letters helps children learn to recognize and name them. Still other teachers intend for the same goal to encompass an understanding of how letters function in a writing system. Some teachers holding this broader view try to reach the goal by teaching children to associate specific sounds with specific letters, while others think this constitutes an inadequate understanding of how alphabet letters function. They teach children to think their way through a spoken word, one sound (phoneme) at a time, and to select letters systematically to code each isolated phoneme.

The particular meaning that different teachers associate with the goal that children will learn about the alphabet determines the practices they judge to be appropriate. Judging appropriateness requires consideration of more than whether children are *capable* of doing something at a particular age. It also includes considering the relation of what is to be learned to the outcome of that learning (that is, learning to read or to spell). Sometimes, when someone says that a particular literacy practice is "developmentally inappropriate" he or she may mean that it is trivial and does not merit much of our instructional time.

Some of the items considered inappropriate for language development and literacy practices in programs for 4- and 5-year-olds (Bredekamp, 1987) perhaps can be faulted more for being relatively trivial than for being inappropriate. For example, 4- and 5-year-olds are certainly capable of reciting the alphabet from memory, but this activity does not contribute importantly to learning to read. It qualifies as inappropriate for this reason. Development (the child's capacity) has little or nothing to do with it.

Recognizing single alphabet letters, on the other hand, contributes greatly to learning to read, though it certainly is not sufficient by itself, as the first-grade teacher observed. *Single* is a key word here, if a meaningfulness criterion is also used to judge the appropriateness of a practice. In meaningful activities, children are able to see and appreciate a connection between what they are learning and some application of it—some reason for its importance or usefulness. If children are exposed to letters and their names through the use of flashcards, such as in the practicum student's game, the purpose of alphabet letters is not obvious. But if children are exposed to letters and letter names in looking at their own names, classroom signs, or titles of storybooks, the purpose of letters is obvious.

As these examples illustrate, several considerations often are made when judging whether a specific practice is developmentally appropriate. These include (1) whether children are *able* to learn something; (2) whether what is to be learned is *important* with respect to some outcome of interest; (3) whether a particular practice allows learning to be meaningful, enabling children to understand for what purpose they are being asked to learn something; and (4) whether the instructional practice is adequate to support learning in a young child whose knowledge is often incomplete and fragile.

This fourth consideration also can be illustrated with the example of recognizing single letters. In teaching letters in isolation, the adult fails to consider that the child does not have in mind the other 25 letters. Thus, the instructional context is simply not adequate for children to learn to discriminate and name individual letters. Teachers also see inadequate context when first graders and second graders stumble in decoding material because their oral vocabularies and background knowledge are not thorough enough to lead to quick translations into actual words. Children get bogged down as they read and cannot retain any sense of meaning as they go. In the latter case, the solution is not as easy as presenting several alphabet letters at once. Teachers can, however, be sure to build vocabulary as they discuss stories that have been read to or by children, and they must provide experiences (such as field trips, science experiments in the classroom, videos, or guest speakers), as necessary, to build background knowledge.

The Focus of the Chapter

This chapter focuses on a very specific aspect of early literacy because only a detailed discussion can help us achieve an understanding of what constitutes developmentally appropriate early literacy practice. Alphabet learning concerns me, first because many preschool and kindergarten teachers ignore this aspect of early literacy and consider it inappropriate, and second, because other early childhood teachers, though providing instruction on this aspect of early literacy, use practices that are problematic like those observed by the practicum student in her kindergarten class, or the game she proposed. Third, many children in urban first-grade classrooms enter without having attended preschool or kindergarten. When this is the case, first-grade teachers wonder how best to teach children about the alphabet.

Although learning about the alphabet, which includes phonemic segmentation, letter-name knowledge, and letter-sound association knowledge, is critical to learning to read, other aspects of early literacy are just as important. These include such things as the development of vocabulary and background knowledge (essential to comprehension and important for facilitating decoding), familiarity with written language (because it differs in structure from spoken language), knowledge of narrative discourse structure (essential for both comprehending and writing stories), and knowledge of print conventions (how to progress through a book and process the layout of print on a page). Alphabet knowledge has been selected because it provides a particular case with which to discuss developmentally appropriate practices, not because learning about the alphabet is the most important aspect of early literacy. It also has been selected because some of the difficulties children experience in learning the alphabet have been misunderstood. Studies of infant capacities shed some light on this topic.

The Young Child's Capacity to Learn About the Alphabet

Three areas of child development are reviewed here: (1) infants' visual discrimination ability, (2) infants' ability to form perceptually based categories, and (3) young children's sensitivity to language at the phoneme level.

Infants' Visual Discrimination Ability

In 1963, Robert Fantz conducted a groundbreaking experiment with newborns. Infants who saw six stimuli looked the longest at a simple human face drawn with black features set against a chalk-white background. A piece of newspaper and a bullseye (two thin white circles inserted on a black background) tied for second place (like the human face, the newspaper and bullseye were patterns). The other three stimuli were not patterns, but solid, colored disks (red, yellow, and white). Infants looked at these the least.

After Fantz's discovery that newborns prefer patterned versus non-patterned stimuli, researchers wondered what exactly infants could see. They wondered what changes infants could notice; could they notice changes in orientation or changes only in form? In a series of studies (Cohen & Younger, 1984), babies 6 to 12 weeks of age were first shown either stimulus 1a or 1b (see Figure 1). The line segments of these two stimuli are exactly the same, but their angles differ. Infants at first were shown one stimulus repeatedly until their attention dropped off—until they became habituated. After habituation, infants were shown one or

Figure 1 Stimuli Used by Cohen & Younger (1984)

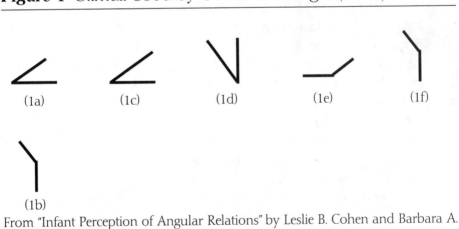

(1a)   (1c)   (1d)   (1e)   (1f)

(1b)

From "Infant Perception of Angular Relations" by Leslie B. Cohen and Barbara A. Younger (1984), *Infant Behavior and Development*, 7, 37–47. Used by permission of Ablex Publishing.

more of four test stimuli. One stimuli (the control) was the habituation stimulus (1c if habituated to 1a). The other three (1d, 1e, and 1f) were variations of the habituation stimulus (1a). One (1d) differed from the habituation stimulus only by orientation. Another (1e) differed only by the size of the angle. In the third (1f), both the angle and the orientation of the lines differed from the habituation stimulus.

Six-week-olds realerted primarily to the same angle shown in a new *orientation*, not to a change in angle size. Twelve-week-olds realerted primarily to a change in angle *size*, not to the same angle shown in a different orientation. The researchers concluded that, at about 2 months of age, infants can combine and integrate lines into simple forms and thus can discriminate among them. Another possibility is that the poor visual acuity of infants under 2 months of age causes lines to blur so that they cannot gauge the distance between them. Whatever the reason, infants older than 2 months focus on changes in composition or form, not on changes in orientation.

Children's subsequent experience in the three-dimensional world maintains their early tendency to disregard orientation when identifying objects (for example, whether a chair is upside-down or right-side up, we call it a chair). But even though young infants and children disregard orientation information when identifying objects, it would be a mistake to assume that they cannot see differences in orientation. They may not be in the habit of consciously recognizing differences in orientation, but research on infant visual perception shows that they are very capable of doing this (for example, Cohen & Strauss, 1979).

The young child can be expected to attend little to the orientation of alphabet letters, not only because doing so violates previous experience in identifying three-dimensional objects, but because it rarely carries important information about a letter's identity. A child can recognize and name most letters, no matter how they are oriented. *M* and *W*, *p* and *q*, and *b* and *d* are the only letters for which identification relies on orientation information. Inadequate knowledge of orientation can cause problems when writing any letter, because each has a conventional orientation (see item 2 in Figure 2), but problems in learning to recognize and name letters are not due to failure to *see* orientation. Figure 2 provides examples of how preschool and kindergarten children can learn letter names, how to form letters, and how letters function.

Figure 2 Practices for Teaching Young Children About the Alphabet

1. Building a model of a trolley station in the block area, a child asks a teacher how to spell the words, *Outbound Green Line*. The teacher dictates *O* and *U*, but vocalizes the *T* and *B* phonemes, leaving the letter selection to the child. Soon, the child asks the teacher to take over the writing, explaining, "It's too much." But the child remains involved, dictating *G, R, E,* and *N,* for *green* and *L, I,* and *N,* for *line,* as the teacher sounds out the words and writes the letters. As the teacher forms *G,* she says, "A line right here makes this letter *G,* not *C.*"

2. When Samantha writes her name on the picture she has drawn, she asks if her *S* looks how "it is supposed to." The teacher explains that it is backward. The teacher writes a correctly oriented *S* on another piece of paper, as Samantha watches. Soon, Samantha writes her name again. But despite having studied the teacher's *S* before starting, she writes her *S* backward once more. She shakes her head no and asks the teacher to help. This time the teacher proceeds differently: "Put your marker right here" (pointing to a spot). "Now, move your marker that way" (pointing again). "Now change directions..." (moving Samantha's hand in the new direction). "Keep gooooing...Stop!" The teacher takes Samantha's hand to guide it in the other direction.

3. A child is playing with alphabet-matching material at a puzzle table. He matches loose letter tiles to letters printed on a background board and then does it again. As the child matches the letter tiles for the third time, a teacher stops by and comments, "That's the other *K.* There's the *T.* Mmm, yes, *N* goes right there."

4. All but six children have been dismissed from music time to go with a teacher to the bathroom and then to snack. To avoid a long wait in the bathroom area, a second teacher keeps a small group to play an alphabet-matching game. First the teacher draws a long vertical line on her paper. One child guesses that the teacher was thinking of *T.* Another guesses *L.* A third guesses *M.* The teacher confirms that she might be thinking of any of these letters. Next, the teacher draws a short horizontal line to the right of the vertical line, at the top. "I was right, *L,*" one child exclaims. The teacher says that it will be necessary to rotate the paper (she rotates it 180 degrees), and then turns the paper over and traces the faint outline showing through from the other side. "*L* is a good guess, but not the letter in my mind."

    The child who suggested earlier that the teacher was thinking of *T* continues to maintain that this letter is in the teacher's mind. Another child thinks it could be *E* or *F.* For the next clue, the teacher starts in the middle of the long, vertical line, and draws a short line to the right. "*F*!" the children shout. The teacher confirms that this is the letter of which she has been thinking.   *(continued)*

Figure 2 Practices for Teaching Young Children About the Alphabet (continued)

5. The children sing the song "Willoughby Wallaby Woo" during music time, and then make up some verses using names of children in the class.

6. A child uses a teacher-made manipulative. Pictures of flowers children have seen on walks and in classroom bouquets donated by parents who have home gardens are mounted on the background board. Velcro-backed name tiles (such as tulips, daffodils, or lilies of the valley) are in a small dish. The child says the name of a flower to himself and then searches for the tile bearing this name. As the child searches the tiles, he can be heard saying, "t," "d," or "l."

Infants' Ability to Form Perceptually Based Categories

After the first studies of visual perception in young infants (for example, Cohen & Younger, 1984), researchers began to wonder if infants could disregard differences and focus on similarities (that is, learn categories or concepts). To probe this question, researchers used not one stimulus in the habituation phase, but a series of stimuli. For example, researchers might show a series of forms composed of straight lines and angles ($<$, $>$, X, Z). In the test phase, researchers would pair an angular form (one such as Y or V, because neither was included in the habituation series) with a form that was not a member of the habituation series category (O, S, ?). If infants formed perceptually based concepts, they would respond only minimally to a member of the habituation series category. But if infants did not form a perceptually based concept, they would realert to both test stimuli.

What researchers found was that the human infant typically realerts far more to the new category test stimulus than to a new exemplar from the habituation category. Remarkably, this capacity has even been found in infants 3 and 4 months old (Eimas & Quinn, 1994). The ability allows the infant to generalize from experience with just a few exemplars to encounters with new members of the same category. In the course of evolution, infants who were skilled at this were more likely to survive because a narrow escape from one instance of danger could be used in the future to avoid danger of a similar kind. Moreover, this capacity prevents infants and adults from drowning in detail. If we could not see commonalities amid differences and use this information to organize and manage the world, we would be completely overwhelmed.

Sometimes it is necessary to pay attention to differences among the members of a category. Even babies can detect small differences between one visual stimulus and another. Many of us also know from our own experience that preschoolers and kindergarten children have the capacity to do the same. The practicum student's 3-year-old niece who could name most letters of the alphabet is not that rare. Thus, when problems occur in preschool or kindergarten children, or even in first-graders who are learning to recognize and name letters of the alphabet, they are most likely due to limitations in opportunity (that is, exposure), not in capacity. Most of us view members of a category (whether dogs or cats, alphabet letters or numerals) as virtually the same, until we have had ample opportunities to compare the members.

The alphabet-matching game (item 3 in Figure 2) is useful for helping children discriminate among letters, especially if each puzzle is made to include letters that are very similar. The alphabet-clue game (item 4 in Figure 2) helps children discriminate among letters that are easy to confuse. Both situations also can provide opportunities for children to learn the name associated with each distinct form (true for the alphabet-matching material only when an adult joins the child). First-grade teachers will find that simply proceeding with writing dictated messages from children, and naming letters as they write words, will work well to help children who are still learning letters. Even commenting about the strokes used to form a letter or the similarity among several letters formed, as the writing proceeds, may be appropriate. But there is no need to delay exposing children to functional writing until all children know alphabet letters. They can gain this information in the context of fuller literacy experiences, as long as teachers are careful to make some information quite explicit.

Young Children's Sensitivity to Language at the Phoneme Level

A third aspect of young children's development that we must consider when judging the child's capacity to learn about the alphabet relates not to graphemes (letters), but to phonemes, the speech segment represented by graphemes. Young children do not naturally notice speech at this level. They *learn* to notice phonemes.

The ability to categorize words based on similarities or differences in a sound segment, and the ability to explicitly segment all of the phonemes in a word, are both good predictors of later success in learning to read (Bradley & Bryant, 1978, 1983; Hoien, Lundberg, Stanovich, & Bjaalid, 1995; Whitehurst, 1995). Sound-categorization skill is demonstrated when children recognize rhyme or alliteration. Games in which a target word is provided and children think of others that rhyme with it or begin with the same consonant phoneme, are examples of sound-categorization tasks. Making up new verses to songs, such as "Willoughby Wallaby Woo" (item 5 in Figure 2), also provides sound-categorization experience.

Explicit segmentation is demonstrated when children isolate the phonemes of a word, one by one in temporal order, to spell it. The teacher demonstrated explicit segmentation when she helped the child make the trolley station sign in the block area (see item 1 in Figure 2). Teachers who assist children in sounding out words they wish to include in stories or picture captions help children learn to segment words. Teachers also can provide explicit demonstrations of phonemic segmentation when they take dictated messages from children, such as when the entire class or a small group of first graders writes a thank-you letter to a parent or guest, or requests information from someone. Teachers should not make the task too tedious by sounding out every word. Selecting some spellings for this kind of explicit attention and involving children in the problem solving can provide the explicit instruction some kindergarten and first-grade children need in order to obtain this skill. This activity is consistent with developmentally appropriate practice because embedding the instruction in functional contexts meets the meaningfulness criterion; children will see the use of the skill. Explicit segmentation is a stronger test of phonemic-level processing than is sound categorization, and it is the better predictor of success in learning to read (Nation & Hulme, 1997). Thus, it is very important that kindergarten teachers and first-grade teachers provide adequate instruction.

In Practice

LETTER RECOGNITION AND NAMING

The following activity is popular among young children.

Mount small snapshots of four or five children in the class in a column on the left-hand side of a tagboard rectangle. Make four or five pictureboards (to accommodate everyone in the class). Be sure to put together on the same pictureboard any names beginning with the same letter. In the space to the right of each photo, draw a straight horizontal line. Laminate the boards and then put a dot of Velcro™ on each line.

Make tagboard nametags to match each picture. Laminate and dot the back of each nametag with Velcro™. Put nametags matching each set of photos in a small container. Place each container with its matching pictureboard on a classroom shelf with other matching/puzzle materials. When children first use the materials, they won't know which name is which. The teacher helps children identify a picture and then he or she segments the beginning phoneme of the child's name. For example, "We need to find the name that starts with M, for Mmm-mm...ichaela's picture. Let's see. This name starts with B, not M. This one starts with R, not M. This one...what does it start with?" (Child answers "M.") "Yes it does! But you know what? That word does not say *Michaela*. It says *Mat*. Mat's name starts with M, but it ends with /tttt/. Let's see. This next one starts with M, and it says...*Mmmm iii ch ae lllll aaaa.*"

This activity provides children with experience in letter recognition and naming, and in isolating the first phoneme in a classmate's name.

The emergence of sound-categorization abilities. Many 4-year-olds can recognize and generate words that rhyme or start with the same consonant phoneme, though it is not uncommon for first-grade teachers to discover that a child in their class has difficulty. These variations seem related to variations in experience, such as opportunities to play word games within the family or in a preschool program, and exposure to nursery rhymes and songs (Fernandez-Fein & Baker, 1995; Whitehurst, 1995).

Variations in language experience during the first 3 years of life also might account for differences in the age at which sensitivity to individual sounds in language emerges. The amount of social and language interaction provided to a baby by adults and the sheer density of language a baby hears varies considerably across differing rearing circumstances (for example, adolescent versus adult mothers, depressed versus nondepressed mothers, and conditions of poverty versus affluence (Hart & Risley, 1989). (See also Schickedanz, Schickedanz, Forsyth, & Forsyth, 1998, chapter 7, for a review.)

Differences in early language environment are related, in turn, to variations in language behavior and development. For example, when

adults interact frequently with infants, the infants babble more than those who are in the company of adults who interact with them relatively little (Oller, Eilers, Steffens, Lyunch, & Urbano, 1994). Similarly, infants whose caregivers talk to them a lot begin to talk earlier and acquire new words more rapidly than do infants whose caregivers talk to them relatively little (Huttenlocher, Haight, Bryk, Seltzer, & Lyons, 1991). Although early-language experiences are not sufficient to develop conscious awareness of rhyme and alliteration (specific experience with rhyme and alliteration is required) the early-language environment either helps or hinders the development of phonological sensitivity.

When teachers discover that children in their classrooms have little ability to respond to sound-categorization tasks, it is important to provide practice in these tasks to help develop the children's experience, rather than assume that a child in first grade, for example, simply lacks the capacity to learn to respond. Even though it is difficult to make up later for less than optimal early experiences with oral language, teachers must keep in mind that differences in children's early instruction are as important as maturational timetables in determining when children acquire various abilities and skills.

The emergence of explicit segmentation ability. This ability emerges after the ability to detect rhyme and alliteration. Many studies show that beginning explicit segmentation ability is present in older 5- and 6-year-olds, and that this ability increases for several years after that (Ball & Blachman, 1991; Content, Kolinsky, Morais, & Bertelson, 1986; Nation & Hulme, 1997; Seymour & Evans, 1994). Several case studies involving middle-class children (for example, Read, 1975; Schickedanz, 1990) indicate that explicit segmentation ability is sometimes present in older 3-year-olds, and very frequently is present in 4-year-olds. In several training studies (for example, Rosner, 1974), low-income 4- and 5-year-olds also have shown beginning levels of phonemic segmentation skill. What this variability suggests is that children's experience is significant. Just as in the case of children's response to sound-categorization tasks, it is also the case that children's ability to engage in explicit segmentation of phonemes is highly dependent on experience.

In many phonemic-segmentation training studies, children represent the phonemes they isolate in a word with chips, not alphabet letters. But several studies (for example, Ball & Blachman, 1991) indicate that coupling phonemic segmentation with the mapping of phonemes to their graphic representations is more helpful in developing reading skill than is phonemic-segmentation without graphic representation. Interestingly, simply increasing children's ability to name letters and to associate sounds with them does not by itself affect early reading skill.

Item 1 in Figure 2 is an example of an instructional practice involving both phonemic segmentation and representation of the phonemes segmented. The teacher demonstrated explicit segmentation as she helped a child spell the words needed for her block-area sign. Item 6 provides an example of a child who segmented the initial consonant phonemes in familiar words (flower names), associated these with letters, and then searched for the specific letters at the beginning of the names printed on tagboard tiles. The child's teacher often demonstrated how to use this kind of material by joining a child in the activity. Children always learned the oral vocabulary first, in the context of unit activities. Then, materials using this vocabulary were made available. Thus, over the course of a year, children became very familiar with how to use these materials.

Kindergarten and first-grade teachers can provide similar demonstrations as they write dictation for a class letter or other message, and teachers can assist individual children who request spellings as they engage in writing each day, by helping them sound out words, phoneme by phoneme. Children often need to collaborate in the segmentation of words before they are able to do this independently. Teachers also might want to provide materials in which Elkonin (1973) boxes are provided to assist children in searching for all the phonemes in words. In keeping with developmentally appropriate practices, it is more desirable on the grounds of the meaningfulness criterion, for example, to provide instruction on explicit segmentation by embedding it in authentic tasks, such as when taking dictation for a class story or letter. However, supplemental practice materials often are needed, as well, especially for work with children in first grade when they have not had previous instruction on explicit segmentation. It is a balance between authentic tasks and skill practice a teacher must try to achieve.

The young child's knowledge of letter names typically provides sufficient letter-sound association information, because letter names contain a sound typically represented by the letter. Thus, young children often need less instruction on letter-sound associations. Instructional time might be spent more wisely on helping children learn to categorize words based on similar sound segments, and to explicitly segment words using authentic contexts where words must be spelled.

Tying Things Together

The purpose of this chapter is to illustrate the use of several criteria to judge the appropriateness of specific literacy practices. It is appropriate to teach young children about the alphabet, although teachers must be careful to use practices that are effective in achieving this goal. Even preschool-age children are capable of learning to recognize and name letters, of engaging in activities involving sound categorization (rhyme and alliteration), and of developing beginning levels of explicit segmentation ability. They can also begin to acquire considerable knowledge about how various lines are composed in drawing letters on paper, and they can develop beginning skill in creating letters themselves through active exploration (Scribbling during toddlerhood and the early preschool years provides children with the opportunity to learn the "relations between the finger movements that guide the tool and the resulting visual feedback," as noted by Eleanor Gibson in 1975.) Some kindergarten and first-grade teachers will feel considerable anxiety when faced with children who have not yet been exposed to these language experiences, and they may feel compelled to provide some explicit instruction on basic alphabet knowledge, while also engaging children in full-fledged reading and writing tasks. In some cases, teachers may feel such panic that they will simplify their programs by cutting out authentic experiences entirely. As developmentally appropriate practices indicate, this is not an especially good way to proceed. A more balanced program will serve children better in the long run because a range of knowledge and skills is needed for children to become competent readers and writers.

References

Ball, E.W., & Blachman, B.A. (1991). Does phoneme segmentation training in kindergarten make a difference in early word recognition and developmental spelling? *Reading Research Quarterly, 26,* 49–66.

Bradley, L., & Bryant, P.E. (1978). Difficulties in auditory organization as a possible cause of reading backwardness. *Nature, 271,* 746–747.

Bradley, L., & Bryant, P.E. (1983). Categorising sounds and learning to read—a causal connection. *Nature, 301,* 419–421.

Bredekamp, S. (1987). *Developmentally appropriate practice in early childhood programs serving children from birth through age 8.* Washington, DC: National Association for the Education of Young Children.

Cohen, L.B., & Strauss, M.S. (1979). Concept acquisition in the human infant. *Child Development, 50,* 419–424.

Cohen, L.B., & Younger, B.A. (1984). Infant perception of angular relations. *Infant Behavior and Development, 7,* 37–47.

Content, A., Kolinsky, R., Morais, J., & Bertelson, P. (1986). Phonetic segmentation in prereaders: Effect of corrective information. *Journal of Experimental Child Psychology, 42,* 49–72.

Eimas, P.D., & Quinn, P.C. (1994). Studies on the formation of perceptually based basic-level categories in young infants. *Child Development, 65,* 903–917.

Elkonin, E.G. (1973). Methods of teaching reading. In J. Downing (Ed.), *Comparative reading* (pp. 551–568). New York: Macmillan.

Fantz, R. (1963). Pattern vision in newborn infants. *Science, 140,* 296–297.

Fernandez-Fein, S., & Baker, L. (1995, March). *Knowledge and experience with rhyme and alliteration in preschoolers from different sociocultural backgrounds.* Paper presented at the Biennial Meeting of the Society for Research in Child Development, Indianapolis, IN.

Hart, B., & Risley, T.R. (1989). The longitudinal study of interactive systems. *Education and Treatment of Children, 12,* 347–358.

Gibson, E.J. (1975). Theory-based research on reading and its implications for instruction. In J.B. Carroll & J.S. Chall (Eds.), *Toward a literate society* (pp. 288–321). New York: McGraw-Hill.

Hoien, T., Lundberg, L., Stanovich, K.E., & Bjaalid, L. (1995). Components of phonological awareness. *Reading and Writing, 7,* 171–188.

Huttenlocher, J., Haight, W., Bryk, A., Seltzer, M., & Lyons, T. (1991). Early vocabulary growth: Relation to language input and gender. *Developmental Psychology, 27,* 236–248.

Nation, K., & Hulme, C. (1997). Phonemic segmentation, not onset-rime segmentation, predicts early reading and spelling skills. *Reading Research Quarterly, 32,* 154–167.

Oller, D.K., Eilers, R.E., Steffens, M.L., Lyunch, M.P., & Urbano, R. (1994). Speech-like vocalizations in infancy: An evaluation of potential risk factors. *Journal of Child Language, 21,* 33–58.

Read, C. (1975). *The categorization of speech sounds in English.* Urbana, IL: National Council of Teachers of English.

Rosner, J. (1974). Auditory analysis training with prereaders. *The Reading Teacher, 27,* 379–384.

Schickedanz, J. (1990). *Adam's righting revolutions*. Portsmouth, NH: Heinemann.

Schickedanz, J., Schickedanz, D., Forsyth, P., & Forsyth A.G. (1998). *Toward understanding children and adolescents*. Boston, MA: Allyn & Bacon.

Seymour, P.H.K., & Evans, H.M. (1994). Levels of phonological awareness and learning to read. *Reading and Writing, 6*, 221–250.

Whitehurst, G.J. (1995, March). *Levels of reading readiness and predictors of reading success among children from low-income families*. Paper presented at the Biennial Meeting of the Society for Research in Child Development, Indianapolis, IN.

CHAPTER 3

"I No EvrethENGe": What Skills Are Essential in Early Literacy?

Beth Roberts

In April of her kindergarten year, Molly was asked to fill out a self-evaluation form (see Figure 1). After giving herself A's in all subject and conduct areas, Molly wrote the following comment: *I No EvrethENGe. I do Not NEEd Iniethenge. I do Not NEEd Ineyh hep bot Nid IneyTheNge.* Her confident assertions are an accurate reflection of her status as a member of the early literacy community. Observations of Molly's engagement with literacy at home and school reveal that she is a reader, a writer, a speller, a storyteller.

Even as Molly has been acquiring the "EvrethENGe" that constitutes the knowledge she brings to her literacy experiences, the scholarly community continues to debate what this "EvrethENGe" is. We go back and forth between calls for an instructional context defined by relevance and meaning in children's early literacy experiences, and calls for the teaching of specific skills, somehow positing these as mutually exclusive positions. Sometimes we linger for awhile in the middle

Figure 1 Self-Evaluation

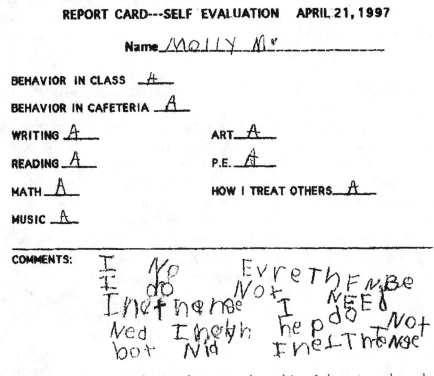

Translation: I know everything. I do not need anything. I do not need any help about anything.

of the instructional spectrum, pleading for balance. All the while, the Mollys of this world pull it all together in their own ways and become members of the community of literacy.

The purpose of this chapter is to describe what we have learned from *children* about the knowledge and skills critical to beginning reading. One point is critical: The learning of concepts and skills (indeed, of anything) takes place within a context, and is related to the development of each individual child (Neuman & Roskos, 1997). This particular chapter focuses on knowledge and skills; discussion of individual development and of context are found in other chapters in this book. In real life, child and context and skills and knowledge cannot be separated so neatly.

To illustrate the essential skills of beginning reading, I have chosen to use writing samples from a kindergartner whose literacy level illustrates the point at which knowledge has come together to facilitate beginning reading and writing. Application of Molly's skills in her writing is evidenced in the selected examples. Of course, Molly has followed a lengthy—in fact, lifelong—progression in acquiring knowledge of language to get to the point where she communicates her meaning so effectively in written form.

Molly's statement is but one brief example of the kind of written products often generated by children in kindergarten. In order to be able to write the piece in Figure 1, Molly has constructed a system of knowledge about language as a means of communication. She has knowledge of the forms and functions of spoken language, of written language, and of the conventions by which spoken language is represented in written form. Furthermore, she knows *that* she has this knowledge. She is *metacognitive* about her knowledge of language. She knows *what* she knows, and she knows *that* she knows it.

In this chapter I will describe the skills Molly has acquired using three categories of knowledge: (1) knowledge of spoken language (speech), (2) knowledge of written language (print), and (3) knowledge of the relation between spoken and written language (the speech/print match). Recognition that words in speech may be represented as individual units in print has been called a "watershed" event (Henderson, 1980, p. 9) in learning to read. Underlying the acquisition of this recognition are several strands of knowledge about the nature of spoken and written language. Following the discussion of development of this understanding, we will revisit Molly's kindergarten writing to see what is made possible by the complex literacy knowledge she has constructed.

Knowledge of Spoken Language

By the time most children enter kindergarten, they have excellent command of the intricacies of spoken language. They use a variety of sentence forms and have a vocabulary of about 5,000 words. Though humans have a genetic predisposition to learn language (Pinker, 1994), each child must individually reconstruct the spoken language system within the context of a language-filled environment. As young children play with spoken language almost from birth, they experiment with and gain control of the phonology, syntax, and semantic elements of their native language. This "play," however, is enormously significant, leading to what Bloomfield (1933) called the "greatest intellectual feat any one of us is ever required to perform" (p. 29), the individual reconstruction of the spoken language system.

Young children's explorations of language enable them to use sounds and words with great facility. Their early speech activities as they name objects lead them to be able to segment words in the stream of speech, despite the fact that spoken words have no audible spaces between them. Motivated by a desire to communicate meaning to others in their world, children begin very early to construct utterances that are effective in getting their needs met.

Children also demonstrate early use of syllable and sound knowledge as they play rhyming games with speech. Even children playing alone sometimes construct nonsense words by changing initial sounds to make rhymes, apparently for the pure pleasure of playing language games.

Using spoken language for specific purposes and being aware that language is composed of different linguistic elements, however, require two different levels of knowledge. Further, learning to read and write requires awareness of language units that goes beyond the awareness required to produce speech (Adams, 1990).

An important line of research has traced the development of children's awareness of the elements of spoken language (for example, Ehri, 1975; Ferreiro & Teberosky, 1982; Karpova, 1966). These studies illustrate the nature of children's evolving hypotheses about the relationship between spoken-language units and the real-world objects and events they represent. Initially, children expect a very concrete relationship between words and what they signify. *Tree*, for instance, might be given as an example of a big word, because trees are big. In children's early development, function words are not recognized as words at all. Over time, children's understanding of the word unit in spoken language becomes more abstract, and full awareness of the word unit seems to develop concurrently with learning to represent word units in writing (Roberts, 1992).

Specific awareness of the phonological elements of speech is critical to beginning literacy. In fact, phonemic awareness has been shown to be the strongest predictor of success in early reading (Adams, 1990). Specific awareness of the sound elements of language develops later than awareness of words as units of speech, and Morris (1992) posits that concept of word facilitates the development of phonemic segmentation in beginning reading.

Just as with concept of word, children develop an awareness of phonemic units of language gradually (Blachman, 1996). For many young children, some level of phonemic awareness develops through their natural and spontaneous use of language. Beyond their normal use of spoken language, children demonstrate a higher level of phonemic awareness as they initiate rhyming games and create nonsense words in their play.

It is when children begin to acquire some knowledge of the names of the letters of the alphabet that their phonemic awareness evolves to the point of being useful in learning to read. Though there is not a one-to-one correspondence between names of the letters of the alphabet and the sounds they make, there is enough similarity between names and sounds that children recognize the relationship, and a working hypothesis enables them to construct initial written representations of words. From then on, a mutually facilitative relationship between awareness of spoken and written language units develops.

Knowledge of Written Language

In many ways, children's discovery of the forms and functions of written language parallels the historical development of written language systems. Children's earliest explorations with writing seem random, as though they are simply making marks on a surface because they are able to do so. At a very young age, however, children begin to be able to distinguish between writing and drawing (Ferreiro & Teberosky, 1982), making circular, connected marks for pictures, and marks composed of lines for writing.

Understanding the abstract, symbolic nature of the writing system requires very sophisticated thinking. Letters stand for sounds that, when put together, represent words, and these words symbolize objects and ideas. Young children's understanding of the nature of written language is initially based on a concrete hypothesis—that written representations stand in a physical relationship to the objects they symbolize. Just as with speech, a child might believe that a large written representation is the name of a large object. The earliest written symbols created by the child may bear no resemblance to actual print, but instead may seem more like a pictorial representation of the object. Nonetheless, the child who creates such a product realizes that an object can, in fact, be symbolized in writing.

Because print is ubiquitous in our society, the scribblings of many very young children take on the characteristics of letters of the alphabet—marks that are separate, with a mixture of circular and linear strokes. Children try many variations on the 26 acceptable forms of the alphabet before settling on combinations of real letters that may be strung together randomly. At this point, the young writers probably still have no idea of the fact that letters stand for the sounds of spoken language. However, they often become very possessive of the letter found at the beginning of their own names, claiming that the letter is "me." They also may develop the hypothesis that letters or letter-like forms stand in a one-to-one relationship to the spoken words they represent, indicating change from their initial idea that written language bears a physical relationship to the signified object.

The child's first written representation of a word using only its beginning consonant is a dramatic moment in the evolution toward literacy. At this point, the child has a rudimentary understanding that letters stand for the sounds of language, though this understanding is probably based on the letter's name rather than its sound. In addition to basic phonemic awareness, this moment shows the child's concept that a word is represented by a single unit of some kind—in this case, a single letter. It is later, with more experience in early reading and writing, that children understand and use the conventions adopted in English to represent words in print, leaving blank spaces between them.

Children must learn the form and structure of printed text—that we read one page at a time, from top to bottom, from left to right. They also must develop the understanding that print is, in a sense, "frozen" and stable on the page, that the reader does not simply make it up as he or she goes along. For many children, this knowledge, too, seems to come about almost incidentally, as they are read to by readers in their preschool worlds (see Chapter 11 for further discussion on children's writing development).

Knowledge of the Speech and Print Match

Adams (1990) says that it is "from speech and through speech that [children] come to understand written language as well" (p. 221). Beyond developing separate understandings of speech and print, as children learn to talk and write they are moving toward an understanding that is critical to beginning literacy: that speech can be symbolized in print, and that there is a one-to-one correspondence between the word units of speech and word units in print.

For children to become successful readers, their early understanding of the nature of written language, as discussed in the previous section, must develop into awareness of the alphabetic principle that underlies English orthography: that the units of written language, letters, map onto units of sound, phonemes (Stanovich, 1992).

Though children begin to acquire literacy with their earliest exposures to written language, weaving together their knowledge of spoken and written language, it is understanding the relationship between speech and print as realized in the alphabetic principle that is the linchpin of "real" reading. Stanovich (1992) summarizes an important body of research when he says that the alphabetic principle must be acquired for children to be able to sound out unfamiliar words and move into fluent reading. When they have command of this understanding, built on their knowledge of the names of letters of the alphabet, young children are able to invent spellings for any words they want to write. This knowledge also facilitates their ability to "finger-point read" texts they have memorized, and to use some minimal cues to learn familiar sight words (Richgels, Poremba, & McGee, 1996).

Research in early literacy has clarified the essential nature of phonemic awareness, conscious attention to the sounds of language, in beginning reading (Adams, 1990; Blachman, 1996; Ehri, 1989). Tacit understanding of the alphabetic principle provides the springboard for developing awareness of how sounds are represented in writing. Children who begin school already knowing how written language works seem to make better use of phonics instruction (McGee & Purcell-Gates, 1997).

Summary of Essential Skills

Young children who live in a literate culture and are supported by a context that encourages the development of literacy often develop the set of skills and understandings that enables them to move smoothly into the community of people who share reading and writing as valued communication experiences, sometimes prior to formal reading instruction. Sophisticated knowledge of the symbolic nature of language and of the convention of representing sound elements of language in print is built on basic understandings of spoken and written language that develop as children interact with others who share their language.

To become readers and writers, children must know that words are the units of spoken language, and that meaningful speech is comprised of words strung together in an orderly way. This speech can be symbolized using the written form of word units. Written words are, of course, composed of letters that stand for sounds. Once children have acquired the names of letters of the alphabet, they are able to choose letter names that approximate the sounds they wish to write. This level of phonemic awareness is a necessary, but not sufficient, condition for decoding unfamiliar words (Blachman, 1996).

Many children have acquired these skills by the time they enter kindergarten because their previous experiences have encouraged literacy development. For other children, more direct instruction in the required skills of literacy is necessary, and well-designed school experiences provide this opportunity.

What We Learn From Molly

The "EvrethENGe" that Molly asserts that she knows in her self-evaluation is a complex body of knowledge about spoken and written language and the relationship between them. She is able to use this knowledge and awareness of the conventions of written language to encode her personal meaning into print.

Molly was a 6-year-old kindergartner when she produced the writing samples in Figures 1, 2, and 3. She is the youngest of five children and has always demonstrated a lively interest in and curiosity about books and stories. She has been read to extensively, most often by her grandfather who lives next door. She attended preschool for 2 years, but public kindergarten was her first 5-days-a-week school experience. Her kindergarten class was characterized by a holistic, literature-based language curriculum, with direct instruction of alphabetic letter names.

Children were given many opportunities to apply their alphabetic knowledge in writing through journals and learning centers, and invented spelling was encouraged in this classroom. Molly was one of the more advanced readers and writers in her kindergarten class, and she was well aware of this. She often watched other children in the class and helped them decide how to spell the words they wished to write.

Outside of school, Molly often chose writing as an activity. She has a small desk at home where she keeps her writing materials. She wrote notes to be mailed to friends and family, occasionally recorded her personal experiences in stories, and stapled together blank pieces of paper to create books, which she then filled with writing and accompanying illustrations (see Figure 2).

These brief samples of Molly's writing display the essential literacy skills she had acquired by the spring of her kindergarten year. An extensive piece, composed in school on a computer within a few days of her self-evaluation is presented in Figure 3.

Molly's writing clearly is built on her foundation knowledge of the form and functions of printed language to communicate intended meaning. The three pieces have three different purposes: self-assessment (Figure 1), telling a story (Figure 2), and reporting on a personal experience (Figure 3).

Concept of Word

All three pieces of writing show Molly's firm concept of word. Her awareness of the individual nature of spoken words is translated into her writing as she appropriately leaves blank spaces between word units. Her concept of word is consistent across the three samples, indicating that she has even acquired awareness of function words, such as *and*, *of*, and *the*, as separate units.

Concepts About Print

Molly's writing is in a form that experienced readers and writers take for granted, but, like other literacy concepts, concepts about print are not acquired all at once (Clay, 1975). The arrangement of her writing on the page, top-to-bottom, left-to-right, with blank spaces separating word units, has evolved from her experience with print in books and classroom examples. In Figure 2, she separates picture and caption and includes her byline as an author and illustrator.

Alphabetic Principle

The letters Molly has chosen demonstrate her awareness of the alphabetic principle—that the sounds of spoken language are sym-

Figure 2 Page From a Homemade Book

Translation: This is the trip to the bottom of the ocean
Submarine
by Molly M.
illustrated by Molly

Figure 3 Report of In-School Experience, Written on Computer

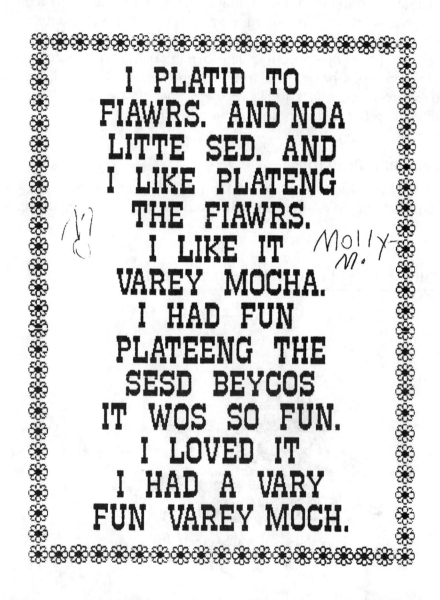

Translation: I planted two flowers. And one little seed. And I like planting flowers. I like it very much. I had fun planting the seeds because it was so fun. I loved it. I had a very fun very much.

bolized by letters in writing. Her writing includes a mixture of invented spellings and sight words that she already knows how to spell.

At the time these pieces were written, Molly's writing ability was
more advanced than her reading. She was able to invent a spelling
for any word she chose, but she read only familiar texts fluently. Her
skills at deciphering new words were limited. She did not apply the
same letter-by-letter strategy to sounding out words in reading that
she used in her invented spellings. The idea that learning to spell seems
to "lead" learning to read has been reported by other researchers
(Chomsky, 1971; Richgels, 1995).

Phonemic Awareness

The sophistication of Molly's invented spelling belies the complexity of her developing phonemic awareness. This awareness is acquired
gradually through experiences with spoken and written language
(Blachman, 1996). Several of the choices Molly has made to spell words
indicate her careful attention to, and in some cases exaggeration of,
the sounds of language. For example, in Figure 3, the first time she
spells *much*, she spells it *MOCHA*, because she says the *CH* sound so
carefully that she hears a vowel sound at the end: *CHA*. In Figure 2,
trip is spelled *chrip*, showing her careful attention to the affricative *TR*
sound at the beginning of the word, a pattern that has been documented in the writing of many young children (Read, 1975). In fact,
Molly asked her mother how to spell *trip*. When told the answer, Molly responded, "I didn't say *tuh-rip*. I said *trip* (with the affricative *TR*
emphasized)!" She then proceeded to write *chrip*, demonstrating that the
knowledge Molly has constructed for herself about the sounds of language is more powerful than the "right" answer offered by her mother.

Instructional Implications

Molly's reading and writing exemplify the best of what happens
when young children have extensive experience with literacy prior to
formal instruction in school. Much of what she has learned has been
experiential and was acquired almost incidentally. She has, as she asserts, mastered the "EvrethENGe" that is both necessary and sufficient

to ensure her status as a reader and writer. She has command of spoken language, understands the nature and conventions of written language, and has synthesized her knowledge of both forms of language to acquire the speech/print match and the alphabetic principle, leading to phonemic awareness. Her clever and creative writing and her confidence in her literacy abilities are the result of what she knows and is able to use. Looking at Molly's work illustrates for us what the "EvrethENGe" of early literacy skills includes. What can we learn from Molly that will help us work with children who do not have "EvrethENGe" they need by kindergarten?

One of the results of Adams's (1990) important book, *Beginning to Read: Thinking and Learning About Print*, has been a renewed call for phonics instruction for beginning readers. The importance of phonemic awareness to beginning reading is clear and is supported by a large body of research (for example, Blachman, 1996; Ehri, 1989; Juel, Griffith, & Gough, 1986; Stanovich, 1986). However, it is equally clear that phonemic awareness is not the only ingredient required for successful transition into reading, and that early literacy experiences in school must not emphasize phonics instruction to the exclusion of the larger literacy picture. In fact, Blachman (1996) emphasizes that phonemic awareness and letter knowledge are necessary but not sufficient conditions for children to learn to decode unfamiliar words.

As has been discussed in this chapter, phonemic awareness is built on understanding the nature of spoken and written language. McGee and Purcell-Gates (1997) note that the phonemic awareness demonstrated in invented spelling is "layered with many, many other kinds of knowledge" (p. 7). For children who come to kindergarten without these layers of knowledge about speech and print, how can instruction best support their development?

The research on this question does not point to a single answer. Some studies (for example, Adams, 1990; Bradley & Bryant, 1983; Stanovich, 1986; Treiman, 1992) have demonstrated that phonemic awareness training programs can be effective for some children. However, Purcell-Gates (1995) and others have shown that, for children who lack basic understanding of functions, forms, and characteristics of spoken and written language, phonemic awareness training is meaningless and is not applied to literacy tasks.

Neuman and Roskos (1997) state that children need literacy instruction that helps them build their conceptual and factual knowledge about the processes of reading and writing. They must see reading and writing used in meaningful ways and experience literacy in their learning environments. Many children, like Molly, acquire literacy knowledge easily and naturally under those conditions. However, all children do not. There are at least two groups of children whose needs must be addressed directly in beginning reading instruction: those who lack the necessary foundational knowledge of language systems, and those who have knowledge of and experience with written language, but have not acquired phonemic awareness.

The needs of the second group of children are perhaps more easily addressed than those of the first, because these children may respond well to direct instruction about the phonetic nature of words in our language (Blachman, 1996; Purcell-Gates & Dahl, 1991). Blachman (1996), however, cautions that, once children have acquired basic phonemic awareness, there is no evidence to support that contin-

ued phonemic training outside a meaningful literacy context is of any value. Many children may even become phonemically aware without direct instruction in an environment that supports exploration of print through focused activities (Richgels et al., 1996).

Teachers must play a key role for the first group of children, those who come to school without the underlying concepts about language that are the foundation for developing phonemic awareness. The necessity of finding out what the children know and building instruction appropriately on each child's knowledge cannot be overstated. This mandate to look at what each individual child knows about literacy makes our adult debates on the "one best way" to develop literacy in all children seem specious. Effective instruction in literacy is instruction that accommodates the child's needs and understandings.

Providing a classroom context that supports development of all beginning literacy knowledge is necessary to meet the needs of children who are at many levels of understanding. This challenge has been stated by Richgels et al. (1996): to teach the essential skills associated with phonemic awareness within a context of meaningful and functional reading and writing. However, there are some characteristics of the literacy environment that, we know, do nurture the development of literacy among young children. It is critical that young children view themselves as effective readers and writers (Dahl & Freppon, 1995), as Molly did. We choose to do things at which we feel competent and avoid those that underscore our weaknesses. Reading is an ability that improves with practice. An environment that provides opportunities to read and write for real reasons, communicating important meanings within a sharing community, supports developing literacy knowledge.

But wanting to read and write, even having real reasons to do so, may not be enough. For many children, direct instruction that focuses on the sound–symbol relationship of written language is necessary to facilitate their progress toward the level of phonemic awareness required for beginning reading. Unfortunately, the reading community has for too long posed the methodology question as an either/or dilemma. Children *either* are provided with real books in a meaningful context for literacy, which makes them *want* to read, *or* they receive skills instruction, which makes them *able* to read if they do not get turned off to the venture. Literacy, however, is too valuable a form of em-

In Practice

CREATING A SPIDER'S WEB

Play the Spider's Web game for practicing phonemic awareness activities. Have children sit in a circle. Say, "Tell me another word that begins the same as *spider*. Roll a big ball of yarn from one child to another as each responds. Gradually, as the ball of yarn is rolled from one child to another, a large spider's web will appear. To roll up the spider's web, simply focus on an ending sound. This activity will give children many opportunities to hear similar sounds again and again.

Of course, many other sound games can be played in the Spider's Web game. Teachers can focus on word families, like *-at* and *-un*, and can help children hear rhyming patterns, or blend beginning sounds with the word family *b-at*. Or a word pair segmentation game can be played. This game begins by reminding children that sometimes a new word can be created by taking away the first sound of a word, such as "if I take *b-* away from *bat* I get *at*." Then roll a ball of yarn to a child and ask, "What sound did I take away?" The child can catch the yarn and say, "b-at, b." If the child has difficulty, model the correct answer, and ask the child to repeat your response (it's important that children hear correct models—increasingly it will not be necessary as they get the hang of it).

Some word families to emphasize are the following:

at	ad
eat	ake
ay	in
and	ing
an	

A Spider's Web game, of course, should not end without a song or rhyme about a spider. Children just can't seem to resist, "I know an old lady who swallowed a fly," one more time. (See Adams et al. [1998] for additional language games.)

Adapted from Adams, M.J., Foorman, B.R., Lundberg, I., & Beeler, T. (1998). *Phonemic awareness in young children: A classroom curriculum*. Baltimore, MD: Paul H. Brookes.

powerment in our society to be so narrowly prescribed. It is clear that the process of constructing meaning in reading and writing requires certain skills and concepts, and as responsible educators it is up to us to make both conceptual knowledge and skills accessible to every child.

From the beginning of this chapter, Molly's knowledge of the spoken and written language systems and the relationship between them has informed our understanding of the components of her literacy attainment. All children can provide this knowledge, if teachers will only ask them. Many forms of assessment, both formal and informal, are available to determine what children know and to inform us as we plan instruction that is appropriate for them (see Chapter 12). I suggest that we ask children what they know. Observe them as they interact with print. Study their invented spelling carefully for insights into their level of phonemic awareness. Watch them as they talk with and play with other children. Listen to them. Find out how they use reading and writing outside the classroom. As literacy educators, we must be as clear about the "EvretENGe" that constitutes an individual child's body of literacy knowledge as Molly is about hers. We can then build instruction that builds on each child's literacy knowledge.

In collecting these data, we will get multiple answers to our questions about what children know and can do; a single instructional solution will not emerge. But from young readers and writers, we can learn EvretENGe we need to know to facilitate their transition into the literacy community. As a community of scholars, we have learned what we now know from children. They have a great deal more to teach us.

References

Adams, M.J. (1990). *Beginning to read: Thinking and learning about print.* Cambridge, MA: The Massachusetts Institute of Technology Press.

Blachman, B. (1996). Early intervention and phonological awareness: A cautionary tale. In B. Blachman (Ed.), *Foundations of reading acquisition and dyslexia: Implications for early intervention.* Mahwah, NJ: Erlbaum.

Bloomfield, L. (1933). *Language.* New York: Henry Holt.

Bradley, L., & Bryant. P. (1983). Categorizing sounds and learning to read: A causal connection. *Nature, 30,* 419–421.

Chomsky, C. (1971). Write first, read later. *Childhood Education, 47,* 296–299.

Clay, M. (1975). *What did I write?* Auckland, NZ: Heinemann.

Dahl, K., & Freppon, P. (1995). A comparison of innercity children's interpretations of reading and writing instruction in the early grades in skills-based and whole language classrooms. *Reading Research Quarterly, 30,* 50–74.

Ehri, L. (1975). Word consciousness in readers and prereaders. *Journal of Educational Psychology, 67,* 204–212.

Ehri, L. (1989). The development of spelling knowledge and its role in reading acquisition and reading disability. *Journal of Learning Disabilities, 22,* 356–365.

Ferreiro, E., & Teberosky, A. (1982). *Literacy before schooling.* Exeter, NH: Heinemann.

Henderson, E. (1980). Developmental concepts of word. In E. Henderson & J. Beers (Eds.), *Developmental and cognitive aspects of learning to spell.* Newark, DE: International Reading Association.

Juel, C., Griffith, P., & Gough, P. (1986). Acquisition of literacy: A longitudinal study of children in first and second grade. *Journal of Educational Psychology, 78,* 243–255.

Karpova, S. (1966). The preschooler's realization of the lexical structure of speech. In F. Smith & G. Miller (Eds.), *The genesis of language.* Cambridge, MA: The Massachusetts Institute of Technology Press.

McGee, L., & Purcell-Gates, V. (1997). So what's going on in research on emergent literacy? *Reading Research Quarterly, 32,* 310–218.

Morris, D. (1992). Concept of word: A pivotal understanding in the learning-to-read process. In S. Templeton & D. Bear (Eds.), *Development of orthographic knowledge and the foundations of literacy.* Hillsdale, NJ: Erlbaum.

Neuman, S., & Roskos, K. (1997). Literacy knowledge in practice: Contexts of participation for young writers and readers. *Reading Research Quarterly, 32,* 10–32.

Pinker, S. (1994). *The language instinct: How the mind creates language.* New York: William Morrow.

Purcell-Gates, V. (1995). *Other people's words: The cycle of low literacy.* Cambridge, MA: Harvard University Press.

Purcell-Gates, V., & Dahl, K. (1991). Low-SES children's success and failure at early literacy learning in a skills-based classroom. *Journal of Reading Behavior, 23,* 1–34.

Read, C. (1975). *Children's categorizations of speech sounds in English.* Urbana, IL: National Council of Teachers of English.

Richgels, D. (1995). Invented spelling ability and printed word learning in kindergarten. *Reading Research Quarterly, 30,* 96–109.

Richgels, D., Poremba, K., & McGee, L. (1996). Kindergartners talk about print: Phonemic awareness in meaningful contexts. *The Reading Teacher, 49,* 632–642.

Roberts, B. (1992). The evolution of the young child's concept of word as a unit of spoken and written language. *Reading Research Quarterly, 27,* 124–138.

Stanovich, K. (1986). Matthew effect in reading: Some consequences of individual differences in the acquisition of literacy. *Reading Research Quarterly, 21,* 360–406.

Stanovich, K. (1992). Speculations on the causes and consequences of individual differences in early reading acquisition. In P. Gough, L. Ehri, & R. Treiman (Eds.), *Reading acquisition.* Hillsdale, NJ: Erlbaum.

Treiman, R. (1992). *Beginning to spell.* New York: Oxford University Press.

CHAPTER 4

How Do We Teach Literacy to Children Who Are Learning English as a Second Language?

Diane Barone

I first started speaking English before I was in kindergarten. By the time I was in kindergarten, I could talk pretty good, good enough for a conversation. It wasn't hard to learn English because my family helped.

I first started writing English in kindergarten. But I could only write letters. I could make just a few words. In first grade, I learned to write sentences and words. In third grade, I learned to write cursive.

What teachers need to know is to not go very fast. My teachers, Mrs. Bray and Mrs. Schneider, are good. They let me read books again and they explained things carefully.

(Kevin, a fifth-grade bilingual student)

I asked Kevin to talk to me about how he learned to talk, read, and write in English when his first language was Spanish. This conversation helped in understanding the importance of learning to talk first and then learning to read and write in a second language. It was clear that writing was very important to Kevin as he learned English. His discussion of instruction was focused totally on writing from the representation of words to the form in which the words were written. He also suggested that teachers who work with students like him should go slow in their conversations and instruction. Perhaps, most important in this conversation was that Kevin's parents helped in the process of bridging his home language of Spanish with his school language of English.

Most of us now realize that students like Kevin are seen frequently in schools. As teachers consider their students, they typically see classrooms that are different from those they experienced in their childhood. Currently in U.S. statistics, one in every three children is from an ethnic or racial minority group. In addition, one in every seven children speaks a language other than English as his or her first language (Miramontes, Nadeau, & Commins, 1997). Clearly, schools will be working more with students from a variety of cultural, socioeconomic, and language backgrounds. Although the students' first language may vary, these students are coming to U.S. schools with the expectation that they will learn English as well as content knowledge. The increasing numbers of these students, who come from a wide variety of home situations that may vary in their support of English literacy learning, help us to understand why it is important to develop strategies to support these students as learners, especially literacy learners in the regular classroom.

In general, children who cannot claim English as their first language have difficulty achieving academic success in U.S. schools (Rossi & Stringfield, 1995). Some of the reasons for this difficulty include the complexities of learning in a second language (Banks & Banks, 1993; Miramontes & Commins, 1991), schools that do not support the home culture (Garcia & McLaughlin, 1995; Neuman & Roskos, 1994), and the low socioeconomic status of many of these families (Connell, 1994). These reasons are important to consider, especially because regular classroom teachers are usually responsible for the education of bilingual students, rather than teachers who are specifically prepared to provide instruction to these students through English as a second language or bilingual programs (Enright & McCloskey, 1985; Garcia,

Montes, Janisch, Bouchereau, & Consalvi, 1993). (See also Chapter 6 on providing culturally responsive literacy instruction.)

In recognition of the difficulties that these students and their class-room teachers often experience, bilingual classrooms generally are rec-ommended as the best learning context. In these classrooms, children can learn to read and write in their first language as they acquire knowledge of English (Crawford, 1989; Ramirez, Yuen, Ramey, & Pas-ta, 1991). In learning situations that include a child's first language as part of the curriculum, the child's home literacy experiences and fam-ily are supported as the child acquires proficiency with a new language (Delgado-Gaitan, 1992; Garcia & McLaughlin, 1995; Mehan, 1982).

Coming to Know a Student Who Is Learning English as a Second Language

Because bilingual classes are not always available to students, class-room teachers have had to develop contexts to support the learning needs of these students. The first area that usually is focused on is wel-coming the child to the classroom. Through this welcoming, the teacher tries to provide a comfortable and safe environment for the child as he or she also tries to determine the child's facility with Eng-lish and perhaps facility with his or her first language as well. In ad-dition to considering the child's abilities with English, it is important to discover if the child has just arrived in the United States. If the child is a recent immigrant, he or she will need to become familiar with the U.S. culture as it is represented in his or her new community, in addi-tion to the new language. For instance, children who have just ar-rived in a community may have recently had experiences with war in their home country (Igoa, 1995). Other children may come to school as the children of migrant workers who frequently move from one school to another. Exploring the family circumstances will help in un-derstanding the child. Additionally, it is important to know the cur-rent living conditions of the family. Often, new immigrants move in with friends or relatives and the housing situation is very crowded. Knowing about these circumstances helps a teacher understand why it is difficult for a child to complete homework assignments.

Exploring a Student's Language Ability

Learning About a Student's First Language

In addition to finding out about the child's home background, teachers discover if the child can read and write in his or her first language. Children who were literate in a first language bring this knowledge to the learning of a second language, and children who could not read or write in their first language need to learn about literacy as they learn a new language. Certainly, learning to read and write as you learn a new language creates a greater challenge. Success in a new classroom should come easier and more quickly for a child who is already literate in one language. A child who is unaware of the reading and writing process will take considerably longer to match this success.

Teachers discover a student's oral-communication ability by observing it on the playground and in small-group situations within the classroom. Wong–Fillmore (1982) observed that students in classrooms composed predominantly of English speakers acquire English faster than when they are in classrooms filled with children who speak the same first language. If students have peers who speak the same first language, the necessity of communicating in the new language is diminished. A tension is created as teachers try to balance the importance of students communicating in their first language as they also provide numerous opportunities for them to converse in their new language—English.

In the best of circumstances, a student will maintain a facility with a first language as he or she acquires a second language. Wong–Fillmore (1991) warns that students who lose their facility with their home language suffer a great disadvantage. These students will have impoverished conversation with their parents and this loss of communication could result in a lessened role for the family in the socialization of their child.

In addition to oral language, teachers explore the reading and writing capabilities of students in both their first language and English when possible. To determine the reading and writing capabilities of a student in his or her first language, a teacher may need to consult outside experts if he or she is not proficient in this language. Often this expert is an older student in the school who speaks the same first language as the student.

Learning About a Student's English Facility

For beginning readers and writers a teacher might learn about a student's reading and writing abilities through journals or book sharing. For example, a student might be asked to write in a journal so the teacher can observe the child's ability to represent words in English. To balance this informal assessment in writing, a teacher might ask this child to talk about a book that he or she has just read. If the child is able to do this easily, the teacher might ask the child to read the story or to read the words that are familiar. It is very important to move beyond word pronunciation to determine a second-language student's reading ability. Most stories that this student reads in school will be based on U.S. concepts and themes. Although a student may be able to pronounce words, this does not mean that he or she has the background experiences to understand a story.

Assessing writing is perhaps easier because students can be asked to write in a journal in either language that they prefer. Over time, a teacher can determine a student's ability to express himself or herself through writing in both languages. An example of this type of writing is shown in Figure 1. Samuel, a first-grade student, wrote about one of his friends having chicken pox. He has mixed both Spanish and English in his writing. From this example, his teacher would know that he is able to communicate easily through writing, that he represents ideas and words completely, and that he still mixes languages when he writes.

The Requirements of Learning a New Language

When thinking about the task of learning a new language, most teachers tend to value the learning of new vocabulary and the syntax or grammar as the most important aspects. Although vocabulary and grammar certainly are important, a language consists of more than these components. Language develops within a culture and provides the means to communicate values, thoughts, opinions, and attitudes. Each language contains nuances that allow for these sophisticated exchanges between individuals and they are often specific to a given language. Words, phrases, gestures, voice inflections, and other elements are often idiosyncratic to a language and provide important clues to

Figure 1 Samuel's Journal Entry

Samuel
(has)
Ranald tiene chicen
PoPs

meaning. Additionally, in order to be able to communicate competently with others, a person must possess the knowledge of the phonology, morphology, syntax, and the lexicon of a language.

Students who are learning English as a second language most often learn English expressions that are used on the playground or in other social situations first (Cummins, 1981). This learning of social language is not surprising as this language serves students' needs best. In addition to language used in social situations, children need to learn academic language. Miramontes and Commins (1991) indicate that academic language takes between 5 and 7 years to develop. Clearly, this is a long period of time that often is not recognized in school environments. Most schools tend to expect that students will become fluent in speaking and thinking in a new language within 1 or 2 years.

In actuality, the process of learning a second language moves through several phases that can be identified by teachers. Tough (1985) provides a guide for teachers to consider when they are working with children learning English as a second language. At first, children will need a period of time to become adjusted to and attuned to the school environment and the new language. Krashen (1982) identifies this time as the silent period in that children generally watch what is happening but are unwilling to talk. After the child begins to feel comfortable in the new school setting, he or she may begin to use English for self-help. Here a child asks for needed materials or starts calling students by name. Following this development, the child starts to use English to join into activities and to comment on what he or she is doing. The next step in learning English involves moving to more abstract thoughts about using English to find out about the world. Children form questions that they would like answered. In the final phase, English is used to extend learning; here the language needs are similar to the needs of children for whom English is their first language. For example, teachers may need to explain a complicated word or concept. Tough's framework provides guidance for teachers who are predominantly teaching in English, not the child's first language.

Most of this discussion has focused on the learning of English in its oral form. Children learning to read and write in a second language face additional challenges. These challenges have been detailed by Miramontes, Nadeau, and Commins (1997). The first of these is that they need to learn to manipulate the symbols of the new language. This involves learning to encode and decode these symbols and their combinations for understanding and expressing ideas in reading and writing. Second, students need to learn to transfer their ideas from one language to another. Here students are becoming facile with the phonetic, syntactic, and semantic systems of a new language. The third task involves the transfer of thinking and conceptualizing in a first language to a second language. This can only happen when a student acquires a large vocabulary and an understanding of the structure of a second language.

Beyond the complexity of learning a second language in general, it also is important to consider the age of the child when he or she arrives at a U.S. school. Collier (1987) examined the test scores of immigrants after they completed an English as a second language program at their school. Students who were between ages 8 and 11 took 4 years to reach the 50th percentile on national standard achievement tests. These students arrived at this performance level faster than immigrant students of other ages. For younger students, ages 5 to 7, it took 5 to 8 years to reach this testing criteria. The reason for this longer period of time was that the majority of the older students were successful literacy learners in their own country before coming to the United States, but younger students were less advanced academically in the country of their birth before coming to the United States. The students at the greatest risk for success in U.S. schools were the oldest students, those students who were age 12 or older. Few of these students ever moved beyond the 40% percentile on achievement tests even after 4 or 5 years of instruction. The oldest students faced the most difficult challenges in learning as they were expected to learn a new language and the sophisticated, abstract concepts that were the routine curriculum of middle school and high schools simultaneously (Miramontes et al., 1997).

By considering these multiple dimensions of language learning, it becomes apparent that children need to acquire more than English vocabulary. Learning a new language is a sophisticated, complex process that requires time and patience (Ovando, 1993).

Instruction for Students Whose First Language Is Not English

Instruction That Supports Both Languages

The following instructional strategies support a student's first language as he or she learns a second language. The goal is to let the student know that the home language is valued and seen to be as important as the learning of English (Cummins, 1986). Additionally, these suggestions offer an opportunity for a teacher to see a student who may not appear particularly proficient in English in a different learning context with different results. For example, when I was participating in a research study in a bilingual class, I was able to watch literacy teaching and learning in a variety of contexts (Barone, 1996). As I observed the teacher reading to her students in English, I noted that the children whose first language was Spanish moved to the back of the group and became very disinterested in the book-reading experience. Then later in the day, when she again read to her students I observed very different behaviors by the children who were learning English as a second language. This time, these students were next to her and they commented consistently about the book's events and characters, while the English-speaking children moved to the back of the group. What contributed to such different behaviors? Most likely, it was because the teacher read to the students in Spanish during the second-book reading event.

The result of these book-reading situations demonstrated that the teacher considered the children as very different learners depending on

the language used for instruction. These situations also highlight the importance of looking at what children can do rather than what they cannot do. Sometimes, when teachers work with students learning English as a second language, they begin to focus on what students cannot do. Miramontes and Commins (1991) suggest that when working with children learning English as a second language teachers should be "actively engaged in focusing on what students *can* rather than *can't* do" (p. 85). By using such a view, "children's existing strategies and knowledge are recognized and accepted, becoming the basis for extending learning" (p. 85).

Freeman and Freeman (1993) describe five strategies that support the first language of students in the regular classroom. Although these strategies support the first language of students, it is not necessary to be a speaker of each student's home language to include them. In some situations, another student or adult who is proficient in the student's first language is needed to provide an English translation. Additionally, these strategies allow the other students in the class to begin to appreciate the richness of language. They can compare languages, and language itself becomes an object of study. The strategies are as follows:

• *Include environmental print written in the student's first language in the classroom.*

Environmental print in the first language supports the student's first language and provides material that the student will read successfully. Support also is given for writing messages in the student's first language and posting them.

• *The school and classroom libraries must include books, magazines, and newspapers written in languages other than English.*

Students can use these materials for gathering information that can be used with the classroom theme, for instance. Students also can bring home these materials so that their parents can read to them.

• *Encourage bilingual students to publish books and share their stories in their home language.*

Although it may not be possible to read a story in a child's first language, older brothers or sisters, parents, friends, or others can provide a translation. When students are allowed to write in their first language in addition to English, they experience success and are willing to write more and to experiment with writing in English.

• *Have bilingual students read and write with aides, parents, or other students who speak their first language.*

It is important, especially for children who are beginning readers and writers, to hear stories read in their primary language. Hearing stories in all languages enriches the literacy experiences for all students.

• *Use videotapes produced professionally or by the students to support academic learning and self-esteem.*

Students can create videotapes that are in English and their primary language. The class serves as an audience for both and is enriched through both presentations.

Instruction That Supports the Learning of English

In addition to the support provided in a child's first language, classroom teachers simultaneously facilitate a student's learning of English. The majority of strategies that follow focus on students who are considered beginning readers and writers. These strategies are gleaned from a variety of experts. Although these strategies are recommended for students learning English as a second language, they also support the learning of all the students in a classroom.

• *Establish literacy routines.*

By establishing systematic routines in the classroom, children learn the ways they will be expected to interact with print and the student responsibilities tied to them. For example, if the school day begins with an exploration of the calendar, children will know where they are expected to sit, how they should respond, who will assume leadership (teacher or a student), and what the content of the discussion will be (Perez & Torres-Guzman, 1992). Other routines might include the organization for reading and writing workshop. If reading and writing workshops occur daily, students quickly begin to understand the expectations associated with these structures.

• *Provide time for children to talk.*

One of the best ways to facilitate a child's speaking and understanding of a new language is to provide numerous opportunities for children to talk. Some of these ongoing situations might be show and tell, peer response groups, or cooperative groupings of children (Lindfors,

In Practice

A PICTURE IS WORTH 1,000 WORDS

For most children in the early grades, but especially for those whose primary language is not English, a picture is often worth 1,000 words. Children have to see the picture before they can understand the meaning of the word.

Some teachers, like Ms. Rodriguez, take advantage of the way many children learn new words. She creates signs in her classroom environment by associating pictures with words. For example, the sign for the Cozy Corner Library includes a picture of someone reading next to the word *library*.

Ms. Rodriguez also makes language concrete for children through her language games. She pairs words with word pictures and finds many of her children constructing meaning for themselves through play. These abstract words are given meaning by pairing them with objects or drawn gestures to emphasize words in context.

She also sends a letter home to parents at the beginning of the school year, encouraging them to use the new "closed caption" option on their television set. All televisions purchased after 1995 have a chip that allows viewers to turn on captions. Though she reminds parents to carefully control the amount children view, watching television while reading the subtitles enables children to read while enjoying their favorite program. Also, research suggests that children learn by seeing the pictures with the print.

1989; Miramontes et al., 1997). (See Chapter 8 for further discussion on organizing the classroom for collaborative activities.)

• *Establish a daily storytime.*

All children benefit from a regularly scheduled time in which the teacher reads stories and other texts to students. For children learning English as a second language, this time provides them with the opportunity to become familiar with U.S. stories and concepts. Additionally, the child becomes familiar with vocabulary that occurs infrequently in oral conversation. Allen (1989) recommends that teachers first introduce concept books to children because the illustrations carefully guide the student to the meaning. After these books, predictable text is recommended which also facilitates a child's acquisition of meaning through repeated phrases and illustrations that closely match text.

• *Use language experience as a strategy.*

Language experience is a highly recommended strategy to use with students learning English as a second language. In using this strategy children communicate predominantly in English; this talk written down then serves as reading material. Also, if the language experience is created around the discussion of a real object, cooking experience, or science experiment, the children should offer many comments that are grounded in the current situation. Through this process, the child is able to connect the abstract words to the real event, thus facilitating understanding (Dixon & Nessel, 1983; Rigg, 1989).

An example of an early-in-the-year dictation is shown in Figure 2. The children were in a first-grade bilingual classroom; half the children had English as a first language and the others had Spanish as a first language. The teacher had the children bring a toy bear to school as part of her beginning unit on bears. The children spent about 15 minutes talking about the bears. This discussion occurred in both Spanish and English. Then the teacher asked the children to tell her specific things that she could write about the bears. Interestingly, the children contributed all their ideas for a dictation in English. The teacher then used this text for beginning reading activities during the week. The children read it each day and the class illustrated it, including illustrations for each sentence. They also tape-recorded their reading of the text. The teacher used the name of each child in beginning dictations to serve as a clue to help children find and read lines of text.

• *Provide opportunities for children to write.*

Children who are learning English as a second language need to be provided many opportunities to express themselves in writing. These children also should be encouraged to write in the language that is most comfortable for them. When they choose to write in English, the teacher should focus on the content of the message and look to any interesting errors as ways to observe and document a child's growth in the new language (Edelsky, 1986). Teachers should encourage journal writing, writing class books, dialogue journals, story writing, and report writing with these children.

Dialogue journals allow for an interactive discussion with a teacher about the content of a book, for instance. Through this type of journal a student is able to negotiate meaning through the responsive writing of the teacher. Over time, it has been observed that students write longer entries that have more conventional elements. The nonthreatening nature of the journal is seen as one of the reasons for this development (Flores & Garcia, 1984; Reyes, 1991; Staton, Shuy, Peyton, & Reed, 1988).

Hudelson (1984) states that students will use knowledge from their first language as they represent words in English. Students will use the pronunciation of a word to help with its spelling. If a child whose first language is Spanish tries to write the word *stop* in English, he or she may write *ESTOP*, basing this spelling on sounds and writing from Spanish. As a student develops in the reading and writing of English, the characteristics from the first language will dissipate and eventually disappear.

Figure 2 Language Experience With the Topic of Bears

Bears

Angela said, "Some bears are big and one is a girl."

Ronald said, "They are cool bears."

Guillermo said, "There are big ones."

Carlos said, "Bad bears."

Chris said, "Happy bears."

Figure 3 Steven's Response to *The Great Kapok Tree*

In Figures 3 and 4, two children in the bilingual class described earlier wrote about the story *The Great Kapok Tree* (Cherry, 1990). Steven
wrote in English: *Four porcupines talking to the boy*. Sammy chose to write
in his first language: Spanish. His teacher provided both an English

and a Spanish translation. He wrote, *I liked when he was cutting the tree and the animals began to say don't cut the tree*. These examples show that the students were able to write about this book, although each preferred to do so in a different language. In this case, this teacher was

Figure 4 Sammy's Response to *The Great Kapok Tree*

proficient in both languages, so she was easily able to decipher what both children wrote. For a teacher without this ability, a conference with an older student who is proficient in both languages would have helped to understand Sammy's writing.

• *Provide thematic instruction.*

One of the biggest challenges for these children is to acquire content knowledge as they are learning English. Often, a concept is shared with a child once and it is then assumed the concept is understood and remembered. For children learning English as a second language, being able to reenter a discussion about a topic or theme allows for a gradual and more permanent understanding of the concept (Perez & Torres-Guzman, 1992). Through the use of themes, students can focus on a central question and locate information in a variety of materials, from books to videos. As they are engaged in this search for meaningful answers to the central question, essential vocabulary is gained (Freeman & Freeman, 1994).

Closing Thoughts

This chapter has focused on ways to support students learning English as a second language within a classroom. Most of the strategies suggested are familiar to classroom teachers, but what is new is the focus on the needs of second-language learners as these strategies are implemented.

What is missing from this discussion is a broader view of the lives of many of the children who are learning English as a second language. In addition to the demands of learning to speak, read, and write in a second language, many of these children also are living in conditions of poverty. Although there are many myths about poor families and their uses of literacy and support of their children in school, there is evidence that counters these beliefs. For example, Taylor and Dorsey-Gaines (1988) found that families living at the poverty level engaged in a variety of literacy events. These families were surrounded with print, although the print rarely contained books for children. The majority of these families value literacy as they see it as the key for their children to be successful and upwardly mobile (Chall & Snow, 1982; Delgado-Gaitan, 1987; Goldenberg, 1984). For some families, their child's ability to get ahead was the primary motive for them to leave their home country and come to the United States. This research highlights the importance of understanding both the literacy events that occur in the home and the beliefs held by the families with respect to the education of their children.

Dyson (1993) shares her observations on this topic in a study she conducted in a primary classroom in an urban setting. She discovered that the children were most successful when the teacher allowed for a permeable curriculum: a curriculum that permitted the home culture to enter the school and the school culture to enter the home. She describes this curriculum as "fluid and fuzzy" (p. 14) in that the child's social world and language are interconnected in school and home or neighborhood events.

Perhaps the most important thing for a teacher to do to support second language learners in his or her classroom is to create an environment that supports all learners: students, families, and teachers. Through such a learning community, all students are thought of as important and their conversations, no matter what language, are seen as critical to the learning process.

References

Allen, V. (1989). Literature as a support to language acquisition. In P. Rigg & V. Allen (Eds.), *When they don't all speak English: Integrating the ESL student into the regular classroom* (pp. 55–64). Urbana, IL: National Council of Teachers of English.

Banks, J., & Banks, C. (1993). *Multicultural education: Issues and perspectives* (2nd ed.). Boston, MA: Allyn & Bacon.

Barone, D. (1996). Whose language?: Learning from bilingual learners in a developmental first-grade classroom. In D. Leu, C. Kinzer, & K. Hinchman (Eds.), *Literacies for the 21st century: Research and practice* (The Forty-fifth Yearbook of the National Reading Conference, pp. 170–182). Chicago, IL: National Reading Conference.

Chall, J., & Snow, C. (1982). *Families and literacy: The contributions of out of school experiences to children's acquisition of literacy*. A final report to the National Institute of Education, Washington, DC.

Collier, V. (1987, April). Age and rate of acquisition of cognitive-academic second language proficiency. Paper presented at the annual meeting of the American Educational Research Association, Washington, DC.

Connell, R.W. (1994). Poverty and education. *Harvard Educational Review, 64,* 125–149.

Crawford, J. (1989). *Bilingual education: History, politics, theory, and practice*. Trenton, NJ: Crane.

Cummins, J. (1981). The role of primary language development in promoting educational success for language minority students. In J. Cummins (Ed.), *Schooling and language minority students: A theoretical framework*. Los Angeles, CA: Evaluation, Dissemination, and Assessment Center of California State University, Los Angeles.

Cummins, J. (1986). Empowering minority students: A framework for intervention. *Harvard Educational Review, 56*, 18–36.

Delgado-Gaitan, C. (1987). Mexican adult literacy: New directions for immigrants. In S.R. Goldman & K. Trueba (Eds.), *Becoming literate in English as a second language* (pp. 9–32). Norwood, NJ: Ablex.

Delgado-Gaitan, C. (1992). School matters in the Mexican American home: Socializing children to education. *American Educational Research Journal, 29*, 495–513.

Dixon, C., & Nessel, D. (1983). *Language experience approach to reading and writing: Language-experience reading for second language learners*. Hayward, CA: The Alemany Press.

Dyson, A. (1993). *Social worlds of children learning to write in an urban primary school*. New York: Teachers College Press.

Edelsky, C. (1986). *Writing in a bilingual program: Habia una vez*. Norwood, NJ: Ablex.

Enright, D.S., & McCloskey, M. (1985). Yes talking!: Organizing the classroom for second language acquisition. *TESOL Quarterly, 19*, 431–453.

Flores, B., & Garcia, E. (1984). A collaborative learning and teaching experience using journal writing. *National Association for Bilingual Education Journal, 7*, 67–83.

Freeman, D., & Freeman, Y. (1993). Strategies for promoting the primary languages of all students. *The Reading Teacher, 46*, 18–25.

Freeman, D., & Freeman, Y. (1994). *Between worlds: Access to second language acquisition*. Portsmouth, NH: Heinemann.

Garcia, E., & McLaughlin, B. (Eds.). (with Spodek, B., & Saracho, O.) (1995). *Meeting the challenge of linguistic and cultural diversity in early childhood education*. New York: Teachers College Press.

Garcia, G., Montes, J., Janisch, C., Bouchereau, E., & Consalvi, J. (1993). Literacy needs of limited-English-proficient students: What information is available to mainstream teachers? In D. Leu & C. Kinzer (Eds.), *Examining central issues in literacy research, theory, and practice* (Forty-second Yearbook of the National Reading Conference, pp. 171–178). Chicago, IL: National Reading Conference.

Goldenberg, C.N. (1984, October). *Low-income parents' contributions to the reading achievement of their first-grade children*. Paper presented at the meeting of the Evaluation Network/Evaluation Research Society, San Francisco, CA.

Hudleson, S. (1984). "Kan yu ret an rayt en Ingles": Children become literate in English as a second language. *TESOL Quarterly, 18*, 221–237.

Igoa, C. (1995). *The inner world of the immigrant child*. New York: St. Martin's Press.

Krashen, S. (1982). *Principles and practice in second language acquisition*. New York: Pergamon Press.

Lindfors, J. (1989). The classroom: A good environment for language learning. In P. Rigg & V. Allen (Eds.), *When they don't all speak English: Integrating the ESL student into the regular classroom* (pp. 39–54). Urbana, IL: National Council of Teachers of English.

Mehan, H. (1982). The structure of classroom events and their consequences for student performance. In P. Gilmore & A.A. Glatthorn (Eds.), *Children in and out of school* (pp. 59–87). Washington, DC: Center for Applied Linguistics.

Miramontes, O., Nadeau, A., & Commins, N. (1997). *Restructuring schools for linguistic diversity: Linking decision making to effective programs*. New York: Teachers College Press.

Miramontes, O., & Commins, N. (1991). Redefining literacy and literacy contexts: Discovering a community of learners. In E. Hiebert (Ed.), *Literacy for a diverse society: Perspectives, practices, and policies* (pp. 75–90). New York: Teachers College Press.

Neuman, S., & Roskos, K. (1994). Bridging home and school with a culturally responsive approach. *Childhood Education, 70*, 210–214.

Ovando, C. (1993). Language diversity and education. In J. Banks & C. Banks (Eds.), *Multicultural education: Issues and perspectives* (pp. 215–236). Boston, MA: Allyn & Bacon.

Perez, B., & Torres-Guzman, M. (1992). *Learning in two worlds: An integrated Spanish/English biliteracy approach*. White Plains, NY: Longman.

Ramirez, J., Yuen, S., Ramey, D., & Pasta, D. (1991). *Final report: Longitudinal study of immersion strategy, early-exit and late-exit transitional bilingual education programs for language-minority children*. San Mateo, CA: Aguire International.

Reyes, M. de la Luz (1991). A process approach to literacy instruction for Spanish-speaking students: In search of a best fit. In E. Hiebert (Ed.), *Literacy for a diverse society: Perspectives, practices, and policies* (pp. 157–171). New York: Teachers College Press.

Rigg, P. (1989). Language experience approach: Reading naturally. In P. Rigg & V. Allen (Eds.), *When they don't all speak English: Integrating the ESL student into the regular classroom* (pp. 65–76). Urbana, IL: National Council of Teachers of English.

Rossi, R., & Stringfield, S. (1995). What we must do for students placed at risk. *Phi Delta Kappan, 77*, 73–76.

Staton, J., Shuy, R., Peyton, J., & Reed, L. (1988). *Dialogue journal communications*. Norwood, NJ: Ablex.

Taylor, D., & Dorsey-Gaines, C. (1988). *Growing up literate: Learning from inner-city families*. Portsmouth, NH: Heinemann.

Tough, J. (1985). *Talk two: Children using English as a second language*. London: Onyx Press.

Wong-Fillmore, L. (1982). Instructional language as linguistic input: Second language learning in classrooms. In L.C. Wilkinson (Ed.), *Communicating in the classroom* (pp. 283–296). New York: Academic Press.

Wong-Filmore, L. (1991). Language and cultural issues in early education. In S.L. Kagan (Ed.), *The care and education of America's young children: Obstacles and opportunities: The Ninetieth Yearbook of the National Society for the Study of Education* (pp. 3–49). Chicago, IL: University of Chicago Press.

Children's Literature Reference

Cherry, L. (1990). *The great kapok tree.* New York: Harcourt.

CHAPTER 5

How Do We Provide Inclusive Early Literacy Instruction for Children With Disabilities?

David A. Koppenhaver, Stephanie A. Spadorcia, and Karen A. Erickson

The research, beliefs, and practices of early literacy have been extended more and more in their application to children with disabilities (Katims, 1991; Koppenhaver, Coleman, Kalman, & Yoder, 1991). This literacy education is increasingly becoming the responsibility of classroom teachers and reading specialists. Remarkable technological advances make this possible by enabling children with physical impairments to compose text through alternative means (for example, modified keyboards or eye-typing), children who cannot speak to communicate with devices equipped with synthetic or digitized speech, and children with spelling difficulties to compose text via picture-based keyboards or spelling-prediction software (Flippo, Inge, & Barcus, 1995). A push by major advocacy groups for inclusive education has been accompanied by a growing research base on the effectiveness of integrated classrooms on communication skill development and learning (Calculator & Jorgensen, 1994; Downing, 1996; Falvey, 1995).

That is not to suggest, however, that the needs of children with disabilities are met easily in the regular classroom; they are not. Children with disabilities force educators to reexamine our teaching philosophies: Do we really believe all children can learn, and, if not all children, then which children? These children demand that we analyze more carefully our instructional goals; why is it that we have been teaching them to name all the letters of the alphabet all these years? These children also require us to consider more thoroughly how accessible our instructional activities are in relation to our students' language and cultural backgrounds, cognitive and communicative abilities, physical and speech development, and world experiences.

We have asked ourselves these and other questions over the past 15 years as we have taught a wide variety of children to read and write. We have conducted classroom research exploring how other teachers address the needs of children with various needs and interests. We have interviewed related services personnel and parents about the support they provide for early literacy learning. We have looked closely at the incredible and often intimidating array of technologies available to support learning, communication, and independent activity in classrooms.

In this chapter, we will introduce two children who we and many other teachers have found especially difficult to teach. One is a first grader, Marc, who by third or fourth grade in many schools where we have worked, would receive a label of attention deficit hyperactivity disorder (ADHD) or learning disability (LD) and receive supplemental instruction in a resource room. In first grade, however, he simply is one of the many children that regular classroom teachers are trying to launch on a successful and motivating school career. The other child is a second grader, Sloan, who, except in a few school systems, is not considered a candidate for inclusive schooling because of the severity of his multiple disabilities and the complex array of technologies he requires for learning, communication, and mobility. Both these examples are composites of two types of children with disabilities. We will highlight the challenges they represent in inclusive classrooms across a single school year, the problem-solving processes involved in teaching students like them, and some of the strategies that have worked for teachers of many similarly challenging students.

The Beginning of School

The first days and weeks of school are filled with a mix of excitement and worry for students and teachers alike: How will I like my teacher? What will we learn about? What kind of students will I have this year? How will I meet all their needs? In this first section, we describe this "getting-acquainted" process for Marc, Sloan, and their teachers.

Marc

Before Marc ever entered a first-grade classroom, his teacher, Ms. Jeule, knew more about his prior school experiences than she knew about most of her other students. His kindergarten teacher had told her how active he was, seemingly always in the middle of everything. He wanted to be in every learning center, and he seemed unable to pick one and stay with it. He often would walk back and forth between two centers, never remaining in either for more than a few minutes. Given other choices, he seldom selected those requiring much time to complete, especially if they involved fine motor tasks such as writing or drawing. At the same time, he seemed as bright as any child in the class. He often remembered minor details like where the teacher had forgotten her planning book or who had been absent earlier in the week.

Ms. Jeule had organized and fine-tuned her instructional program carefully throughout her first 4 years in the classroom. Her students spent time each day in four core learning experiences—class meetings, small-group and independent reading, writers' workshop, and math and science centers—where they engaged in self-directed learning of concepts and processes that Ms. Jeule had introduced in earlier lessons.

After reading the reports from Marc's kindergarten teacher, Ms. Jeule worried about how he would manage to work within this framework. During the first month of school, her concerns were confirmed as all of Marc's past behaviors seemed to repeat themselves. Because virtually every one of her classroom activities had a fine motor component or focus, Marc's avoidance of fine motor tasks was especially noticeable. He appeared to be particularly frustrated by writers' workshop, in which his fine motor delays rendered his handwriting nearly illegible, and his undeveloped knowledge of letter–sound correspondences made it difficult for him to detect even a single sound in most of the words he wanted to write. For example, the children wrote first drafts in which they were directed to write the sounds that they heard in words they did not know how to spell. Marc wanted to write, *I went for ice cream last night*, and repeated the sentence aloud. For each word, he searched the entire alphabet for letters that he thought might appear in one of the words. By the end of this lesson and arduous strategy, Marc's paper read, *I C*. As this process repeated itself over days and weeks, Marc grew increasingly unwilling to write, to read his writing aloud, or to show it to other students during sharing time. Before the end of September, Marc regularly avoided writers' workshop altogether.

Marc appeared to be on task more regularly during silent reading time. However, he picked the same picture books with very little text in only a few topic areas including horses, outer space, and trucks. When questioned about his reading, he often would relate elaborate, highly descriptive narratives that resembled the books' illustrations, but seldom shared similarity to the actual text. When Ms. Jeule pressed him for text-based responses, he often became very angry and would refuse to participate further.

Small-group reading lessons were the most difficult for Marc. When Ms. Jeule brought small groups of students together to teach a minilesson or monitor their reading progress, Marc consistently stumbled when attempting new vocabulary. When asked what letters were contained in the word, he would say the alphabet aloud and yell out the letter he thought it might be. It usually took three or four attempts for each letter in the word. Other students would tell him the rest of the letters, and he grew more and more anxious. When asked which sounds matched the letters, he would blurt out the first sound that came to his mind. Marc's classmates grew impatient with him during these small-group minilessons. During the reading of the text itself, Marc was rarely able to read any of the words that his group had just learned. When it was his turn to read aloud, he often would guess at the words and refuse to sound out those he could not recognize. A peer would then read the unknown word for him.

By the end of September, Marc told his parents he disliked school, and Ms. Jeule could find little evidence of progress. Test results indicated that Marc did not qualify for exceptional children's services of any kind. The evaluator explained that Marc's IQ was 97, well within normal limits. Because he was only beginning first grade, his achievement had not fallen significantly behind his peers. The evaluator explained that Marc, like many other students, might qualify later for learning–disability services, but probably not until after third grade when the gap between his potential abilities and actual achievement had grown larger, and his achievement had fallen substantially behind his peers.

Sloan

Sloan's motorized wheelchair banged against the doorway as he made his way into his new classroom. Now in second grade, he would have a new teacher, a new team of therapists, and only a handful of classmates who had been in his first-grade class. The only familiar team member was the consultant special–education teacher. Just 5 months ago, Sloan had only gestures, facial expressions, and vocalizations to communicate his basic needs, fears, and joys. Now, because of the coordinated efforts of his parents and a former speech-language pathologist (SLP), he had a new communication device to serve as his voice. He could touch pictures on his device to produce messages preprogrammed by his mother and the SLP, but the physical impairments caused by his cerebral palsy made it difficult for Sloan to touch the picture he wanted, and it was difficult to predict and program all of the messages he might need or want to say. Sloan still lacked a way to say exactly what was on his mind. The instructional team hoped that despite the test scores indicating language abilities at the 2- to 3-year-old level and moderate mental retardation (IQ of 45), Sloan could learn to read and write well enough to meet his face-to-face communication needs.

The thud of Sloan's wheelchair startled his new teacher, Ms. Carroll, who was finishing last-minute plans at her desk. Sloan's special bus was delivering him to school 15 minutes early this week so that he could travel down uncrowded halls to his room. Starting the next week, a peer would meet him at the front door and they would navigate the halls together. Ms. Carroll introduced herself, "Hi, Sloan. I'm glad to see you again. Remember, we met last May?" Before Sloan could respond, 23 other children came through the door to start a new school year.

The other children searched the cubbies for the yellow school buses with their names written on them and then looked for the desks bearing their names. When all the children were seated, Ms. Carroll suddenly realized that Sloan was still waiting. She introduced Sloan to the rest of the children and showed him to his special table at the side of the room.

Ms. Carroll next carefully explained the class rules and the daily schedule to the class. She emphasized the overflowing baskets of books they would get to read this year and the new computer they would get to use in the writing center. While the children chattered excitedly about computers they had used before, Ms. Carroll worried about learning to operate it. Then she looked at Sloan's special desk with adjustable legs and a slanted top, the standing frame that filled his materials storage area, the class bathroom now crowded by his changing table, and the bolster chair that he would sit in during group time. A great deal of equipment had accompanied this one young boy.

Ms. Carroll passed out individual writing folders that already had several sheets in the back pocket and one stapled to the inside front cover. She talked about the importance and joys of writing and read a few of her favorite pieces from previous students. Sloan should have been able to participate in the planned brainstorming lesson, but would need help through a communication device to the computer. Ms. Cole, his personal assistant, would help Sloan with his equipment and transportation but also help each of the other students with their work.

Now 35 minutes into the school day, Sloan was about to be involved actively in the classroom activity for the first time. As Ms. Cole prepared the computer, she asked Sloan to drive his power wheelchair to where she was sitting. By the time Sloan arrived at the computer, the other children had already written down six possible writing topics: three things they liked and three they disliked. Ms. Cole turned off Sloan's chair and pushed it up to the computer cart. She plugged in the cable as the directions said and double clicked on the talking word-processor icon. Then she asked Sloan, "Can you tell me the name of one thing you like?" Sloan looked down at his device and touched the picture of a swimming pool. His device said, "I swam in my pool every day this summer. I liked it a lot." Simultaneously this message appeared on the computer screen, and each word was highlighted automatically and spoken aloud. Ms. Cole smiled and replied, "I like swimming also. Can you tell me one thing you dislike?" Sloan did not respond. Ms. Cole looked at the pictures on Sloan's device and asked, "Sloan, is there a message on your device that you could use to write about the thing that you don't like?" Ms. Cole made a mental note to tell the SLP and Sloan's mother that she needed more pictures and words for activities like this.

The other children had completed long lists of possible writing topics, and Sloan had one. But it was only the first day of school, the communication device had been connected successfully to the computer, and Sloan did participate in the lesson, if only in an abridged manner. As Ms. Carroll explained how to use the lists in the students'

daily writing, Sloan was trying to turn around in his chair to see the teacher. Ms. Cole made another mental note: "Turn the computer around so Sloan faces the instructor."

Thursday afternoon of that week, the instructional team met, including Ms. Carroll, Ms. Cole, the special-education consultant teacher, the SLP, the occupational therapist, the physical therapist, and Sloan's mother. Each week, they were scheduled to meet for 45 minutes to talk about instructional lessons and necessary modifications.

Ms. Carroll was the team leader. In meetings prior to the beginning of school, she had expressed concerns about her lack of training and experience with children with disabilities. She told the team that she would need help planning for the day-to-day activities and in evaluating whether or not she was meeting Sloan's needs. The related services personnel explained that they could help with Sloan's seating and positioning, assistive equipment needs, and communication device use in the classroom. The special-education consultant teacher shared a lesson planning sheet and explained that she could provide instructional assistance if Ms. Carroll would use the form as a guide in identifying the goals of activities, target vocabulary, and themes or lessons that were the focus each week. Ms. Carroll also learned that Sloan did not do the same thing as the other children or even produce the same products; he had to learn the same lesson content.

Ms. Carroll asked for clarification in how she might get started in using the planning sheets. The consultant began with self-selected silent reading, an activity that was repeated each day with a similar goal. The goals of the activity, building reading fluency and interest, could be entered permanently on the planning sheet along with the adaptations for Sloan: books on computer with speech feedback and highlighting that would allow Sloan to read independently once he was taught a few keyboard commands; easy books with repeated lines, predictable text, or short texts linked closely and clearly to the pictures; books on slides that Sloan could read independently using a switch to "turn" pages; and the opportunity and means for self-selection of the materials that he could access independently. As the meeting adjourned, Ms. Carroll left feeling overwhelmed by the extra work Sloan represented and frustrated by what she viewed as a less than successful first week.

Beginning the Year With a Student With Disabilities

It is often difficult initially to determine how children with disabilities are similar in their needs to other students in a mainstream class, particularly when many of their differences are so obvious or when we have not taught many students with disabilities. When beginning-of-the-year administrative tasks are piled on top of the growing challenges of ordinary classroom management, teachers may naturally be wary of including children with disabilities in their classrooms. We have found two general strategies useful in getting started with these students.

The first, and most important, strategy is that of focusing on instructional goals rather than activities. When we think about a child with severe physical disabilities participating in an activity like writing a 100-word narrative, it can be overwhelming, and the adaptations meaningless. For example, technology would allow a teacher to preprogram a single computer key to enter a 100-word narrative when it is touched, but what would the child learn or accomplish unless the goal is touching the key? When we consider that our instructional goal may be creative expression, sequential information presentation, or accurate description, it becomes possible to consider alternate routes to the same destination, and our adaptations are created with the idea of allowing the child to achieve the same learning outcomes as his or her peers. Schumm and her colleagues (Schumm, Vaughn, & Harris, 1997; Schumm, Vaughn, & Leavell, 1994) have described a more elaborate planning pyramid that teachers of adolescents with disabilities have found useful in this process. However, we find the basic planning sheet quicker and easier when teams are trying to work together to meet a child's communication needs or when an individual teacher is trying to plan a particular lesson.

Second, we have found it helpful to interpret either nonperformance or nonconventional behaviors as indicative that something is missing in the activity that would enable the child to be successful. For example, when a student like Marc moves quickly from one center to another and does not stay with any learning activity, we investigate the possibility that the activities are not organized clearly enough or structured sufficiently to enable him to work independently. We consider pairing him with a peer; reading the directions aloud to him;

or providing direct instruction in the requisite actions, thinking processes, or communicative behaviors. When a student like Sloan vocalizes unintelligibly or does not respond to a question, we examine the available vocabulary on his device, the complexity of the question, the length of time he is being given to respond, or the background knowledge required for successful response. We find that this hypothesis-testing approach leads us to a more constructive problem-solving process than the assumption that the students failed to perform because they are incapable.

Balancing Instruction and Inclusion

Inclusion begins after teachers gain familiarity with the abilities and differences of their students, center their instructional planning on learning goals, and adopt a hypothesis-testing framework for classroom problem solving. Successful classroom teaching becomes more regular, and the instructional program begins to address multiple needs simultaneously and more seamlessly.

Marc

Ms. Jeule found her balance of individual reading and writing opportunities and teacher-guided reading instruction a useful starting place for Marc to begin learning the necessary skills for reading and writing. She decided to take advantage of Marc's willingness to read independently and added more science-related magazines, picture books, and nonfiction texts to the classroom library. She also worked with Marc and his classmates to create easy-to-read books on topics Marc liked by writing short text to accompany magazine pictures.

Within Marc's small-group minilessons, she increased her emphasis on systematic word study because these students still needed to work on recognition and use of the letter–sound system in words. Word groups that shared similar onsets (for example, *cat, can,* or *car*) or rimes (for example, *cat, hat,* or *fat*) were presented each week. Many instructional lessons required the class to listen for the different sounds within these words and to push candy tokens forward for each sound they heard. Marc's group used the tokens to count crayons in the box, jars of paste on the shelf, and words in sentences they heard. They clapped the syllables in their names, listened to nursery rhymes, and made up their own silly rhymes. Eventually Marc began to demonstrate his awareness of syllabic and phonemic units within words. In his writing, he was using more and more letters to represent sounds, even if they were not always correct. The rest of small-group reading time was spent reading short selected texts that gave students the opportunity to practice reading those words that they had worked with. Ms. Jeule used many of the student- and teacher-made books and repeated line books she found in advisory lists (for example, Morrow, 1989, pp. 209–224). When students read aloud, Ms. Jeule initially had allowed other students to chime in and correct one another when a word was missed or read incorrectly. However, Marc and some of the other students became overreliant on classmates to assist when coming across unknown words. Recognizing this pattern, Ms. Jeule taught the students to think metacognitively about decoding unfamiliar words. She guided them to create strategies to employ for this purpose: looking at the letters of the words, reading to the end of the sentence, thinking of similarly spelled words and their pronunciation, sounding out the word until a reasonable attempt was achieved, and then checking for meaning within the sentence. The strategies were put on small index cards and laminated for each student to use as a bookmark. At first, Ms. Jeule had to remind the students of the list of strategies often, but eventually all of the students learned to assist one another by using the list independently as needed.

The entire class met each week to have the word groups introduced. Words were placed alphabetically on the wall for all students to see (Cunningham, 1991). Ms. Jeule would spend a short time each day in a word-review activity. For example, the class would sort a group of words according to a spelling pattern, vowel sound, or semantic feature. In previous years, Ms. Jeule had been able to conduct these activities with little preparation. However, this year she found that Marc often was anxious to answer a question and would blurt out an incorrect response immediately, even if it was something that he had worked on recently and begun to master. As his incorrect responses mounted, Marc began to refuse to answer questions. Ms. Jeule decided to tell Marc during small-group time which word he would be asked about later. This helped Marc to focus on this word, consider his response, and respond correctly in the whole-class activity. Ms. Jeule also began to use review activities that required students to be actively engaged in writing the words, rearranging individual letter cards to spell the words, and correct their own mistakes in each word. Marc was better able to remain on task, respond correctly, and learn from his mistakes in these activities.

A word-study center was set up where students played word games with the weekly lists. Mystery Word Match (Cunningham, 1991) required Marc and a partner to use shorter lists of words to guess each other's two- or three-syllable word. Ms. Jeule had provided them with sample sentences on index cards. Each sentence had a blank for the mystery word, which was written on the back of the card. Ms. Jeule created activity folders for the different ability levels within her class, and students worked within their assigned activity set. Some of the games created for Marc's use included listening to an audiotape of instructions and prompts to successfully complete particular word games. These taped instructions kept him from leaving immediately for another station, and the novelty of the tape recording captured his interest. Questions and prompts from the small-group instruction were recorded on the tape to help Marc work independently with these types of problems and gradually internalize the problem-solving strategies.

Writers' workshop activities were modified to help Marc with three particular problem areas: letter formation, spelling, and getting his thoughts on paper. Marc had good oral-language skills, and the actual composition process was not the main area of concern, but rather his handwriting and spelling difficulties. Magnetic letters and words were made available to create sentences when the focus was getting his ideas on paper. Ms. Jeule found that the magnetic poetry kit provided words, word endings, and phrases that Marc used easily for this purpose. At other times Marc was allowed to use a tape recorder to dictate his composition. In both cases, Ms. Jeule then would assist in transferring his composition to paper. All the students were responsible only for correctly spelling those words that the class had placed on the word wall. All other words within his compositions were sounded out and a best attempt was made to record as many sounds as were in the word.

In Practice

STORYBOOK PARTNERSHIPS

Children with disabilities need to be and feel like vital members of the class-room community. There is no better way to do this than to form partnerships with other children in the classroom.

Ms. Jacobs regularly schedules 15 minutes each day in her kindergarten class for recreational reading time. Though many children are just beginning to read, she tries to pair those who may just be learning about concepts of print with those who are already reading independently. Each pair becomes partners for the next 2 weeks.

During the 15-minute period, one of the partners will become the designated "reader" and will read the book to his or her partner, and then the other will take a turn (Ms. Jacob found that letting the children take turns reading the whole book to each other enhanced children's comprehension more than letting each child read a page). Though many of her children are "preconventional read-ers," they are encouraged to read as if their teacher might be reading them a sto-ry. Rather than ask for assistance from the teacher, children are invited to invent or get help from their partner in recognizing new words, encouraging children's independence and camaraderie with others. This is a time for friends to infor-mally read a self-selected book together and to help one another in the process.

After recreational reading, the children come together in a group and share their favorite stories. It is also a time when all children, regardless of their dis-abilities, can join in experiencing the joys of literacy.

From Neuman, S.B., & Soundy, C. (1991). The effects of "storybook partner-ships" on young children's conceptions of stories. In J. Zutell & S. McCormick (Eds.), *Learner factors/teacher factors: Issues in literacy research and instruction* (pp. 141–148). Chicago, IL: National Reading Conference.

Computers were available in the classroom for Marc during other times when getting ideas on paper was the central goal. The media librarian helped Ms. Jeule to find the Write Out:Loud talking word-processing program and Co:Writer word-prediction software. Write Out:Loud increased Marc's awareness of what he was writing by reading it back aloud to him. Co:Writer reduced his word-finding difficulties by providing him with word choices based on the first letter of each word he typed and its location in the sentence. Finally, the librarian explained that a sans-serif word-processing type font (for example, AvantGarde) might benefit Marc's reading and writing. She explained that many students found the "ball-and-stick" letters easier to identify because they were similar to the manuscript printing they wrote.

Another center was set up to help Marc and other students work on the manual issues of writing. Tracing paper, sandpaper, changing color markers, and other tools were available for Marc to work with on the manual creation of letters.

Sloan

In just 8 weeks, Ms. Carroll and her students had adopted many management routines that made Sloan's inclusion easier. A student met him at the door each morning and helped him through the crowded hallway to the classroom. Then the child helped Sloan out of his coat, emptied his backpack, and retrieved notes from home, lunch money, and homework. Sloan kept everything on his wheelchair tray and drove around the room, stopping first at the blackboard where he responded to his friend's yes or no question to order lunch. Next he stopped at the homework basket where his friend deposited his homework, and then he stopped by Ms. Carroll's desk to deliver the notebook that went back and forth between home and school each day so that the adults in each environment could hear the important news that Sloan's developing communication skills prevented him from conveying fully.

His tray now empty, Sloan made his way to his own table that was now placed in a cluster with four other children's desks. Classmates were already busy negotiating the morning sign-in sheet that awaited them. This morning it read, *Please sign in and tell me what you think is going to happen in the last chapter of* Stone Fox (Gardiner, 1983). While the sheet was circulated, Sloan looked through the pages of pictures on his communication device until he reached a page with the letters of his name. The letters, arranged in alphabetical order, were all lower case, and Sloan was learning to touch the shift button before selecting the first letter. Ms. Cole noted as she wrote, "Not perfect, but we're getting there."

The conversation at the table now had turned to the question about the story. The children were arguing about whether the boy in the story would win. Sloan did not typically participate in these conversations because his communication system still lacked sufficient vocabulary, but today he had an opinion. He was vocalizing and making unintelligible sounds that his peers could do little more than acknowledge. With Ms. Cole busy and Ms. Carroll helping another group settle a dispute, Sloan was on his own. While his group continued their discussion, he navigated through his communication device to the page with categories listed. The SLP had been helping him learn to categorize information during the social-studies lessons. During these lessons, the SLP also showed him the other categories that were on the page and modeled their use. The SLP even had other children who were working in Sloan's group use the device to choose topics of conversation from the categories of information they were learning. For example, the children selected *person* or *place* using the device and then added something like *food* to initiate a new conversation.

This morning Sloan reached the category page and selected *person*. When the device showed him pictures of specific examples within that category, Sloan selected *boy*. The children in his group stopped talking and asked, "What did you say?" He hit the picture again, and the device repeated, "Boy." One peer said, "What about the boy? Do you think he wins the race?" Sloan responded with a wide smile and eyes pointed upward, his gesture for "yes." Another peer said, "We all agree," and wrote the group's prediction on the sign-in sheet. Sloan and his classmates had learned to communicate and listen to one another.

Later, when the children were getting ready for writing workshop, Ms. Cole reminded Sloan to drive to his computer. A classmate followed him, plugged his communication device into the computer, and double clicked on the talking word-processing program to get it started. Whenever Sloan was asked to compose text, he selected what appeared to be unrelated words in random order. The team had decided that part of the problem was that Sloan had significant syntax problems and limited experience linking related thoughts and ideas. They wanted to provide him with models without encouraging him to copy others' words and sentences. Consequently, they established the routine that Ms. Cole continued to follow by asking Sloan to pick a writing topic. Sloan selected a message from his communication device (for example, "Let's go to the mall. I like hanging out at the pet store."). Ms. Cole then wrote a few short sentences on a related topic, reading her text aloud as she wrote to indicate what she was thinking and the processes she was using in writing. After she finished, she read it all again, put it away, and said, "Okay Sloan, now it's your turn to write." Sloan then composed by using a combination of invented spelling from his alphabet page and whole words and phrases selected from the categories page and other pages like it. He wrote: *Let's go the mall. I like hanging out at the pet store. I lk dog. I hf cat.*

By this third month of school, Sloan was beginning to link thoughts and ideas in simple sentences. He was beginning to demonstrate some knowledge of letter–sound correspondence through his selection of initial letters in his invented spelling, and he was learning about the process of combining all the communication techniques available to him to construct messages.

Balancing Instruction and Including Children With Disabilities

One of the central challenges in the inclusive classroom is meeting the needs of the individual child with disabilities while addressing overall instructional goals and not detracting from the education of the other students. One critical component that often is overlooked or underused is home-school communication. Parents know their child far better than teachers can hope to in the course of a single school year. They can save teachers time in searching for solutions by interpreting a child's nonperformance or nonconventional response. They can provide insight into the child's interests or problem-solving strategies that have led to success or failure at home or in the community. Most important, they can support our classroom program at home if they understand the goals we are attempting to address and their application in the child's life now and in the future. We have met few children with severe learning difficulties who thrive on a school-only program. The successful nonspeaking children we have met have communication devices programmed both at school and at home. (See Chapter 7 for further discussion on fostering children's early literacy development through parent involvement.)

Another powerful yet overlooked or underused resource is the collective energy of other students in the class and school. Classrooms are complex environments. Teachers and their assistants occasionally miss school days. An individual may forget to turn on the computer in the morning. A child's needs can remain unmet if a teacher is attending to another activity. Learning is far more likely to proceed unimpeded in classrooms where 23 students know the routines for starting the computer, connecting the communication device, interpreting nonconventional behaviors, and turning in homework. All these types of management routines require initial investments in training but pay dividends in fewer interruptions, unimpeded learning, and greater teacher comfort over the school year. Likewise classmates provide powerful and diverse models when they use a child's communication device to ask a question or answer the teacher, or when they complete a collaborative writing assignment with a child with disabilities who uses spelling-prediction software or a talking word processor.

End of the Year

One other strategy that we have found particularly important to successful inclusive instruction of children with disabilities is a tolerance for difference. This is much easier said than done. We expect quick responses to what we think are routine questions in the classroom. We interpret physical behaviors as clear and accurate representations of cognitive capability. We interpret democracy as meaning the same rules apply identically to the all students. We view those who are different as "less fortunate." None of these beliefs, nor the behaviors that accompany them, are useful in teaching, supporting independence, fostering communication, or creating classrooms where all students can learn. For example, in late May, Ms. Jeule met with

Marc's parents to review the school year and consider recommendations for him in the following year. The many words posted on the wall represented the most immediate and obvious evidence of Marc's success. Although he still required many verbal hints for the irregular words, he had mastered many basic decoding rules. More important, he was applying these rules as an independent reader. Although his parents were concerned by the often illegible handwriting he produced, Ms. Jeule shared writing samples clearly illustrating the progress he had made in letter formation. More important, Ms. Jeule explained to Marc's parents how his difficulties and strategies had helped her to reexamine her instructional goals for all her students. She now carefully considered writing-activity preparation and set-up, the availability of a wide range of writing tools, and project evaluation in relation to the specific goals, set-up, and available tools. She planned to incorporate these ideas into her classroom the next school year, even if she did not have a student like Marc.

On the last day of the school year, Sloan's group gathered around the computer to respond to the morning sign-in question, *What was your favorite thing about second grade?* Each child typed his or her name with the standard computer keyboard and then typed a response to the question. When it was Sloan's turn, he already had the alphabet page displayed on his communication device. He touched the shift key and typed *S-l-o-a-n*. He selected the screen about feelings and touched the picture, *I like*, and then selected the school subjects page and touched *reading* and then *writing*. The children in his group looked at one another with surprise, recognizing that Sloan had just responded without a model or anyone's help. In unison, the peer group called for the teacher. Ms. Carroll looked at the computer screen, and she remembered how fearful she had been at the beginning of the year that she would not be able to meet Sloan's needs. She recalled her mixed emotions about the computer, and she remembered how she had excluded Sloan that first morning as she anxiously awaited Ms. Cole's arrival. She recollected her struggles with the teacher consultant to find a mutually understood way to communicate goals, adaptations, and plans. She contemplated how very different she had thought Sloan was from the rest of the children. But now she felt a sense of accomplishment as she stared at the computer screen bearing the clear message, *Sloan I like reading writing.*

The Importance of Inclusive Literacy Instruction for Children With Disabilities

Recently a colleague asked, "Wouldn't it be nice if we stopped talking about special education and regular education and instead talked about education?" We agree. School is not defined in any dictionary as a place for the instruction of only children who have average intelligence, who can walk, who can speak English, and who are perfect models of classroom behavior.

The importance of inclusive instruction for children with disabilities is that they receive instruction from the school personnel who have the greatest knowledge of literacy theory and practice, the most training, and the greatest print-specific resources. They are surrounded by models of varied print use, purposeful reading and writing, frequent peer interaction and support, and the expectation that children can, should, and will learn to read and write. They also are surrounded by the children who are and will be their neighbors, colleagues, clients, friends, and peers throughout school and life.

The importance of inclusive instruction to nondisabled children is that they experience a more accurate representation of the diversity of daily life. They learn new ways of communicating. They see and use a wider variety of assistive and instructional technology. They gain a greater appreciation of the often camouflaged capabilities underlying some children's more obvious disabilities and differences. They have many and varied opportunities to practice behaviors that are respectful and considerate of human differences.

The importance of inclusive instruction for early literacy educators is that children with disabilities provide us with a window on the effectiveness of the rest of our instructional program (Erickson, 1995). They show us the limitations of our instructional methods and materials. They remind us to stay focused on the goals and not the activities of daily instruction. They clarify for us that teaching is not teaching unless children are learning. They force us to think about the kinds of scaffolding that all children require in order to generalize skills. Ultimately they make us better teachers, and that benefits everyone.

References

Calculator, S.N., & Jorgensen, C.M. (Eds.). (1994). *Including students with severe disabilities in schools: Fostering communication, interaction, and participation.* San Diego, CA: Singular.

Cunningham, P.M. (1991). *Phonics they use: Words for reading and writing.* New York: HarperCollins.

Downing, J.E. (1996). *Including students with severe and multiple disabilities in typical classrooms: Practical strategies for teachers.* Baltimore, MD: Paul H. Brookes.

Erickson, K.A. (1995). *Literacy and inclusion for a student with severe speech and physical impairments.* Unpublished doctoral dissertation, University of North Carolina, Chapel Hill.

Falvey, M.A. (Ed.). (1995). *Inclusive and heterogeneous schooling: Assessment, curriculum, and instruction.* Baltimore, MD: Paul H. Brookes.

Flippo, K.F., Inge, K.J., & Barcus, J.M. (Eds.). (1995). *Assistive technology: A resource for school, work, and community.* Baltimore, MD: Paul H. Brookes.

Katims, D. (1991). Emergent literacy in early childhood special education: Curriculum and instruction. *Topics in Early Childhood Special Education, 11,* 69–84.

Koppenhaver, D.A., Coleman, P.P., Kalman, S.L., & Yoder, D.E. (1991). The implications of emergent literacy research for children with developmental disabilities. *American Journal of Speech-Language Pathology, 1*(1), 38–44.

Morrow, L.M. (1989). *Literacy development in the early years: Helping children read and write.* Englewood Cliffs, NJ: Prentice Hall.

Schumm, J.S., Vaughn, S., & Harris, J. (1997). Pyramid power for collaborative planning. *Teaching Exceptional Children, 29*(6), 62–66.

Schumm, J.S., Vaughn, S., & Leavell, A.G. (1994). Planning pyramid: A framework for planning for diverse student needs during content area instruction. *The Reading Teacher, 47,* 608–615.

Children's Literature Reference

Gardiner, J.R. (1983). *Stone Fox.* New York: HarperCollins.

Additional Teacher Resources

Cunningham, P.M., & Allington, R.L. (1994). *Classrooms that work: They can all read and write.* New York: HarperCollins.

Don Johnston Developmental Equipment (1000 N. Rand Rd., Bldg. 115, Wauconda, IL 60084. Tel. 800-999-4660. Fax 708-526-4177. E-mail: djde@aol.com) manufactures software and hardware supporting learning and communication of children with disabilities including Co:Writer, Write:OutLoud, Ke:nx, and the Discover Switch.

Erickson, K.A., & Koppenhaver, D.A. (1995). Developing a literacy program for children with severe disabilities. *The Reading Teacher, 48,* 676–684.

Erickson, K.A., Koppenhaver, D.A., Yoder, D.E., & Nance, J. (1998). Integrated communication and literacy instruction for a child with multiple disabilities. *Focus on Autism and Other Developmental Disabilities, 12*(3).

IntelliTools (55 Leveroni Ct., #9, Novato, CA 94949. Tel. 800-899-6687. Fax 415-382-5950. E-mail: info@intellitools.com) manufactures software and hardware supporting communication and learning of children with disabilities, including Intellikeys, Intellitalk, and Intellipics.

The National Center to Improve Practice (55 Chapel St., Newton, MA 02158-1060. Tel. 617-969-7100. Fax 617-969-3440. E-mail: ncip@edc.org) conducts research and development in the education of children with disabilities, has a wide variety of print and multimedia materials for teachers and parents of children with disabilities, and maintains a Web site on literacy and children with disabilities (http://www.edc.org/FSC/NCIP/Tour/Intro.html).

Roller, C.M. (1996). *Variability not disability: Struggling readers in a workshop classroom.* Newark, DE: International Reading Association.

CHAPTER 6

How Can We Provide for Culturally Responsive Instruction in Literacy?

Patricia A. Edwards and Heather M. Pleasants

As educators think about what it means to be a culturally responsive literacy teacher in the schools of today, they often think back to the ways in which their own teachers or colleagues have addressed culture in their classrooms. Some of these teachers may have identified and used different manifestations of culture such as food, artwork, and dress in order to teach students about the various meaning of culture. Teachers remember themselves as students constructing Pilgrim hats and Indian headdresses out of construction paper at Thanksgiving. Some may even have memories of making a flag from another country, doing a report, and cooking a dish from that country and bringing it to class to help celebrate an "International Day."

In other classrooms, teachers may have addressed culture by adopting a "color-blind" attitude. When equipped with this attitude, teachers often say that they "don't see black or white" or that they "see only students" (Nieto, 1992, p. 109). This way of thinking about diverse students is based on the good intentions of teachers who want to provide classrooms that are fair and equitable by seeing everyone in their classroom simply as human beings.

Although these perspectives on culture's place in the classroom seemed adequate in the past, they are insufficient for today's students. As the children entering school are recognized as increasingly diverse, teachers have become more sophisticated in their understanding of culture and the meaning of culture in the classroom (Byrd, Lundenberg, Hoffland, Couillard, & Lee, 1996). Many teachers have acknowledged that culture is made up of much more than food, artwork, or ways of dressing ourselves. In fact, teachers understand, as Cushner, McClelland, and Safford (1996) do, that

> Culture can be likened to an iceberg—only 10 percent of the whole is seen above the surface of the water. It is the 90 percent of the iceberg that is hidden beneath the surface of the water that most concerns the ship's captain who must navigate the water. Like an iceberg, the most meaningful (and potentially dangerous) part of culture is the invisible or subjective part that is continually operating on the unconscious level to shape our perceptions and our responses to these perceptions. It is this aspect of culture that leads to the most intercultural misunderstandings. (p. 50)

Teachers also understand that adopting a color-blind attitude toward students is not the answer to becoming culturally responsive literacy teachers. Although being color blind toward students is one way of attempting to build a fair, impartial, and objective classroom environment, it can also lead to classrooms in which differences are seen as deficits. In attempting to see all students as the same, teachers can inadvertently treat students unfairly by "denying the differences in students that help make them who they are" (Nieto, 1992, p. 109).

An important theoretical perspective on addressing culture in the classroom has been outlined and developed by Giroux (1992), and is best captured by the idea that teachers function as "border crossers" in the classroom. This perspective encompasses the notions that students' and teachers' cultures play a critical role in the learning process, teachers are the bridge between the environment of the school and the other parts of children's worlds, and teachers should make every effort to include and integrate students' cultures into their teaching. In relation to literacy instruction, teachers who see themselves as border crossers integrate literature into their teaching that reflects a variety of cultural influences, and they attempt to understand and then build on the strengths of children that originate in varying cultural practices. Based on border-crossing teaching practices, theory, and research, it is our position that culturally responsive literacy instruction can first be defined through the ongoing collection, understanding, and utilization of information and skills that relate to the cultural diversity of students. This can then be used to provide students with the foundations necessary to entice and inspire them to become good readers and writers, and to empower them academically and socially. Further, culturally responsive teaching "is not color-bound or language-specific but subsumes all diversities to ensure sensitivity to and responsibility for all learners" (Huber, Kline, Bakken, & Clark, 1997). Culturally responsive teachers develop certain skills and actively seek out and use information and resources that will allow them to tap students' interests in reading and writing, thereby making reading and writing development relevant to students' academic and social lives. This kind of teaching is not achieved quickly or easily, but through conscious effort and dedication to understanding students and creating positive interactions with them.

What Do We Know About Culturally Responsive Teachers?

Our current understanding of what it means to be a culturally responsive teacher has been greatly informed by case studies of teachers who have perfected this approach toward the cultures of their students. Foster (1993), in her work on the culturally relevant practices of exemplary African American teachers, has identified some general patterns of interaction that characterize effective teaching practices. For example, she states that "excellent African American teachers embrace cultural patterns of collectivity, incorporating them into classroom activities" (p. 577). Further descriptions of what culturally responsive teachers do in their teaching practices have been prevalent

(Henry, 1994; Ladson–Billings, 1994); these practices have included the promotion of mutual respect, the construction of a culturally pluralistic classroom environment, an explicit concern and care expressed for students as individuals, and a promotion of critical reflection and thinking about life beyond the classroom (Byrd et al., 1996).

In conjunction with the existence of examples of teachers who are culturally responsive, research that has examined how culture influences interactions in the classroom has contributed to our definitions of culturally responsive teaching. Much of this research has given us specific ways that culture influences the interactions and communication between teachers and students. As might be expected, young children in particular are best taught to read in situations compatible with those of their home culture. Au and Mason (1983) for example, investigated this issue with students of Polynesian-Hawaiian ancestry. Teachers who insisted that Hawaiian children speak one at a time in answering their questions had great difficulty in conducting effective reading lessons. On the other hand, teachers who allowed the children to cooperate or speak together in answering questions were able to lead lessons that were more successful. In the research of Erickson and Mohatt (1982), it was found that teachers of Odawa Indian students were most effective when they avoided exercising direct social control over students. According to their findings, teachers were likely to have more difficulty if they gave students direct orders, singled them out in class, and waited for all students to do the same thing at the same time. In contrast, teachers were likely to have fewer difficulties if they gave directions in a less direct way, questioned children individually or in small groups, and allowed the students to shift from one activity to another in a gradual fashion.

Heath (1982) also provided evidence for the idea that culturally different children may not be familiar with classroom communication routines. She compared the use of questions in three settings: homes in Trackton, a working-class black community; homes of white teachers in a community close to Trackton; and the classrooms that included children from both communities. In the classrooms and teachers' homes, Heath found that teachers often asked questions for the purpose of training children. The children were expected to give answers already known by the adult. When the child was looking at a book, questions might include What's that? or Where's the puppy? In Trackton, on the other hand, children generally were not asked questions for which an adult already knew the answer. Rather, they were asked open-ended questions with answers unknown to the adult. Subsequently, until teachers began using both questioning styles, many children from Trackton were given negative evaluations by teachers.

In Practice

A PARENT BOOK CLUB

At McKinley School, parents regularly get together two mornings a week for an hour-long book club. Along with the librarian and a bilingual specialist, they read popular children's literature and talk about the texts. Because many of the parents are not fluent readers, the leaders try to include several different genres of children's text, such as predictable stories (with memorable lines), episodic predictable stories (with short episodes and a few predictable lines), and narrative stories. Coffee and doughnuts are always available for those parents who may not have had time for breakfast. After they read the story chorally (which is available in either Spanish or English), the leaders focus on three key questions:

■ What do you want your child to take away from this text?
■ What kinds of questions or comments do you think will stimulate a discussion?
■ How might you help your child revisit this book?

Each parent then visits his or her child's classroom and reads the new story. Some of the favorites include the following:

Brown, M. (1972). *The runaway bunny*. New York: Harper & Row.
Carle, E. (1969). *The very hungry caterpillar*. New York: Philomel.
Freeman, D. (1968). *Corduroy*. New York: Viking.
Galdone, P. (1975). *The little red hen*. New York: Scholastic.
Guarino, D. (1989). *Is your mama a llama?* New York: Scholastic.
Keats, E.J. (1971). *Over in the meadow*. New York: Scholastic.
Keats, E.J. (1976). *The snowy day*. New York: Puffin.
Mayer, M. (1975). *What do you do with a kangaroo?* New York: Scholastic.
Piper, W. (1954). *The little engine that could*. New York: Platt & Munk.
Slobodkin, E. (1947). *Caps for sale*. Reading, MA: Addison-Wesley.
Zolotow, C. (1972). *William's doll*. New York: Harper & Row

From Neuman, S.B. (1996). Children engaging in storybook reading: The influence of access to print resources, opportunity, and parental interaction. *Early Childhood Research Quarterly, 11,* 495–514.

Although much of the research concerning differing communication styles between teachers and students is associated with race and ethnicity, communication differences also are influenced by social class. Bernstein (1977) found that people of lower-class backgrounds often used a "particularistic" language style that assumed that listeners have a familiarity with intents and meanings. Conversely, middle-class families often use a more abstract or "universalistic" language style in which meaning and context are made explicit (Knapp & Wolverton, 1996). In other words, when students from lower-class and middle-class backgrounds respond to teachers' questions, lower-class children are more likely to give answers based on the presumption that the teacher has the same background knowledge as they do. On the other hand, middle-class children often do not make this assumption, and qualify their answers by providing more contextual details. These different ways of communicating can have obvious implications for classroom interaction, especially when teachers from middle-class families expect students from lower-class families to respond in specific ways during instructional conversations.

Researchers also have begun to report on the importance of teacher-parent communication for culturally responsive teaching. Cazden et al. (1980) point to the importance of "cariño," or a caring relationship, as seen in the interactions of one first-grade teacher and her Mexican American students. Speaking in Spanish, the teacher communicated a sense of caring by using terms of endearment in addressing the children, reinforcing norms of politeness and respect, and in showing her knowledge regarding the cultural practices of their families. Similarly, teachers who have researched the various "funds of knowledge" contained in Latino households have gained a much deeper understanding of parents and students and have shown parents that they can be a valued part of their child's academic life (Gonzales et al., 1995). (See Chapter 7 for further discussion of fostering early literacy development through parent involvement.)

Presently there exists a great deal of information about teacher education programs designed to produce culturally responsive teachers (King, Hollins, & Hayman, 1997), about what culturally responsive teaching looks like in practice, and about what types of interactional approaches work best with students from particular cultures.

What has been missing from the research literature are the processes by which teachers can become culturally responsive. In this chapter, we hope to provide further guidance toward achieving culturally responsive literacy teaching by examining one particular kind of communication between teachers and parents. We begin by presenting a look at what teachers have done in the past in order to foster an understanding of their students and parents.

What Have Teachers Done in the Past?

Currently, and in years past, every good teacher of reading and writing knew that one way to get to know his or her students and their parents was to ask parents a series of questions about their home literacy practices and environment. Teachers believed that these questions would lead to them becoming more culturally responsive. The problem with this strategy then and now is that many teachers have asked parents a series of questions that require simplistic answers, such as, How many hours per week do you routinely spend reading stories to your child? Do you read your child the newspaper, comic books, library books, magazines, or a book of his or her choice? Have you set aside a certain time every day to read to your child?

At first glance, these questions seem to be beneficial tools for understanding families and how they support their children's academic and social success. Unfortunately, when teachers ask these types of questions, many parents answer with one-word responses or provide answers that they think teachers want to hear. As a result, even though teachers may receive bits and pieces of information about home literacy environments, many vital questions may remain unasked and unanswered. Leichter (1984) has noted that efforts to understand and assist families often have used school-based models and outcome-based measures of school achievement to understand how families can be useful to students. These models and outcome measures often are translated by teachers into the kinds of questions listed earlier. This may mean for teachers and parents that discussions of a child's literacy development remain one dimensional. Although this one dimension may reveal some of the important artifacts and activities needed as a foundation for literacy development, other important information remains hidden (Anderson & Stokes, 1984).

In contrast to a unidimensional model, Leichter contends that conceptions about the ways in which family environments condition the child's experience with literacy can be clustered into three broad categories, as follows:

- Physical Environment: The level of economic and educational resources, the types of visual stimulation, and the physical arrangements of the family set the stage for the child's experiences with literacy.

- Interpersonal Interaction: The child's literacy opportunities are conditioned by moment-to-moment interpersonal interaction with parents, siblings, and others in the household with respect to informal corrections, explanations, and other feedback for the child's experiments with literacy.

- Emotional and Motivational Climates: The emotional relationship within the home, parental recollections of their experiences with literacy, and the aspirations of family members condition the child's experiences with literacy. (p. 40)

Information related to these three categories can enable teachers to see and understand the complex cultural and social worlds their students inhabit. Unfortunately, in their daily interactions with students, teachers often must make judgments about students without the benefit of such knowledge. We felt that one way to bridge the gap between home and school and between the cultures of students and teachers was to begin designing what Potter (1989) calls a "participatory role" for parents. In order to provide this role for parents, we undertook a yearlong study of first-grade parents' stories of literacy. In this chapter, we define parent stories as narratives gained from open-ended interviews that draw from Leichter's categories as a framework. In these interviews, parents respond to questions designed to provide information about traditional and nontraditional early literacy activities and experiences that have happened in the home. Parent stories are further defined through their ability to construct for teachers a multilayered picture of home literacy environments. By using stories as a way to express the nature of the home environment, parents can select anecdotes and personal observations from their own individual consciousness to give teachers access to complicated social, emotional, and educational issues that can help to unravel for teachers the mystery around their students' early literacy beginnings. It is our belief that a key to unlocking the importance of culture may be contained within the stories and experiences surrounding a child's home life.

Many parents have vivid memories about their children's early literacy, including the routines they did with their children, specific interactions, observations of their children's beginning learning efforts, ways in which their children learned simply by watching them, descriptions of "teachable moments" they had with their children, and descriptions of things about their children that may not be obvious to the teacher but would help their children's performance if the teacher knew. Additionally, parents also may have scrapbooks, audiotapes, videotapes, photographs, or other artifacts that help explain their children's literacy history. Through the presentation of this knowledge and these kinds of artifacts, parent stories can provide teachers with the opportunity to gain a deeper understanding of the "human side" of families and children, including why children behave as they do, the origins of children's ways of learning and communicating, knowledge of some of the problems and possibilities parents have encountered, and how these problems and possibilities may have impacted their children's views about school and the schooling process.

Description and Rationale for Our Study

In the fall of 1995, we met with a group of 12 first-grade teachers. All of the teachers are white and have taught first grade for at least 10 years. We asked the teachers to identify a group of students who were having difficulty learning to read and write. It is our belief that first grade is a good place to start investigating experiences at home and how these experiences impact students' literacy development.

Few teachers have the opportunity to obtain the history of a child's literacy development from the parent's point of view. Our decision to collect stories was guided by our knowledge that teachers need opportunities to gain detailed information from parents. It was further guided by previous research on stories as a medium for collecting rich and detailed data (Jensen, 1989; Vygotsky, 1934/1978). Our primary intention was that knowledge from the parent stories could be used to provide teachers with new ways to constructively think about and gain information about students' lives.

A Case Example: Mrs. Vasquez, Sharon, and Kayle

In the following section, we first share Mrs. Vasquez, the first-grade teacher who considers Kayle to be at risk for failing first grade. Mrs. Vasquez has questions and concerns about Kayle that would not be easily answered by obtaining purely descriptive, objective information from Kayle's mother. Following Mrs. Vasquez's comments are excerpts from Sharon Graham's (Kayle's mother) parent story. We have selected her parent story for the chapter because it nicely illustrates how parents' information can unearth the diversity that children bring to school—a diversity that is often misunderstood. After presenting this case, we discuss some of the complex and sensitive issues surrounding the use of parent stories. In addition, we provide some of the strategies that teachers can employ in order to use parent stories to gain understandings of the contribution of home activities and parent-teacher communication in the academic success of children. Through Sharon's story, we will demonstrate how parent stories connect the home and the school, and can be an important part of creating culturally responsive literacy teaching.

Teacher Concerns About Kayle's School Life

The following statements about Kayle were taken from a conversation the first author (Edwards) had with Mrs. Vasquez.

In my opinion, Kayle comes to school overdressed. Can you believe that his mother dresses him in white shirts? Every time I ask him to do anything (be it writing his name, letters, counting, art assignments) and he feels that he cannot do it successfully, he cries. His constant crying is extremely annoying to me. When I look at Kayle, several questions go through my mind—Why does he cry so much? Why does he feel that he has to know how to do everything perfectly, and why won't he just try to complete the task? In my classroom, I'm not asking children to be perfect. I'm simply asking them to try and take risks. After all, they are first graders, no teacher expects first graders to do everything perfectly. If a child does not try, practice, or take risks, how will they learn? In my conversations with his mother, she appears to be a good mother. You can tell that she loves and adores her son. She dresses him nicely, and she makes it a point to give him breakfast every morning. All of the questions that I normally ask parents, she has provided satisfactory answers. Maybe I'm not asking the right questions. There must be something that the mother knows that will help me relate better with Kayle.

Through this excerpt, it is clear that Mrs. Vasquez would like some information from Kayle's mother that would help her better understand Kayle's behavior at home. The information Mrs. Vasquez was seeking was gained through asking Sharon questions pertaining to her knowledge of the experiences, activities, and relationships in which Kayle has been a participant at home. Below we present a first look at Sharon and her son Kayle.

Snapshot: Sharon and Kayle

Sharon Graham is the only daughter in her family. She is 32 years old and unmarried. Her family owns a trucking business and Sharon works for the family business, which makes it possible for her to have a flexible work schedule. Sharon was extremely excited when she got pregnant and her mother, father, and grandparents shared in her excitement. In the following statement Sharon describes the emotions she and her family shared.

> When I found out I was pregnant…I prayed for a boy and that's what I got…and the grandparents were so ecstatic. Everyday for me was just happiness. I was happy the whole time.

Because she is a single parent, it is extremely important to Sharon that she be with her son in the evenings. According to Sharon

> I remember my parents working very hard—they didn't really take the time out to sit and read. I can't remember having any books being there except for the ones I would bring home. And they didn't really have an interest like I think they should have. Like we have to have today.

Though she recognizes that her own parents could have participated in more literacy activities with her, Sharon has undergone her own struggle to be more involved in Kayle's life. She admits the following:

When he was younger, I didn't read as much as I should have, but now it's a daily thing that we do. I think that could be considered fun...I read to him more like, biblical stories and things like that. He had an interest at age 2 of just looking at the pictures, and then from my sounding, he could tell if something was funny or something, he liked the different ranges of voice that I would use.

Because Sharon is unmarried, her younger brother assumed the role of father for Kayle. Sharon appears to be appreciative of this, however, her brother's influence on Kayle's life might not be as positive as Sharon seems to think. Below Sharon describes her appreciation of her brother:

I've been a single parent since Kayle's birth. And my brother has always been there and he's been like, I guess, I never wanted to say, father figure because it wasn't his father, but other family members consider him a father figure, but to me he is more of Uncle Chris. And from the day I had my son Kayle, my brother was in the room, in the delivery, and they just bonded. My brother is a real lady's man, so I can think of incidents when my brother would take him out to the mall and stroll him around just to get attention from girls; they would say "He's so cute!" I knew he was using my son! So now, my son has been interested in girls from an early age. I know that Uncle Chris cannot do any wrong in my son's eyes. My brother is in the army, National Guard, and I found my son getting interested in the army, things like that.

Sharon acknowledges that Kayle's father does not participate in his life. However, the way in which she answers Kayle's questions about his father is positive.

I think just really, the most important thing is that he does not have a father. I live with my parents, his grandfather is there, but still I think that he's going to be a little shy when those father day events come up or parent day and there's just me. We talk about it, I ask, "Honey, am I doing OK? Do you feel bad that your father is not here? Is it something that you want to talk about?" He says no. And every now and then his father will call but they rarely see each other. It's funny, today he asked to call, so I let him call. He's welcome to call any time. But his father isn't there, but I don't push him. So I think that may affect him. But again, I'll have my brother there when it comes to that or grandpa, so I'll try to fill that void.

Making a Man: Sharon and Kayle's Relationship

Sharon has had an extremely close relationship with Kayle from the time he was very young; she has treated him as if he were her "little man." Evidence of this is found in her description of their relationship:

> The things we do for fun would be just talking, we might come up to the school and fly a kite, uhm, oh, I take him traveling, he's been to the Bahamas and Florida. The movies, other things we do to have fun, he really enjoys picking out his own school clothes. I get a kick out of that.

> We live up north in a resort town. From the ages of 2 to 4, I didn't know anybody there. We depended on each other for conversation...so routinely, we just talked every day. Decided where we were going to eat. We did laundry, that was a routine thing. He was so good at that, we'd go to the Laundromat. That was good.

Sharon's way of interacting and socializing with her son has both positive and negative elements. In some ways, it appears that she has taught him important social skills but has also inadvertently encouraged Kayle to behave in ways that are not age appropriate.

> Baths. (I enjoy) giving him baths. He still enjoys it today. Lotion him down. I'm just going to be frank. With black skin you have to keep your skin moisturized. Being a boy he's not shy. Lotion him down, it reminds me of an older man, getting a massage. From head to toe. So that's a routine.

Interestingly, although the activities that Sharon does with Kayle could be interpreted as activities in which two married adults participate, these activities have enabled him to develop skills that will be useful in academic tasks at school:

> He finally got into cutting coupons. He was the first one to realize what we needed in the house, and he would cut coupons and we would do the grocery shopping together, so that was our routine thing.

Defining Kayle

In Sharon's reflections on her son, what comes through most clearly is the contrast between Kayle's exposure to an adult world and Sharon's sheltering behavior toward him.

In the beginning, I think that's when you…it's your first child and everything is just a learning experience. I knew it took my son a long time to walk. Because he never learned to crawl, I was always holding him and things like that. After he did learn to walk, it was his baby sitter that taught him to learn to walk. I just remember putting him against the wall and encouraging him and having this big smile and being joyful. In all his learning experiences, even today, we have to show him enthusiasm. When he accomplishes something, just give him a clap.

Based on the comments Mrs. Vasquez expressed about Kayle's reluctance to take risks, it appears as if Kayle's reliance on his mother might be transformed into reliance on immediate feedback from his teacher. Sharon's explanation of what Kayle needs in the classroom supports this idea.

He likes to be recognized the utmost when he accomplishes something. So she might really encourage him when he does do something right, or learns something new. Keep that praise going, energetic. It will just make him go a little further when you show excitement.

Sharon's Recollections of School

Sharon remembers skipping first grade and being placed in the second grade, but she has vague memories of why she skipped first grade. However, the following memory sheds light on her experiences as a learner:

I remember in the English books how you have a page of words and you're supposed to fill in the sentences with one of the words here. I would never try to figure out how I do that. And the teacher was never coming around to explain it to me, so I was putting any word there and one of the kids would tell me that's wrong. So I can remember experiences learning from the kids instead of the teachers because they were a higher level. And I remember feeling embarrassed.

From this reflection on her schooling, one cannot help but wonder if Kayle may feel similarly as he tries to understand how to do classroom tasks, and if his mother has inadvertently reinforced this behavior. In support of this idea, another one of Sharon's memories sheds light on her childhood feelings, the boundaries she believes teachers should not cross, and her thoughts on teachers allowing children to experience childhood.

> Not to burst their bubbles. I remember in second grade I was told by my teacher there was not Santa Claus and I went home crying to my parents. Because she just figured you were in second grade, you were older, you should know that there is no Santa Claus. And I think some things have to be left up to the parents. And I remember being so hurt, crying, running all the way home. And I remember my mom going up to that school giving that teacher hell. I guess little things like that, they're still young enough they should still have some childhood. I don't know if they do this, I haven't had any experiences like that with my son, but I guess I would want them to know, let's not make them grow up too fast.

These comments again are indicative of the conflict Kayle may feel through concurrently being sheltered and being treated as an adult. In response to her own emotional needs, Sharon may have forced Kayle to grow up quickly, without giving him the message that it is all right to be a child, to explore, and, as Mrs. Vasquez says, to take risks.

Concerns and Questions: Sharon's Knowledge of Kayle's School Experiences

As is often true of first-grade parents, the struggles Kayle has in school seem to be foremost on Sharon's mind.

> My son is mixing up letters now. The first thing that comes to my mind is dyslexia. I don't know if it's that he's still learning. I don't know if it's obvious that D's and B's in lower case are simple. I don't know. But we constantly go over it all the time. My experience is that I've seen him just develop a pattern of writing. For instance, before he came to kindergarten, I went to these teacher stores and thought, what should I buy to get him ready? And I found out whatever I tried to do, it just would never sink in, I could never teach him to write, I tried and tried. But what I learned from school, they have a method for each letter, it's almost like a story. Bring the loop down to make a J, or something, dot that T, something weird like that. I would have never thought of that.

Although she feels that she has not been successful in helping Kayle with his writing, she has been proactive in her efforts to help her son. This information is critical for educators' thinking about children who are at risk, because it is often assumed that a child's at-risk status is caused partially by disinterested and passive parents or caregivers. On the contrary, Sharon displays her willingness to be involved and informed about what is happening with Kayle at school.

> Weekly they go to the library at school. I find myself getting upset because some of the books that he's bringing home are not first-grade level, they're more higher. And the words are too big. I want him to pick out books like Dr. Seuss, the ones I remember. So I feel my role is to really stay informed. I come up to all the events that I hear.

In addition to being a proactive parent, Sharon mixes her praise of teachers with suggestions for creating a more positive working relationship between parents and teachers.

> I would just encourage teachers to try to bridge that gap between parents and teachers. Not to scare them, but let them know what's happening today. To do things different when you come across something that may interfere. Again, I have to commend teachers. They are awesome. I could have never taught my son as far as where he is today. So I really have grown to admire them.

Sharon's reflections on her communication with Mrs. Vasquez reveal that her emphasis on better teacher-parent communication may originate in one experience in which Sharon felt disinvited from being involved in Kayle's academic life.

> Then last but not least, something interesting came across, but they didn't act on it with me. I think the ethnic part of education has to be built up more. Something came across, I was real surprised in this class, about a month ago, he took a letter home asking parents if they wanted to participate in their ethnic group and come and do a presentation about it. Of course I wanted to. I never heard anything back, maybe they got another parent.... I think it's so important for my son, being a black male to know about some of the other black people in history. So I hope they integrate more the ethnic program.

In this last segment from Sharon's story, it is easy to see just how critical the information from parent stories can be. With the realization of how Sharon had been affected by not being invited to Kayle's classroom, Mrs. Vasquez can take the needed steps to reinforce a parent–teacher relationship that otherwise may have become strained or even severed.

Addressing Parent Stories and the Issues Surrounding Them

When we first began the task of identifying and making sense of the important themes in Sharon's parent story, we could not help but notice the fact that her story was not linear, but winding, overlapping, and complex. Indeed, as Metzger (1986) has noted,

> Stories go in circles. They don't go in straight lines. So it helps if you listen in circles because there are stories inside stories and stories between stories and finding your way through them is as easy and as hard as finding your way home. And part of the finding is the getting lost. If you're lost, you really start to look around and listen. (p. 104)

As we continued the process of working with Sharon's story, we realized that we had found several different pathways into Kayle and Sharon's home. The pathways contained within parent stories can offer teachers a new way to craft an understanding of children who are culturally diverse. This is possible because parent stories allow teachers to identify what it means, specifically, when we use the words *home literacy environment* to talk about students' success or lack of success in school. By thinking about parent stories in this way, teachers are able to look at the issues, problems, and strengths of homes that influence the literacy development of young children. These explorations are the first step toward making connections between parent stories and how they can be used to better educate every child. It is also a step toward shaping culturally responsive teaching.

In our thinking about how parent stories can be used in a culturally responsive way, three key questions have guided our thinking: What should teachers do with parent stories? How can teachers build on what children bring to the classroom? and How can we improve classroom practice through parent stories? We address each of these questions separately in the next section of this chapter, and in doing so we hope to provide teachers with ways to think about the potential applications of parent stories.

What Should Teachers Do With Parent Stories?

Once collected, parent stories have several important uses. For example, a common fear many teachers express when planning interactions with parents from different cultural backgrounds is that they may somehow alienate or offend those parents. By asking a parent if they would like to tell their parent story in order to aid in their child's instruction, a teacher not only creates an opportunity for parents to feel valued, but also makes it possible for a line of communication to be opened. Consequently, during and after the collection of parent stories, teachers can gain insight into cultural practices that may prove instrumental in easing any cultural incongruities that may exist between their own culture and that of the parents with whom they interact. Parent stories can also be used by teachers in order to develop instructional plans for students. Instead of making guesses about what instruction might be best for individual students, teachers can view students through the lens provided by parent stories and then make decisions about instruction that are more individually and culturally appropriate. This is exemplified clearly in the parent story that we have presented in this chapter—while Mrs. Vasquez was trying to institute a classroom environment in which her students felt free to take risks, Sharon's ways of interacting with Kayle inhibited his risk-taking abilities. With the knowledge provided from Sharon, Mrs. Vasquez could modify her approach to working with Kayle in order to ease him into the culture of the classroom.

Another important use of parent stories is as a resource for teachers in their thinking about whether a child should be referred for special services. By reading parent stories, teachers are supplied with ideas of what they can do in the classroom and they also are made more aware of what goes beyond the bounds of their time and ability. Perhaps most importantly, once teachers have a parent's story, they have a starting point for discussing with parents both concerns about a students' academic and social progress, and ideas for how parents can better help their children to be successful.

How Can Teachers Build on What Children Bring to the Classroom?

Without communicating with parents and receiving information from them, teachers have little idea of what kind of teachers parents are, and they may have even less knowledge about what has been taught to children (and why) before they enter school. Parent stories can be the beginning of cooperative communication between parents and teachers that will lead to understanding what areas a child needs to work on in the classroom and at home. Once this communication has been established, parent stories create a meaningful role for parents and allow them to be recognized as a child's first teacher. Relatedly, parent stories can help teachers discover what parts of a parent's teaching are congruent or incongruent with what goes on in the school. With this knowledge, teachers are then enabled to discuss with parents ways in which they can help their child at home.

How Can We Improve Classroom Practice Through Parent Stories?

Unfortunately, when diverse children come into the classroom environment, teachers are often expected to teach without connecting the child to the environment of the home. Despite this expectation, most teachers realize that they need extra help in teaching children, but are at a loss when it comes to identifying precisely what kind of help they need. Parent stories can be used to help teachers pinpoint what children need in terms of subject matter foundations, social skills, and can even be useful when teachers seek help from local community and social service agencies in order to meet the needs of diverse children (Shaver, Golan, & Wagner, 1996). Instead of throwing instruction up in the air and hoping that every child will catch what they need, parent stories can give teachers a greater sense of agency in working with diverse children. Another implication parent stories have for classroom practice is realized when teachers have conflicts with students or parents. Through parent stories, teachers can talk about these conflicts with more than just intuitive knowledge about how best to prevent future conflicts. For example, with the knowledge provided from

Sharon's story, Mrs. Vasquez can be better prepared to deal with the possible feelings of alienation that Sharon felt when she was not invited to the classroom.

Finally, parent stories bring to light the differences between the home and the school. Although narratives have been written about family poverty and other adverse conditions (Taylor & Dorsey-Gaines, 1988) teachers have not been able to reflect on narratives that relate directly to the environment and circumstances surrounding their own classroom and the school in which they teach. Perhaps stories will begin to uncover the richness of families, and also highlight the richness that teachers might not have been able to recognize previously.

We understand that although some of the information in the excerpts from Sharon's and other parent stories may be viewed as positive, other ideas and experiences can appear negative or counterproductive to the education of the children highlighted in the stories. However, regardless of how they are perceived initially, these stories reflect the realities of many school children who grow up in what are typically described as at-risk environments; these realities must be confronted and dealt with. Additionally, though teachers may recognize the value of parent stories, they may be reluctant to collect them because of the lack of control teachers have over what happens in the home or because they have no specialized training to collect parent stories. What must be made clear in these situations is that teachers frequently make judgments about students and their families without the benefit of information from the families being evaluated. What seems best for teachers and the families they serve is knowledge based not in teachers' suppositions, but in the realities of the lives of parents and their children. Lastly, teachers also may feel that they are crossing the boundaries of families' right to privacy if they attempt to talk with parents about the home environments of students. However, if teachers are to educate all children and become culturally responsive in the process, they must more fully understand the families of their students, they must begin to develop creative ways to help the children in their classrooms become ready to learn, and they must take action in order to deal with the strengths, problems, and issues that children bring to school.

References

Anderson, A.B., & Stokes, S.J. (1984). Social and institutional influences on the development and practice of literacy. In H. Goelman, A. Oberg, & F. Smith (Eds.), *Awakening to literacy* (pp. 24–37). Exeter, NH: Heinemann.

Au, K., & Mason, J.M. (1983). Cultural congruence in classroom participation structures: Achieving a balance of rights. *Discourse Processes, 6*(2), 145–167.

Bernstein, B. (1977). *Class, codes and control: Vol. III. Towards a theory of educational transmission.* London: Routledge & Kegan Paul.

Bryd, J., Lundenberg, M.A., Hoffland, S.C., Couillard, E.L., & Lee, M.S. (1996). Caring, cognition, and cultural pluralism: Case studies of urban teachers. *Urban Education, 31*(4), 432–452.

Cazden, C.B., Cavrasco, R., Maldonado-Guzman, A.A., & Erickson, F.C. (1980). The contribution of ethnographic research to bicultural education. In J. Alatis (Ed.), *Current issues in bilingual education* (Georgetown University Roundtable on Language and Linguistics). Washington, DC: Georgetown University Press.

Cushner, K., McClelland, A., & Safford, P. (1996). *Human diversity in education: An integrative approach.* New York: McGraw-Hill.

Erickson, F., & Mohatt, G. (1982). The cultural organization of participation structures in two classrooms of Indian students. In G. Spindler (Ed.), *Doing the ethnography of school.* New York: Holt.

Foster, M. (1993). Educating for competence in community and culture: Exploring the views of exemplary African–American teachers. *Urban Education, 27*(4), 370–394.

Giroux, H. (1992). *Border crossings: Cultural workers and the politics of education.* New York: Routledge, Chapman & Hall.

Gonzalez, N., Moll, L.C., Tenery, M.F., Rivera, A., Rendon, P., Gonzales, R., & Amanti, C. (1995). Funds of knowledge for teaching in Latino households. *Urban Education, 29*(4), 443–470.

Heath, S.B. (1982). Questioning at home and school: A comparative study. In G. Spindler (Ed.), *Doing the ethnography of schooling: Educational anthropology in action.* New York: Holt, Rinehart & Winston.

Henry, A. (1994). The empty shelf and other curricular challenges of teaching for children of African descent: Implications for teacher practice. *Urban Education, 29*(3), 298–319.

Huber, T., Kline, F.M., Bakken, L., & Clark, F.L. (1997). Transforming teacher education: Including culturally responsible pedagogy. In J.E. King, E.R. Hollins, & W.C. Hayman (Eds.), *Preparing teachers for cultural diversity* (pp. 129–145). New York: Teachers College Press.

Jensen, J.M. (1989). Introduction. In J.M. Jensen (Ed.), *Stories to grow on: Demonstrations of language learning K–8 classrooms* (pp. xv–xx). Portsmouth, NH: Heinemann.

King, J.E., Hollins, E.R., & Hayman, W.C. (1997). *Preparing teachers for cultural diversity.* New York: Teachers College Press.

Knapp, M.S., & Woolverton, S. (1996). Social class and schooling. In J.A. Banks & C.A.M. Banks (Eds.), *Handbook of multicultural education*. New York: Macmillan.

Ladson–Billings, G. (1994). *The dreamkeepers: Successful teachers of African American children*. San Francisco, CA: Jossey–Bass.

Leichter, H.J. (1984). Families as environments for literacy. In H. Goelman, A. Oberg, & F. Smith (Eds.), *Awakening to literacy* (pp. 38–50). Exeter, NH: Heinemann.

Lightfoot, S.L. (1978). *Worlds apart: Relationships between families and school*. New York: Basic Books.

Metzger, D. (1986). Circles of stories. *Parabola, 4*(4).

Nieto, S. (1992). *Affirming diversity: The sociopolitical context of multicultural education*. White Plains, NY: Longman.

Potter, G. (1989). Parent participation in language arts programs. *Language Arts, 66*(1), 29–43.

Shaver, D., Golan, S., & Wagner, M. (1996). Connecting schools and communities through interagency collaboration for school-linked services. In J.G. Cibulka & W.J. Kritek (Eds.), *Coordination among schools, families, and communities: Prospectus for educational reform* (pp. 349–378). Albany, NY: University of New York Press.

Taylor, D., & Dorsey-Gaines, C. (1988). *Growing up literate: Learning from inner-city families*. Portsmouth, NH: Heinemann.

Vygotsky, L.S. (1978). *Mind in society: The development of higher psychological processes*. (M. Cole, V. John-Steiner, S. Scribner, & E. Souberman, Eds. and Trans.). Cambridge, MA: Harvard University Press. (Original work published in 1934)

CHAPTER 7

How Can We Foster Children's Early Literacy Development Through Parent Involvement?

Peter Hannon

The new conceptualization of early literacy learning that informs the chapters of this book has not only changed how we see children but also has profound consequences for how we see parents. More than 20 years of research has revealed that young children know more about literacy, and know it at an earlier age, than had been recognized. They do not acquire all this knowledge on their own; they are helped by parents and other family members. Educators need to understand how this takes place and how to identify the implications for early literacy education.

The literature on early literacy development, by emphasizing children's accomplishments—the way, for example, that they actively construct literacy and knowledge of written language—sometimes portrays an almost magical unfolding of literacy development. This can be a misleading representation of the term *emergent literacy*. It only takes a moment's reflection to realize that early literacy learning is a highly social activity, mediated by people who care about children's development and who are as eager to introduce them to literacy as to other important features of the world that they are entering. Literacy development does not occur by itself. The key social group in which most young children's learning takes place is, of course, the family, and it is caregivers in the family—principally parents—whose role is crucial.*

Parents are generally very active in promoting their children's early literacy development. In Western industrialized countries this is true for preschool children in families across a wide range of socioeconomic levels (Hannon & James, 1990). Although almost all parents attempt to assist literacy development in some way, they do not all do it in the same way, to the same extent, with the same concept of literacy, or with the same resources (Hannon, Weinberger, & Nutbrown, 1991; Heath, 1983; Taylor, 1983; Taylor & Dorsey–Gaines, 1988; Weinberger, 1996; Wells, 1987). The variation in extent of parent involvement can be enormous; for example, shared storybook experiences can range from just a few episodes or none at all before school entry to several thousand. Hannon and James (1990) found that most parents of preschool children would appreciate support from preschool teachers but often do not get it. Significant numbers of parents, nevertheless, do deliberately teach their children specific aspects of reading or writing (Farquhar, Blatchford, Burke, Plewis, & Tizard, 1986; Hall, Herring, Henn, & Crawford, 1989; Hannon & James, 1990). Most learning is probably incidental—arising, as Weinberger (1998) states, through encounters with literacy before school, "often unrecorded and transient, but nevertheless powerful and cumulative in their effect" (p. 39).

Research also has given us a fuller appreciation of the nature of the early literacy development that parents foster—the "roots of literacy" which, Goodman argues, often go unnoticed (Goodman, 1980, 1986). Particularly interesting is what children learn from environmen-

---

* In what follows, *parent* should be read as referring to children's principal caregiver in the home, including grandparents, stepparents, older siblings, significant adults, and biological parents. Likewise *family* refers to the social group in which the child is cared for and grows up, be it nuclear, single parent, or extended.

tal print—a major feature of the print-rich cultures of the Western world—which for some children may be more influential than books. Children's writing development also can be traced back to their early years, especially if one looks at what they learn about the function of writing and its form (Hall, 1987; Teale & Sulzby, 1986). Other aspects of early literacy learning that have been highlighted by researchers, and that obviously depend on parents, include phonological awareness (Goswami & Bryant, 1990), understanding of narrative and story (Meek, 1982; Wells, 1987), and decontextualized talk (Snow, 1991). This development starts well before the beginning of classroom literacy learning and, after school entry, continues outside and inside the classroom.

By the time children enter school they have had numerous family literacy-learning experiences. Studies show that the extent of these learning experiences, their nature, and how they relate to school literacy are of great importance for children's later academic achievement. Simple measures of literacy development at school entry (for example, the ability to recognize or form letters or handle books) are powerful predictors of later achievement—better, arguably, than other measures of ability or oral language development (Tizard, Blatchford, Burke, Farquhar, & Plewis, 1988; Wells, 1987). Other predictors from as early as 3 years old include knowledge of nursery rhymes (Maclean, Bryant, & Bradley, 1987) and having favorite books (Weinberger, 1996). Much of the variation in children's abilities at school entry is due to what parents do or do not do in the preschool years. After school entry, there are numerous studies (reviewed, for example, in Hannon, 1995) that show that home factors and family-literacy experiences continue to exert a powerful influence on children's capacity to engage successfully with the school curriculum. In short, it is clear that achievement in early literacy education depends on factors outside the classroom.

There is a considerable challenge—even a dilemma—here. Teachers want to do their utmost to provide successful early literacy education for children, yet success depends greatly on people and factors outside the classroom and beyond their control. There is a limit to what can be achieved in the classroom alone, but given that teachers cannot simply hand over all their responsibilities to parents, what can they do?

Responding to the Challenge

One way to respond to factors outside the classroom is to ignore the challenge—to focus just on the classroom on the grounds that teachers are not responsible for what happens outside. Historically, this has been the dominant tradition in elementary schooling in most countries where mass compulsory schooling was established in the 19th century. Schools took responsibility for imparting literacy to children and parents were supposed to let this happen. This may have worked in an era when large numbers of parents had limited literacy and when written language was less pervasive in everyday life. However, in today's conditions this practice fails to take account of the true nature of early literacy learning and amounts to a form of *parental exclusion*.

Parental exclusion is by no means uncommon. It is rarely acknowledged as such or planned deliberately, and it may be accompanied by a rhetoric that insists that the parent is the child's first teacher and that the school relies on parent support. Exclusion usually is an unintended consequence of practices that may seem obvious and sensible to schools, such as those listed in Figure 1.

Another response to the challenge is *limited involvement* for parents. For example, parents might be invited into a second-grade classroom to help with children's oral reading. Suppose six parents accept the invitation but of these only two or three are able to maintain their commitment for more than a few weeks. This is certainly involvement (and of value to those concerned) but it remains limited in being confined to a small percentage of the children's parents—usually mothers not in full-time employment. It also is limited in being focused on children's classroom literacy learning rather than their home learning. Another example of limited involvement might be a school policy that officially encourages children to take home classroom reading books but that in fact is implemented so weakly that most children in most classes may only take advantage of it once or twice a year.

Is it realistic to expect schools to move beyond parental exclusion or limited involvement to fuller involvement? The answer is yes, but only if we are prepared to rethink crucial issues related to the early literacy curriculum, our understanding of the parent role in children's early development, school policies, and teacher professionalism. The

Figure 1 Some Unintended Ways of Excluding Parents

- Deny parents access to the classroom (e.g., on the grounds that if they all came at the same time there would not be enough space).
- Rely exclusively on classroom reading materials that parents cannot obtain for themselves (e.g., basal reading programs).
- Do not allow classroom books or other literacy materials home (e.g., on the grounds that they would be lost or damaged).
- Show no interest in children's home literacy activities.
- Limit information about the school's literacy program (e.g., to one part of principal's pre-entry address to parents).
- Treat parents' estimations of their children's progress skeptically.
- In conversation with parents use unexplained technical terms (e.g., decoding, digraph, miscue, or psycho-motor) whether or not they are strictly necessary.
- Gently dissuade parents from taking on a teaching role with their children (e.g., on grounds that they should not be overanxious or pressuring).
- If parents help in the classroom, steer them away from direct participation in literacy activities (e.g., to washing paint pots or baking) and away from working with their own children.
- Smokescreen the above with regular statements about the importance of parents in children's education.

---

assumption in this chapter is that the evidence of parents' influence on children's early literacy learning is so compelling that we must try to overcome obstacles to involving parents in early literacy education. The aim of what follows is to set out a conceptual framework that can underpin new practice, offer practical ideas, and indicate how research is helping the development of good practice.

A Conceptual Framework for Practice

Parental involvement is most likely to be effective if it is based on clear thinking about aims and methods. Some basic distinctions and concepts can help. It is worth distinguishing children's *home literacy learning* from their *classroom literacy learning*. It is the former that has been shown to be so significant by the new conceptualization of literacy learning. This should be no surprise. In the early years children obviously spend much more active time at home than in classrooms. Also, as Figure 2 suggests, home literacy learning may be more powerful than classroom learning in certain respects.

From this viewpoint, work with parents focused on children's home literacy learning has more potential than that focused on classroom learning. For example, it might be better for schools to support parents in shared storybook reading at home (perhaps by sending school books home) than to have them come into school to support children's classroom reading. Both are possible, but it is a mistake to think that they are the same thing or that parent involvement always means getting parents into school.

Whichever context of literacy learning is to be the focus, involvement requires some work with parents, that is interaction between teacher and parent, preferably including some face-to-face dialogue. In some involvement programs the location for work with parents is in children's homes (for example, through home visits), but this can be expensive in staff time and is a method to be used sparingly. Work with parents sometimes can be accomplished more efficiently if it is located in schools (for example, literacy workshops for groups of parents). It is important not to confuse the *location* of work with its *focus*. The parent workshop located in a school, for example, could focus either on children's home learning or on their classroom learning. Figure 3 on page 128 offers a way of conceptualizing focus and location to show that there are four basic possibilities for action.

Home Literacy Versus Classroom Literacy

Being serious about home literacy learning brings up another difficult issue—the ways in which *home literacy* differs from *classroom literacy*. The new conceptualization of literacy has shown how home literacy is embedded in social practices and values that obviously vary between social contexts and groups. For early childhood educators the idea that there could be more than one kind of literacy—specifically

Figure 2 Possible Characteristics of Children's Literacy
Learning at Home and in School

HOME LEARNING   **CLASSROOM LEARNING**

Ways in which home literacy learning might be more powerful

High adult–child ratio.	Low adult–child ratio.
Close relationship with adults.	Distant relationship with adults.
Extended conversations possible.	Limited opportunities for conversation.
Shaped by interest and need.	Shaped by curricular objectives.
Natural problems.	Contrived problems.
Often seems effortless.	Often seems to require effort.
Often spontaneous.	Timetabled.
Flexible duration.	Fixed duration.
Vertical age group likely.	Horizontal age group likely.
Child sometimes in teaching role with younger children.	Very few opportunities for child to act as a teacher.

Ways in which classroom literacy learning might be more powerful

May not encounter concepts in the easiest order for learning.	Planned progression through subject matter.
Special resources not usually available.	Supported by special resources.
Opportunities vary with home background.	Opportunities more equal.

Other differences

Adults as models.	Adults as instructors.
Use of print media and television media often extensive and uncontrolled.	Use of audio-visual and printed materials subordinated to teaching objectives.
Recognition of children's achievements reflects many values.	Recognition of children's achievements reflects school objectives.
Rarely assessed formally.	Often assessed formally.

Figure 3 Focus and Location of Work With Parents

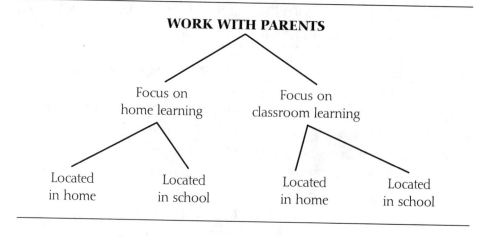

that there might be valid alternatives to school literacy—is still rather novel. Yet it is clear that certain aspects of classroom literacy are rarely part of home literacy (such as taking tests or writing stories), and there are aspects of home literacy that are not prominent in classrooms (such as reading comics, studying the Bible, or writing shopping lists). At the same time, there is a significant overlap between the two environments in the cognitive demands of different literacies (for example, in knowing graphophonic correspondences or appreciating the idea of audience). Practical ways of dealing with home-school boundaries will be discussed later in the chapter.

A Model of the Parent's Teaching Role

Underlying every form of parent involvement is a model of the parent's teaching role. It is worth making this explicit. In some forms of involvement, the parent is a classroom helper working under the teacher's supervision in nonprofessional areas of literacy teaching. In other cases, often in the special-needs area, parents are given the role of technician (explicitly so in the past by Ryback & Staats, 1970) and asked to implement a tightly specified instructional program. Some schools refer to parents as partners—a high aspiration if partnership is taken to mean joint decision making and sharing of risks and profits.

I have suggested elsewhere (Hannon, 1995) that a useful model of the parent's role can be based on what parents often already do to foster their children's literacy development. This model is partly a matter of logical necessity, and partly a reflection of widely accepted theoretical perspectives. It involves the four concepts of *opportunities, recognition, interaction,* and *model* and hence can be referred to as ORIM.

In the early years, parents can provide vital literacy learning *opportunities* by having suitable materials for children's drawing or scribbling activities; by encouraging literacy–related sociodramatic play; by alerting them to, and helping them interpret, environmental print; by engaging them in nursery rhymes that aid speech segmentation and phonological awareness; by sharing storybooks and other written materials; by having other printed matter such as books, encyclopedias, and newspapers in the home; by creating space for literacy activities by rationing television viewing; and by enabling children to use libraries and newspapers to participate in trips or holidays that provide further literacy demands and opportunities.

Parents can provide unique encouragement for children in their *recognition* and valuing of children's early achievements in, for example, handling books, reading, understanding logos, and writing. Recognition of early literacy learning involves the kind of praise, celebration, and awareness of development that parents provide in other areas of development such as talking, walking, and social skills.

Parents need to *interact* with children—supporting, explaining, and challenging them to move on from what they know about literacy to do more. An important form of interaction is involving children in real literacy tasks in which they can make a meaningful contribution (for example, adding their "writing" to a greeting card, turning the pages of a book, or selecting shopping items by brand name) thereby enabling them to do today with an adult what tomorrow they will be able to do independently. But *interaction* can take many forms, including pointing out, direct instruction, demonstration, dialogue, games, and sociodramatic play. It can be informal or structured.

Finally parents act as powerful *models* if and when children see them using literacy, for example, in reading newspapers for information or enjoyment, in writing notes or shopping lists, in using print to find out things, in following instructions, in earning a living that involves paperwork at home, and in generally demonstrating how written language is linked to a wide range of adult purposes in the home, community, and workplace.

The ORIM model is most useful in thinking about parent involvement focused on home literacy learning, but it is applicable to classroom literacy learning too (and to most areas of learning at any age). However, rather than applying ORIM to all literacy learning, it is helpful to disentangle various strands of literacy development. What counts as a strand of literacy is largely a matter of convenience. Three main strands to be considered are *reading, early writing,* and *oral language* (others can be distinguished as necessary, for example, semiotic awareness). Strands can always be unpicked further into substrands. For example, in the reading strand, it is vital to recognize the importance of children's engagement with environmental print as well as reading books and other texts. Key substrands of oral language include phonological awareness, storytelling, decontextualized talk, vocabulary, and talk about written language. The metaphor of strands is helpful in suggesting that these elements are at the same time separable and intertwined. For each strand of literacy, parents have the potential to provide opportunities, recognition, interaction, and a model (see Figure 4). Each cell in this matrix refers to an aspect of parental support for early literacy learning (for example, providing a model of reading or providing appropriate interaction in writing activities).

The matrix is a way of linking helpful concepts. It is not in itself a theory of literacy development (despite, of course, being informed by such theories). It can help describe existing patterns of family literacy—in particular it helps in seeing what families do rather than what they supposedly fail to do. More important is the framework's potential as a map of involvement possibilities. One can ask in relation to each cell in the framework, How could work with parents support their role here? This is not meant to be prescriptive, stipulating what families ought to do. Rather it is a matter of enlarging parents' conception of what they *could* do, thereby increasing their choices and awareness of what power they have. This framework is a heuristic device for generating an involvement program. It provides a convenient checklist for thinking through what might be done with parents in relation to

Figure 4 A Map of Involvement Possibilities

		STRANDS OF EARLY LITERACY		
		Reading	Writing	Oral language
PARENTS PROVIDE	Opportunities			
	Recognition			
	Interaction			
	Model			

any selected strand of literacy. Reviewing all the cells makes a full coverage of possibilities more likely.

This consideration of the parent's role means that the teacher's role needs some rethinking. It is not helpful to think of classroom teachers being the only, or even the principal, teachers of literacy. The teacher's role should include accomplishing some things in collaboration with, and through, parents. To work effectively with parents they may need new knowledge, understanding, and skills. They need to appreciate the power of home literacy learning, understand the parent's role, and understand what they can do to support parents in that role. In some cases, support for parents will have to include adult literacy education. There are implications for professional development here that we have only just begun to address (Nutbrown, Hannon & Weinberger, 1991; Hannon & Nutbrown, 1997). (See Chapter 13 for further discussion of teachers growing as professionals.)

Early in this chapter the term *family literacy* was used (Taylor, 1983) to refer to the context of interlinking literacy activities of family members within which so much of children's literacy learning takes place in the early years. Recently, however, the term has been used more narrowly to refer to a particular kind of literacy-oriented program in which early education for children is combined with adult basic education for parents. These programs are undoubtedly of value but perhaps only for certain families, not as a universal solution. Parent involvement should be part of early literacy education for all children, regardless of whether their parents are thought to need, or are prepared to accept, adult basic education. (Also, parents should have access to adult basic education whether or not their children are in an early-education program.) We should be clear, then, that parent involvement in early literacy education need not be *family literacy* in the narrow sense of that term.

From Theory to Practice

Returning to the question in the title of this chapter (How can we foster children's early development through parent involvement?), I suggest four levels of involvement for educators to consider: (1) avoiding unnecessary parent exclusion, (2) linking home and school literacies, (3) developing home-focused programs for school-age children, and (4) developing home-focused preschool programs. I argue that all schools should work at the first and second levels, most should work at the third level, and some should work at the fourth level.

Avoiding Unnecessary Parent Exclusion

This level of involvement is simple; it means reviewing the kinds of school practices that are listed in Figure 1 on page 125 (plus any that readers are able to add). The basic question to be asked is, What are we doing that tends to exclude parents from early literacy education in our school, and is it really necessary? As an example, take the first point listed in Figure 1. If parents are barred from entering classrooms during the day (or at the end of the day), they are likely to have less insight into their children's classroom literacy experiences and how they could be involved in their learning. We need to ask if the practical difficulties are insurmountable. How likely it is that all parents would want to come in at exactly the same time? Would they want to stay for long periods? Could there be different open days during the week for different children? Could different parents be offered their own special times each week when they are welcome to stay with their children? If all else fails, could a video of children's classroom experiences be loaned to parents? I do not suggest that what is done here is the touchstone of parent involvement; it is only one of the areas in

which unnecessary exclusion can be turned into something more positive. All such practices should be subjected to the same scrutiny.

Linking Home and School Literacies

This level of involvement is only a short step from the first. There are many ways in which home literacy learning and classroom literacy learning can be linked and can strengthen each other. The most obvious is encouraging classroom activities to go home, at least occasionally (for example, so that children can finish a piece of writing). Another way is not just to permit parents to come into the classroom but actually to encourage them to get involved in specific classroom activities. Parents can be involved with children sharing books, adding captions, making books, helping with drawing or writing tables, adding to classroom print displays, writing or reading with a computer, supporting literacy-related sociodramatic play, teaching nursery rhymes, identifying and collecting logos and signs, and occasionally providing a model of reading or writing themselves. This kind of involvement is valuable but still somewhat limited because it is often about parents providing opportunities rather than recognition, interaction, or a model of literacy. It also is limited because only a minority of parents come into school and often not those whose children would benefit most. Parents in school may not work with their own children and, even if they do, they are not in their most powerful teaching context (the home) shaping children's home learning.

It can be valuable to have school literacy spreading into the home and family context but ways also can be found to bring home literacy into the classroom context. For example, many young children do some writing or drawing at home. Why not use a special pinboard to display their work in the classroom? They also could be encouraged to bring in examples of texts read at home—magazine pages, packaging, or mail—to emphasize that home literacy learning is valuable and can contribute to classroom literacy and vice versa. Classrooms open to literacy in this way are much more effective in being culturally responsive to the families and communities they serve. However, as Edwards (1995) points out, there is scope for teachers to learn from parents as well as for parents to learn from teachers about the two worlds of literacy.

In Practice

AN ENVIRONMENTAL PRINT WALK

We know young children's literacy development is helped by meaningful encounters with environmental print. Most families, in the course of everyday activities, provide children with such opportunities—in the home or neighborhood. Families can provide recognition of children's growing achievements in noticing familiar texts and what they mean. The family members' interaction with children around environmental print will affect what children learn from it. Children also learn if they see family members providing a model of using environmental print to accomplish various goals.

One way to work with families to increase their awareness of their power to influence development in this strand of literacy is an "environmental print walk" (Nutbrown & Hannon, 1997). Walk around the neighborhood of your school and note examples of print. Map out a route from one example to another and devise some kind of quiz, checklist, or worksheet for children to complete in cooperation with family members. The worksheet can include instructions or questions like the following: Find a sign that begins with the letter *P*; How could you find out what street you're on? and What's that store trying to sell us? Make the tasks appropriate for children's ages and abilities and parents' literacy levels. Explain to families that children can learn by seeing examples of print, being praised for whatever they can decipher, having the meaning and purpose of it explained to them, and seeing other family members use print. Individual families can be sent out on walks, but it can be more fun to make it a special summer evening event at a time when many working parents can join in. If the walk finishes at a picnic site or playground, so much the better. Afterward point out to families that they can do this type of activity for themselves. Tell parents they may be surprised what their children are learning!

Developing Home-Focused Programs for School-Age Children

In this level there is a deliberate, systematic, and sustained attempt to influence children's home literacy learning. Unlike the second level this might require extra teacher time or a different allocation of time. The most common form of such involvement is regularly sending school books or other reading materials home for parents to share with their children. In relation to ORIM we can see this as focusing on the reading–books strand, chiefly by increasing opportunities in the home. Some programs go further and seek to influence parent–child interaction. I (1995) have distinguished open and prescriptive approaches. In the latter, parents are involved in following a prescribed method of book sharing, for example through the paired reading technique (Topping & Lindsay, 1991) or pause, prompt, and praise (Glynn & McNaughton, 1985). These tend to focus on children's word–reading development. A concern with broader aspects of storybook reading is urged by Edwards (1989, 1995) and from different perspectives by Goldsmith and Handel (1990) and Arnold and Whitehurst (1994). The main implication for practice is that it is desirable to go beyond merely assisting parents to provide more opportunities to helping them reflect on and, if they wish, change their interaction around and during reading sessions. Nor should we overlook the R and M of ORIM. Parents can be helped to recognize children's literacy development in book reading, and it can be pointed out to parents that they can be a powerful model of literacy (Neuman, 1996).

Book reading is what people think of first in relation to school-age home-focused parent involvement. Other strands of literacy have been overlooked but deserve to be considered too. In relation to writing, one initiative has been reported by Green (1987) who describes a project in which parents of kindergarten children were shown three ways to help them at home (by acting as a scribe, by writing to children, and by encouraging children to write themselves). The oral language strand of early literacy development also has been neglected, although Wade (1984) has reported an initiative in which there was an attempt to enhance young children's storytelling ability.

In level three, parent involvement, there is considerable scope to develop practice across the various cells of the ORIM matrix. What classroom teachers choose to do will depend on their school's priorities and the resources available. Figure 5 suggests some key questions that can be used as a basis for planning action.

Developing Home-Focused Preschool Programs

We know that the preschool period is important in early literacy development. Can schools and early childhood programs work with parents before school entry? The approaches described earlier can be adapted for parents of preschool children (bearing in mind that what counts as *preschool* in one educational system will be *school-age* in another). Preschool parent involvement appears to have considerable potential and, if resources can be found, definitely should be considered in schools and communities where young children are likely to have low achievement in literacy. It is not a matter of "fixing" families and their children before school entry as much as giving parents options in supporting early literacy learning and equalizing children's

Figure 5 Working With Parents: 10 Key Questions

1. Is the focus to be children's home learning, school learning, or both?
2. Is the work with parents to be carried out in school, at home, or in both locations?
3. What is to be the target age range of the children and duration of the program?
4. Is the program to be selective or comprehensive?
5. Which strands of literacy are to be addressed?
6. Which aspects of the parents role are to be supported?
7. What resources will be needed to initiate and maintain the program and where will they come from?
8. How will the program be explained to families?
9. What is the timetable for implementation?
10. Will the program be evaluated? If so, how?

access to the school curriculum. It should also be accompanied by careful review of the experiences of the children and families after children start school, because preschool programs should never be regarded as a substitute for high-quality culturally responsive curricula.

One of the most effective forms of parent involvement at this level is helping parents to create more book-reading opportunities in the home. McCormick and Mason (1986) have described a program in which children had "little books" mailed to them in the months before they started kindergarten. In a British project described by Swinson (1985), parents of preschool children (ages 3 to 4) were encouraged to read to their children from books made available from a school. There were two initial meetings for parents to discuss home reading to children and general advice on good practice. The project ran for most of a school year. Book clubs for parents in schools have shown to be highly effective in promoting children's receptive language and concepts of print (Neuman, 1996). These initiatives are very simple and straightforward yet have been shown to produce measurable gains. The Pittsburgh Beginning With Books Project has provided packs of books for much younger children, without parent-teacher interaction, but on a much larger scale with thousands of children (Locke, 1988; Segel & Friedberg, 1991). There has since been a similar initiative on a smaller scale in the United Kingdom (Wade & Moore, 1993). In the Australian West Heidelberg Early Literacy Project a home-visiting initiative led to a program in which preschools sent books home and supported parents, through meetings in school and other means, in reading to their children (Toomey & Sloane, 1994).

Preschool parent involvement has focused very much on the reading-books strand in literacy, and mostly on parents providing opportunities, and there is scope to do much more. One attempt to cover all the cells in the ORIM matrix is the Raising Early Achievement in Literacy Project in Sheffield, England, which is currently working with teachers to develop and evaluate a parent-involvement program (Hannon & Nutbrown, 1997; Nutbrown & Hannon, 1997). In relation to the writing strand, for example, the Project has used ORIM to generate practical ideas for parent involvement such as those listed in Figure 6. The same questions generate ideas for other strands.

Figure 6 Applying ORIM to the Writing Strand

How can we help parents provide more opportunities?

• Suggest parents provide a small space (temporary or permanent) where children can draw and write. • Show photos of children writing at home. • Show possibilities of literacy–related sociodramatic play. • Point out writing possibilities with household materials (e.g., packaging or junk mail). • Provide starter packs of writing materials. • Use home visits to introduce variety in materials (e.g., lined paper or forms) and implements (pencils, felt tips, chalk, or paintbrushes). •

How can we enhance parents' recognition of early achievement?

• Show examples of how children's writing develops from earliest mark making to conventional script. • Use overhead projector presentations and wall displays. • Run workshops on writing development. • Invite parents to sort examples of writing into possible developmental sequence. • Encourage a home scrapbook of children's writing to show changes over a 1–2 year period. • Refer to writing when talking to parents about their child's activities during a preschool session. • Use "literacy jigsaw" to focus attention on writing achievements. •

How can we support and extend parents' interaction with their children?

• Encourage parents to involve children in writing tasks (greeting cards, shopping lists, and notes). • Invite parents to participate in shared writing sessions in school. • Emphasize value of accepting early approximations. • Give away the concept of scaffolding. •

Can we suggest how parents could provide a model of using written language?

• Use workshops, displays, everyday conversations, home visits, and leaflets to emphasize that children learn about writing from watching writers write. • Talk with parents about the influential models they provide in writing notes, greeting cards, or shopping lists; filling in forms; or doing domestic paperwork at home. • Use workshop to list other models that their children see (other adults, characters in books and television, secretaries, servers, and preschool teachers). • Ask parents to note all the different models of writing their child might see in a day. • Encourage parents to "scribe" for children. •

What We Know About What Works

The clearest evidence concerns home-focused programs (levels three and four). For school-age parent involvement, there have been numerous studies of the effects of both open and prescriptive approaches to parents hearing school-age children read at home, almost all of which have been demonstrated to produce gains (Hannon, 1995). The findings are more consistent for prescriptive approaches that tend to be implemented in limited-duration programs. The evidence is also very encouraging for preschool programs. Almost all studies cited earlier have reported gains.

The research literature to date is much less helpful in telling us whether one kind of program is better than another. There are methodological difficulties in comparing programs that differ in aims, literacy focus, target group, age range, and duration. There is very little evidence about long-term effects, and we do not yet know what can be gained by combining different programs or having programs with a broader scope in terms of ORIM than those tried so far. We do not know what is the limit to what can be achieved through parent involvement. Nevertheless, enough is known for classroom teachers and schools to be confident that well-planned parent involvement has positive outcomes.

What We Should Do

The challenge identified at the beginning of this chapter concerned four critical areas—the literacy curriculum, the parent's role, school policy, and rethinking professionalism. In each of these areas there are clearly things to be done. In relation to the curriculum, we need to be clear about the nature of school literacy while at the same time acknowledging the relevance and validity of children's home literacy. The early literacy curriculum should be open enough to permit, and even encourage, home-school links. In relation to the parents, it is important to recognize that they have considerable power to influence early literacy learning, particularly in the home, but at the same time they may appreciate support in key aspects of their role. In relation to school policy, the need is to be clear about aims and what level of commitment to parents is appropriate. Different levels of involvement will require different levels of staff time and funding. Finally, in relation to professionalism the issue is one of redefining or extending the teacher's role. To involve parents is not to give away teachers' professional expertise but to take on the challenge and stimulation of working with adults and young children in the conviction that anything that teachers believe they can accomplish alone, they can do better in collaboration with parents.

References

Arnold, D.S., & Whitehurst, G.J. (1994). Accelerating language development through picture book reading: A summary of dialogic reading and its effects. In D.K. Dickinson (Ed.), *Bridges to literacy: Children, families, and schools* (pp. 103–128). Cambridge, MA: Blackwell.

Edwards, P.A. (1989). Supporting lower SES mothers' attempts to provide scaffolding for book reading. In J. Allen & J.M. Mason (Eds.), *Risk makers, risk takers, risk breakers: Reducing the risks for young literacy learners* (pp. 222–250). Portsmouth, NH: Heinemann.

Edwards, P.A. (1995). Combining parents' and teachers' thoughts about storybook reading at home and school. In L.M. Morrow (Ed.), *Family literacy: Connections in schools and communities* (pp. 54–69). Newark, DE: International Reading Association.

Farquhar, C., Blatchford, P., Burke, J., Plewis, I., & Tizard, B. (1985). A comparison of the views of parents and reception teachers. *Education 3–13, 13,* 17–22.

Glynn, T., & McNaughton, S. (1985). The Mangere home and school remedial reading procedures: Continuing research on their effectiveness. *New Zealand Journal of Psychology, 14,* 66–77.

Goldsmith, E., & Handel, R. (1990). *Family reading: An intergenerational approach to literacy.* Syracuse, NY: New Readers Press.

Goodman, Y.M. (1980). The roots of literacy. In M.P. Douglas (Ed.), *Forty-fourth Yearbook of the Claremont Reading Conference* (pp. 1–12). Claremont, CA: Claremont Reading Conference.

Goodman, Y.M. (1986). Children coming to know literacy. In W.H. Teale & E. Sulzby (Eds.), *Emergent literacy: Writing and reading* (pp. 1–14). Norwood, NJ: Ablex.

Goswami, U., & Bryant, P. (1990). *Phonological skills and learning to read.* Hove, UK: Erlbaum.

Green, C. (1987). Parental facilitation of young children's writing. *Early Child Development and Care, 28,* 31–37.

Hall, N. (1987). *The emergence of literacy.* London: Hodder & Stoughton.

Hall, N., Herring, G., Henn, H., & Crawford, L. (1989). *Parental views on writing and the teaching of writing.* Manchester, UK: Manchester Polytechnic School of Education.

Hannon, P. (1995). *Literacy, home and school: Research and practice in teaching literacy with parents.* London: Falmer.

Hannon, P., & James, S. (1990). Parents' and teachers' perspectives on preschool literacy development. *British Educational Research Journal, 16*(3), 259–272.

Hannon, P., & Nutbrown, C. (1997). Teachers' use of a conceptual framework for early literacy education involving parents. *Teacher Development, 1*(3), 405–420.

Hannon, P., Weinberger, J., & Nutbrown, C. (1991). A study of work with parents to promote early literacy development. *Research Papers in Education, 6*(2), 77–97.

Heath, S.B. (1983). *Ways with words: Language, life and work in communities and classrooms.* Cambridge, UK: Cambridge University Press.

Locke, J.L. (1988) Pittsburgh's Beginning with Books Project. *School Library Journal,* February, 22–24.

Maclean, M., Bryant, P., & Bradley, L. (1987). Rhymes, nursery rhymes, and reading in early childhood. *Merrill-Palmer Quarterly, 33*(3), 255–281.

McCormick, C.E., & Mason, J.M. (1986). Intervention procedures for increasing preschool children's interest in and knowledge about reading. In W.H. Teale & E. Sulzby (Eds.), *Emergent literacy: Writing and reading* (pp. 90–115). Norwood, NJ: Ablex.

Meek, M. (1982). *Learning to read.* London: The Bodley Head.

Neuman, S.B. (1996). Children engaging in storybook reading: The influence of access to print resources, opportunity, and parental interaction. *Early Childhood Research Quarterly, 11,* 495–514.

Nutbrown, C., & Hannon, P. (Eds.). (1997). *Preparing for early literacy education with parents: A professional development manual.* Nottingham, UK: NES-Arnold.

Nutbrown, C., Hannon, P., & Weinberger, J. (1991). Training teachers to work with parents to promote early literacy development. *International Journal of Early Childhood, 23*(2), 1–10.

Ryback, D., & Staats, W. (1970). Parents as behaviour therapy technicians in treating reading deficits. *Journal of Behavior Therapy and Experimental Psychiatry, 1,* 109–119.

Segel, E., & Friedberg, J.B. (1991). "Is today Liberry Day?" Community support for family literacy. *Language Arts, 68,* 654–657.

Snow, C. (1991). The theoretical basis for relationships between language and literacy in development. *Journal of Research in Childhood Education, 6*(1), 5–10.

Swinson, J. (1985). A parental involvement project in a nursery school. *Educational Psychology in Practice, 1*(1), 19–22.

Taylor, D. (1983). *Family literacy: Young children learning to read and write.* Exeter, NH: Heinemann.

Taylor, D., & Dorsey-Gaines, C. (1988). *Growing up literate: Learning from inner-city families.* Portsmouth, NH: Heinemann.

Teale, W.H., & Sulzby, E. (Eds.). (1986). *Emergent literacy: Writing and reading.* Norwood, NJ: Ablex.

Tizard, B., Blatchford, P., Burke, J., Farquhar, C., & Plewis, I. (1988). *Young children at school in the inner city*. London: Erlbaum.

Toomey, D., & Sloane, J. (1994). Fostering children's early literacy development through parent involvement: A five-year program. In D.K. Dickinson (Ed.), *Bridges to literacy: Children, families, and schools* (pp. 129–149). Cambridge, MA: Blackwell.

Topping, K., & Lindsay, G. (1991). The structure and development of the paired reading technique. *Journal of Research in Reading, 15*(2), 120–136.

Wade, B. (1984). Story at home and school (Educational Review Publication Number 10). Birmingham, UK: University of Birmingham, Faculty of Education.

Wade, B., & Moore, M. (1993). *Bookstart in Birmingham* (Book Trust Report No. 2). London: Book Trust.

Weinberger, J. (1996). *Literacy goes to school*. London: Paul Chapman.

Weinberger, J. (1998). Young children's literacy experiences within the fabric of daily life. In R. Campbell (Ed.), *Facilitating preschool literacy* (pp. 39–50). Newark, DE. International Reading Association.

Wells, G. (1987). *The meaning makers: Children learning language and using language to learn*. London: Hodder and Stoughton.

CHAPTER 8

How Do We Motivate Children Toward Independent Reading and Writing?

Lesley Mandel Morrow and Linda B. Gambrell

What do we know about motivating children to want to learn? Motivation is the process of initiating, sustaining, and directing one's own activity. It also means returning to and continuing to work on a task with sustained engagement (Maehr, 1976; Wittrock, 1986). If we transfer this general definition of motivation to describe readers and writers, we would say that motivated readers and writers are individuals who choose to read and write on a regular basis for long periods of time, for pleasure and information. Both literature about motivation and our observations in research suggest many combinations of settings and activities to motivate children to learn.

We had been working with Mrs. Youssef and other early childhood teachers in the same school concerning the design of social and physical contexts to motivate children to read and write. We tried to apply motivation theory to the design of classroom environments, activities, and settings for learning that would promote independent reading and writing. In Mrs. Youssef's first-grade classroom, we designed a literacy center that included many choices of activities; we then visited regularly to observe children using the center. Mrs. Youssef had modeled the use of the materials in the center and now was providing time for children to use them. Children could choose from many activities and decide whether to work alone or with others. We observed the following.

Children were curled up on the rug in the literacy center, leaning on pillows with books they had selected to read silently. Don and Lea, squeezed tightly into one rocking chair, shared a book. Natalie, Shakiera, and Dharmesh were snuggled in a refrigerator box that was painted to make it more attractive. Furnished with stuffed animals to make it cozy, it created a private spot for the children. They took turns reading the same books.

Isabela and Veronica were using the felt board and story characters for *The Three Bears* (Galdone, 1975), taking turns reading and manipulating the figures. Each time they came to the phrase *Who's been sitting in my chair?* they read together.

Four children were listening on headsets to a tape of *The Little Engine That Could* (Piper, 1954). Each child held a copy of the book and chanted along with the narrative when they came to part that read, *I think I can, I think I can.*

Mat and Tim were at the Author's Spot writing a book about snakes, and bouncing ideas back and forth. Some children were checking books out of the classroom library to take home to read.

Tashiba had four copies of a story that she handed out to other children. She made a circle of chairs where the group sat as she pretended to be the teacher. She read to the others, stopping occasionally to ask if anyone else wanted a chance to read. Mrs. Youssef sat in the circle with the children, taking her turn at reading when Tashiba called on her (Morrow, 1996).

The room was filled with productive activity. The children were motivated to read and write because the environment was rich with accessible literacy materials. Students had responsibility for choosing activities and deciding whether to work alone or with others in an atmosphere that was self-directed and social.

Motivational Contexts for Learning

Skinner and Belmont (1993) revealed that teachers who have clear goals promote motivation. In addition, teachers should provide support in the form of scaffolding and positive reinforcement. Erickson (1995) found that when children were given responsibility for their learning they were more likely to be motivated to work toward a goal than children who were in situations that were controlled by the teacher. These controlled situations are characterized by an overemphasis on rules, procedures, and time restraints for completing projects. Students need some autonomy and opportunities in which they can raise questions and search for answers. Often they focus better on activities requiring higher-order thinking. Children are motivated to accomplish goals with challenging activities in settings where they have some control and the opportunity for social collaboration with peers.

Oldfather (1993) and Turner (1995) suggest that the social constructivist theory has implications for learning settings that tend to be motivating. The social constructivist views learning as an active process in which knowledge is constructed by individuals, based on their personal experiences and prior knowledge. Learning is a social process where learners construct knowledge together (McCombs, 1991). In classrooms that incorporate this theory into practice, learning is student-centered around topics of interest to children. Students are encouraged to take risks, express ideas, and have choices as to what they will learn and how they will go about achieving goals. Children are involved in directing many of their learning experiences and have input into the evaluation of their performance (Bandura, 1989; Ford, 1992).

Csikszentimihalyi (1990) suggests that an activity will be motivating if it is challenging, but not beyond the skill of the learner. The challenge must be such that it results in perceived success. Children must experience success to be motivated to continue work on a task. Teachers offer students guidance and support to help with challenging activities.

The following list summarizes the kinds of activities that have been found to motivate learning:

1. Activities with materials that are easily accessible.
2. Activities that are facilitated by teachers who model, guide, and scaffold information to be learned.

Morrow and Gambrell

3. Activities that provide for choices of materials and experiences for learning.

4. Activities that challenge, but can be accomplished.

5. Activities that give the learner responsibility and some control over the learning process, such as self-direction, self-selection, and pacing of learning activities.

6. Activities that are meaningful and functional by using authentic materials and settings.

7. Activities with conceptual orientations that add interest to what is being learned.

8. Activities involving social collaboration among peers and adults.

9. Activities that offer time for practicing skills learned in settings that are independent of the teacher.

10. Activities that offer the child a feeling of success.

Based on this review of motivation theory, several elements emerge as most important. Access to materials and choice of materials that are challenging and offer opportunities for success have been found to promote motivation. Young children engage in reading and writing in a sustained manner when they have access to literacy materials and literacy-enriched centers with authentic tasks and themes (Morrow, 1992; Neuman & Roskos, 1993). The physical environment of classrooms is the natural place for providing access to materials to motivate reading and writing.

Another element that emerged as extremely important to motivation is social engagement in learning. In the following section we will discuss how the physical environment is a social setting for learning in which students have the opportunity to practice skills learned with peers and adults. They are settings where students have autonomy to make decisions about their learning.

Physical Contexts That Motivate Reading and Writing: Making Materials Accessible

Motivation theory suggests that access to materials, in this case reading and writing materials, will encourage students to engage in literacy activities in a voluntary and sustained manner. Therefore the physical environment in a classroom can play an important role in motivating children to read and write. When designing classrooms, many elements of motivation theory should be considered, including the meaning and function of the materials for students. Materials should be connected to content-area subjects or a theme to add interest. There should be many choices of materials and activities that provide a challenge and lead to success. The environment needs to be designed for social interaction among peers and adults, and materials must be accessible so that students can use them easily.

Historically, philosophers who studied early childhood development described the importance of preparing the environment with manipulative materials to foster learning in real-life environments (Froebel, 1974; Rusk & Scotland, 1979). Montessori (1965) advocated carefully prepared classrooms to promote independent learning with every material in the environment having a specific learning objective.

Research has demonstrated how the physical design of classrooms affects children's behavior. Rooms partitioned into small spaces facilitate verbal interaction and cooperative play among peers more than rooms with large open spaces (Field, 1980). Children in carefully arranged rooms have shown more creative productivity and greater use of language-related activities than children in randomly arranged rooms (Moore, 1986). Literacy-enriched dramatic-play areas based on themes have stimulated literacy activities and the enhancement of literacy skills (Morrow & Rand, 1991; Neuman & Roskos, 1992). Dramatic play with story props has improved comprehension of stories, including recall of details and the ability to sequence and interpret (Mandler & Johnson, 1977). Enhancing physical designs of literacy centers increased children's use of materials in the centers and their literacy achievement as well (Morrow, 1992).

Arranging the Classroom to Motivate Reading and Writing

The following plan is suggested as a guide to effectively arrange a classroom. Literacy-rich classrooms contain centers dedicated to content areas, such as social studies, science, math, art, music, dramatic play, block play, and literacy (see Figure 1 on the next page). Centers are accessible for children and contain general materials for each content area and materials specific to topics being studied. Literacy materials are included in all centers, and centers are designed so children can use these materials independently or in small groups. The materials are labeled and stored on shelves or in boxes. Each piece has a designated spot so that teachers can direct children to specific items and children can find and return them easily. Early in a school year, centers hold a small number of items; new materials are added as the year progresses. It is extremely important to note that when new items are placed in centers, teachers must introduce their purpose, use, and placement (Montessori, 1965).

The room design should support whole-group, small-group, and individual instruction. A conference table provides space for small-group and individualized instruction for skill development. The table is placed in a quiet area of the room and is situated so the teacher can see the children who are working independently at centers.

Centers are positioned so areas where quiet work is typical (literacy, math, social studies, and science centers) are away from more noisy, active environments (dramatic play, blocks).

Visually Accessible Environmental Print

Literacy-rich classrooms are filled with functional print. Signs communicate information, for example, Quiet Please and Please Put Materials Away After Using Them. Charts labeled Helpers, Daily Routines, Attendance, and Calendar simplify classroom management (Morrow, 1997a; Schickedanz, 1993). A notice board is used to communicate with the children in writing. Experience charts display new words generated from themes, recipes, and science experiments. Environmental print must be used, however, or it will go unnoticed. Children are encouraged to read it, copy it, and to use the word labels in their writing.

The Literacy Center

Children read and write more in classrooms with literacy centers than children whose classrooms do not have them (Morrow, 1992).

Figure 1 Early Childhood Classroom Floor Plan

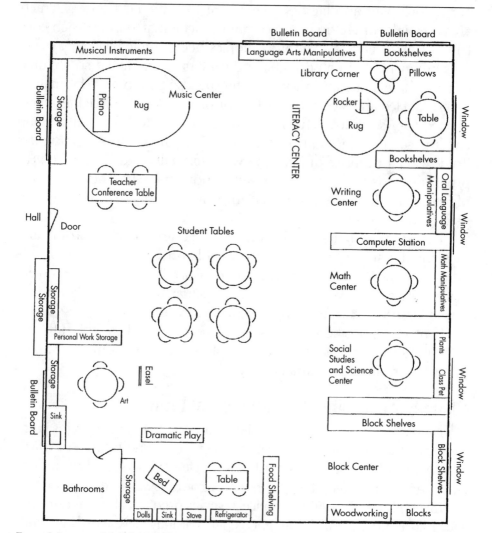

From Morrow, L.M. (1997). *Literacy development in the early years: Helping children read and write* (3rd ed.). Boston, MA: Allyn & Bacon. Used with permission.

The literacy center includes space and materials for writing, reading, oral language, and listening (see Figure 2 on page 152). It should be visually attractive with children having easy access to books, and children should be involved in designing, managing, and developing the rules for using the center.

Morrow and Gambrell

Materials from the literacy center can be used in other parts of the room. Because many activities in the literacy center take place on the floor, it should have a rug and pillows or beanbag chairs. A rocking chair allows for comfortable reading, and children enjoy holding stuffed animals as they read. Books are stored in open-faced shelving for displaying titles about themes being studied. Regular bookshelves also are used to house five to eight books per child at three to four grade levels. Books are color coded by categories and represent different genres of children's literature such as picture storybooks, poetry, informational books, magazines, biographies, fairy tales, novels, cookbooks, joke books, and craft books. Books also are placed in baskets with labels representing differing levels of difficulty. Interest in the books is kept high by rotating them regularly, and by permitting children to check books out of the classroom to read at home. Literacy manipulatives such as felt boards with story characters, puppets, and taped stories with headsets have motivated children to engage in storytelling, storybook reading, and writing (Morrow, 1997b). Word-analysis games are included as well.

The Author's Spot

The writing portion of the literacy center, called the Author's Spot, includes a table and chairs and writing materials such as colored markers, crayons, pencils, paper, chalk, and a chalkboard. Various types of paper are available. Most of the paper is unlined newsprint ranging in size from 8 × 11 to 24 × 36. Index cards are used for recording "very-own words" that are stored in index boxes. Folders, one for each child, are used to collect writing samples. A computer is a necessary component of the Author's Spot.

Materials for making books are essential, including paper, a hole punch, a stapler, and construction paper. Blank books prepared by the teacher, keyed to themes, invite children to write. A bulletin board for children to display selected pieces of their writing is important, as well as a message board used to exchange notes among members of the class and the teacher. Mailboxes, stationery, envelopes, and stamps for children's incoming and outgoing mail may be placed in the writing center.

Figure 2 The Literacy Center

From Morrow, L.M. (1997). *The Literacy Center: Contexts for Reading and Writing.* York, ME: Stenhouse Publishers. Used with permission.

Integrating Literacy Materials Into the Content Areas

Programs that motivate early literacy development include an integrated approach to literacy learning. Books to read, materials to write with, things to listen to, and activities to talk about are incorporated into subject–area teaching. Literacy activities have more meaning when they are integrated into content areas (Dewey, 1966). These content themes encourage students to use new vocabulary and ideas, and provide a reason for reading and writing. With each theme studied, new books, posters, music, art projects, dramatic–play materials, and scientific objects are added.

Mrs. Green's first–grade class, which is an excellent example of how to use literacy materials in content areas, was studying nutrition. She extended the theme to all learning centers and encouraged reading and writing by adding the following materials and activities:

Science center. Materials for nutrition projects were added such as recipes and the ingredients needed to prepare them, foods to be classified for nutritional content, and foods to be tasted. There were journals to record food eaten daily to account for their nutritional value, and books about good nutrition.

Social studies center. Pictures of food were placed on maps to show where they were produced. Recipe books and recipes from home sent by parents representing different cultures were added.

Math center. Various foods, such as macaroni or beans were added and used as counters. Counting books that contained foods, and blank books for children to create their own number books about different foods also were included.

Literacy center. Books, magazines, and pamphlets about good nutrition were added to the library section of the center. The Author's Spot had boxes for index cards for collecting nutritional recipes from other countries.

Art center. Play dough for making pretend foods and a recipe poster for making the play dough was added to the art center. Dry foods to make collages (macaroni, peas, and seeds), and fruit and vegetables for printing with paint were added as well.

Music center. Songs on tape about nutrition were included in this center such as *Chicken Soup With Rice* (Sendak, 1962).

Block center. Blocks were used to design places where food comes from, such as farms and supermarkets. The following items also were added to this center: farm props (small plastic animals and plants), supermarket props (empty food boxes, receipts, play money, and bags), and posters displaying food information.

Dramatic-play area. This area was turned into different ethnic restaurants and included menus, receipts, order forms, recipes, 3 × 5 cards for new recipes, cookbooks, empty food boxes, signs found in restaurants, a cash register, play money, food posters, cooking magazines, and clothing for servers.

Social Contexts for Motivating Reading and Writing

Allowing children to participate in social contexts is one of the most important motivating factors for reading and writing. With the environment in place providing accessible materials, choice of activities, and materials that are meaningful and functional, the teacher needs to provide time for students to interact socially in literacy activities. For this to occur successfully, teachers must model and guide the use of activities and materials. When children work in social settings productivity increases because they explain things to one another, listen to one another's explanations, and arrive at joint understandings (Johnson & Johnson, 1987). In social collaborative settings, peers offer support and help to one another (Forman & Cazden, 1985), and students accomplish more together than they could do alone. The ultimate goal for social interactive settings is for students to learn to be self-directed, make decisions, work together, stay on task, and be accountable for completing activities. Initially children need guidance when working in these settings, but with experience they participate with less formal structure.

Organizing for Social Collaborative Activities

In preparation for social collaborative reading and writing activities, students need guidelines such as the following: Decide who you will work with, select only one or two activities to do in a given period, handle materials carefully, speak in soft voices, put materials back in their place, try new activities, stay with a group or partner to complete tasks, and record completed tasks in a log.

Rules for social collaboration may include the following:

- When working in groups or with partners, select a leader to help get started, be sure that everyone has a job, share materials, and take turns talking.

- Helpful things to say to one another may include the following: I like your work; You did a good job; Can I help you?

- Check your work and how well you cooperated by asking yourself the following: Did you say helpful things? Did you help one another? Did you share materials? Did you take turns? Did you all have jobs?

When introducing collaborative activities, some teachers assign children to centers or activities. Eventually, teachers can allow children to choose peers with whom to work and what activities to do. The role of the teacher during this time is to model behavior, work with individuals and small groups, and act as a facilitator in the classroom.

What Happens During Social Collaborative Activities

Preparing the environment for social collaborative activities allows children to engage in practicing and refining a variety of literacy skills. For example, children may write their own stories and then prepare felt characters to present them. Children improve reading comprehension by discussing stories and retelling stories in various ways such as tape recordings, puppet shows, or dramatic presentations. The use of manipulative literacy materials allows children to read and write in different ways and satisfies their individual learning styles. When collaborating, children help one another read words, come up with ideas, and spell. Learning also occurs through social conflicts when students disagree about spelling a word, or what should happen next in a story they are writing. Conflict enables children to study the options and negotiate a compromise in order to reach a decision (Piaget & Inhelder, 1969).

Illustrations of Social Learning Settings

The following are settings that promote independent, self-directed, social engagement in reading and writing.

Partner Reading and Writing

Ms. Keefe, a first–grade teacher, includes partner reading and partner writing in her classroom. Children select a partner for reading and writing for a week-long period. At the end of this time they select a new partner to work with. We observed Ms. Keefe's room when she initiated partner reading. The exercise was tied to the study of an author, Arnold Lobel. After Ms. Keefe read one of the author's books, partners could select a Lobel book. The format involved each pair of students finding a comfortable spot in the classroom, a reviewing of the book by looking at the pictures first, and discussing what they thought it might be about prior to reading. Then the children took turns reading. When the reading was done, the children reflected on what the story had been about and how closely their predictions matched the book.

Ms. Keefe also engaged her children in partner writing. She always began her day with a story she read aloud to the children based on a theme being studied. The day we observed she read *Arthur's Tooth* (Brown, 1978) because it was dental-health week. Ms. Keefe suggested that the children write about an experience they had with their teeth, such as going to the dentist or losing a tooth. Children found partners and discussed what they were going to write about. Each gave the other some input before writing. After writing, the partners read their stories to each other. Then they suggested ideas for change or additions to their partner's work. The partners made the suggested revisions and then read their stories to each other again.

Buddy Reading and Writing

Buddy reading and writing is similar to partner reading and writing, but buddies are children from different grade levels working in pairs. In this setting the older child will read to the younger child and is coached about being a mentor; however the younger child will read

In Practice

THE POWER
OF COLLECTION

Children love to collect things—to line up objects and delight in what they have to offer. Collections can be powerful motivators for literacy, too, as Mr. Roller quickly discovered with his bustling kindergartners.

Together the teacher and class decided to build a large collection of bookmarks for their classroom, so they gathered bookmarks from neighborhood libraries, bookstores, and family and friends. To show off their collection, they made a bookmark border around the entire room, low enough for everyone to see and touch.

From time to time Mr. Roller would pause and comment on the display, pointing out colors, special words, and different sizes and shapes, and admiring the beautiful tassels that some of the bookmarks had. Sometimes he asked the children for their ideas about how to arrange and rearrange the collection in different and interesting ways.

The teacher also encouraged the children to make their own bookmarks for the collection. With the children's help, he made a bookmark-making place in the art area of the classroom and stocked it with plenty of supplies: assorted paper, writing tools, stencils, stamps, sequins, glitter, and stickers. Children enjoyed creating with these materials while at the same time encountering basic ideas about written language. They explored print, manipulated writing tools, compared language, questioned and argued about word spellings, and indulged in simple problem-solving activities with print.

As collections go, the bookmark collection got to be pretty big—but the literacy awareness it stimulated in Mr. Roller's kindergartners was bigger still.

as well. Buddies also are encouraged to write together using the partner-reading format described earlier.

Literature Circles

Literature circles are another social setting for motivating reading. They are groups of three or more children and are formed for children to discuss books they have read with one another. The teacher models literature-circle activities so they can be carried out successfully. With young children, literature circles will be more successful if topics are raised for discussion by the teacher. Topics might include telling the parts of a story that they liked best, the parts of the story that they did not enjoy, and how they might have ended the story in a different way. After practicing in these circles with the teacher, the children should be able to carry out these discussions alone with an appointed leader to help the organization of the session

Thematically Enriched Dramatic Play

An observation of Ms. Roberts first-grade class illustrates how activities modeled by the teacher motivate reading and writing when children use materials in social settings that have meaning, a function, and concept orientation. With each thematic unit, Ms. Roberts helps her children design the dramatic-play center to reflect the topic being studied. When learning about animals, the students in her room decided to create a veterinarian's office. The class visited a veterinarian to help with their planning. They created a waiting room with chairs and a table filled with magazines and books in the dramatic-play center. Ms. Roberts suggested including pamphlets about good health practices for pets, which she had obtained from the veterinarian. The children made a variety of posters, including one that listed the doctor's hours, one that said, No Smoking, and one reading Check In With The Nurse When You Arrive. The nurse's table contained forms for patients to fill out, a telephone, telephone books, appointment cards, and a calendar. There were patient folders, prescription pads, white coats, masks, gloves, cotton swabs, a toy doctor's kit, and stuffed animals. Blank paper, a stapler, pencils, markers, colored pencils, and crayons were placed in the area as well. The classroom computer was relocated in the dramatic-play area for keeping patient records and other files. The center's design was a collaborative effort by the teacher and children.

After preparing the environment with her students, Ms. Roberts modeled the use of the materials. She suggested, "While waiting for your turn to see the doctor, you can read to your pet and the nurse can ask you to fill out forms. The receptionist can talk to patients on the phone about problems with their pets, schedule appointments, and write out appointment cards. He or she can write bills, accept payments, and give receipts. The doctor can write prescriptions and patient reports." Later, Ms. Roberts joined the children in the dramatic-play area, pretending first to be the nurse and then the doctor, so that she could model the types of literacy behavior she hoped the children would try.

A week later, the children were fully engaged in this center. Jonnell sat in the waiting room reading the story *Caps for Sale* (Slobodkina, 1993) to her pet monkey. Damien joined her with his pet rabbit and listened. He asked if he could have a turn reading. Before they were finished, the nurse called Jonnell to come and answer questions about her monkey's problems. When Jonnell finished filling out forms, she watched the two pets for Damien while he spoke with the nurse. Katie was acting as the doctor, examining a pet cat that was brought in by Emily. Katie wrote the animal's name and the owner's name in a file folder and then picked up the prescription pad. She told Emily, "You see this. Now this says that you make sure that this teddy bear takes 100 pills every hour, until he feels better. Keep him in bed with covers, and be sure to give him lots of juice." Then she wrote down *100 PLS EVRY OWR* on the pad.

Ms. Roberts was aware of the importance of the physical environment and social learning to help develop literacy skills by motivating children to communicate in various ways.

Concluding Remarks

The room designs discussed in this chapter, with interesting, accessible materials and activities that are guided by the teacher, should develop literacy through positive and successful experiences. The social context allows for practicing skills, selecting activities, and taking responsibility for learning. These are all motivating elements that will help to ensure the development of lifelong voluntary readers who choose to read for pleasure and for information.

References

Bandura, A. (1989). *Social foundations of thought and action: A social cognitive theory.* Englewood Cliffs, NJ: Prentice Hall.

Csikszentimihalyi, M. (1990). Literacy and intrinsic motivation. *Daedalus, 119*(2), 115–140.

Dewey, J. (1966). *Democracy and education.* New York: Free Press.

Erickson, H.L. (1995). *Stirring the head, heart, and soul.* Thousand Oaks, CA: Corwin Press.

Field, T. (1980). Preschool play: Effects of teacher/child ratios and organization of classroom space. *Child Study Journal, 10,* 191–205.

Ford, M.E. (1992). *Motivating humans.* Newbury Park, CA: Sage.

Forman, E., & Cazden, C. (1985). Exploring Vygotskian perspectives in education: The cognitive value of peer interaction. In J. Wertsch (Ed.), *Culture, communication, and cognition. Vygotskian perspectives* (pp. 323–347). Cambridge, UK: Cambridge University Press.

Froebel, F. (1974). *The education of man.* Clifton, NJ: Augustus M. Kelly.

Johnson, D.W., & Johnson, R.T. (1987). *Learning together and alone* (2nd ed.). Englewood Cliffs, NJ: Prentice Hall.

Maehr, M.L. (1976). Continuing motivation: An analysis of a seldom considered educational outcome. *Review of Educational Research, 46,* 443–462.

Mandler, J., & Johnson, N. (1977). Remembrance of things parsed: Story structure and recall. *Cognitive Psychology, 9,* 111–151.

McCombs, B.L. (1991). Unraveling motivation: New perspectives from research and practice. *The Journal of Experimental Education, 60,* 3–88.

Montessori, M. (1965). *Spontaneous activity in education.* New York: Schocken Books.

Moore, G. (1986) Effects of the spatial definition of behavior settings on children's behavior: A quasi-experimental field study. *Journal of Environmental Psychology, 6,* 205–231.

Morrow, L.M. (1992). The impact of a literature-based program on literacy achievement, use of literature, and attitudes of children from minority backgrounds. *Reading Research Quarterly, 27,* 250–275.

Morrow, L.M. (1996). *Motivating reading and writing in diverse classroom: Social and physical contexts in a literature-based program* (NCTE Research Report No. 28). Urbana, IL: National Council of Teachers of English.

Morrow, L.M. (1997a). *Literacy development in the early years* (3rd ed.). Boston, MA: Allyn & Bacon.

Morrow, L.M. (1997b) *The literacy center: Contexts for reading and writing.* York, ME: Stenhouse.

Morrow, L.M., & Rand, M. (1991) Promoting literacy during play by designing early childhood classroom environments. *The Reading Teacher, 44,* 396–402.

Neuman, S.B., & Roskos, K. (1992). Literacy objects as cultural tools: Effects on children's literacy behaviors in play. *Reading Research Quarterly, 27*(3), 202–225.

Neuman, S.B, & Roskos, K. (1993). Access to print for children of poverty: Differential effects of adult mediation and literacy-enriched play settings on environmental and function print tasks. *American Educational Research Journal, 32,* 801–828.

Oldfather, P. (1993). What students say about motivating experiences in a whole language classroom. *The Reading Teacher, 46,* 672–681.

Piaget, J., & Inhelder, B. (1969). *The psychology of the child.* New York: Basic Books.

Rusk, R., & Scotland, J. (1979). *Doctrines of the great educators.* New York: St. Martin's Press.

Schickedanz, J.A. (1993). Designing the early childhood classroom environment to facilitate literacy development. In B. Spodek & O.N. Saracho (Eds.), *Language and literacy in early childhood education: Yearbook in early childhood education, Vol. 4* (pp. 141–155). New York: Teachers College Press.

Skinner, E., & Belmont, M. (1993). Motivation in the classroom: Reciprocal effect of teacher behavior and student engagement across the school year. *Journal of Educational Psychology, 85,* 571–581.

Turner, J.C. (1995). The influence of classroom contexts on young children's motivation for literacy. *Reading Research Quarterly, 30,* 410–441.

Wittrock, M.C. (1986). Students' thought processes. In M.C. Wittrock (Ed.), *Handbook of research on teaching* (pp. 297–314). New York: Macmillan.

Children's Literature References

Brown, M. (1978). *Arthur's tooth.* Boston, MA: Little, Brown.

Galdone, P. (1975). *The three bears.* Boston, MA: Houghton Mifflin.

Piper, W. (1954). *The little engine that could.* New York: Platt & Munk.

Sendak, M. (1962). *Chicken soup with rice.* New York: HarperCollins.

Slobodkina, E. (1993). *Caps for sale.* New York: Scholastic.

CHAPTER 9

How Do We Teach Literature to Young Children?

Lea M. McGee

Sharing literature with children is a much-enjoyed and frequent activity in many families. Some parents immerse their young children in experiences with literature soon after birth, and activities with books continue to be a central part of family activities throughout the childhood years (Taylor, 1983; Taylor & Dorsey-Gaines, 1988). Research has shown that young children benefit in many ways from frequent activities with books. They have larger, more literate vocabularies and learn to read better than children who have few book experiences (Dickinson & Tabors, 1991; Wells, 1986). More importantly, book-reading interactions during the preschool years actually seem to provide children with opportunities to learn how to understand stories as well as with models of literary language and structures usually not found in daily speech (Cochran-Smith, 1984; Purcell-Gates, 1988). Sharing good stories provides children with many opportunities to learn how to talk about and understand stories in ways that we expect in the mainstream literary culture. Children learn to construct story meanings using a variety of meaning-making strategies.

Learning How to Mean: Understanding Literary Language, Characters, and Events

In the following book-reading interaction between 18-month-old Kristen and her mother, they share a favorite story, *The Three Little Pigs* (Galdone, 1970). Kristen's understanding of the story reflects her level of language and cognitive development. Her mother accepts Kristen's responses to the story and extends her understanding.

Kristen: (brings the book, sits on her mother's lap, and turns the book so the cover is facing right-side-up.)

Mother: The three little pigs, (points to each of the pigs on the cover of the book). (Kristen opens the book and turns several pages while her mother is talking.)

Kristen: (gazes at a picture and points to a picture of a tree) Tee (looks up at her mother).

Mother: Yes, it's a tree.

Kristen: (points to another tree in the picture) Tee (looks up at mother again).

Mother: Um, um, (points to each of the little pigs in the illustrations) Here are the little pigs. Bye, bye mama (waves her hand). We're going to build us a house.

Kristen: (laughs, waves at the mama pig in the illustration and turns the page.)

Mother: Look. The first pig... (Kristen turns page).

Mother: Oh, oh, I see that wolf (points to the wolf, eyes get larger as if in fright).

Kristen: (turns page and points to wolf) oh, oh.

Mother: Oh, oh. He huffffed and puffffed (blowing on Kristen) and he blewwww that pig away. Very bad, isn't he? (in different tone directed toward Kristen as an aside).

In this interaction Kristen used several meaning-making strategies to construct her own understanding of the story. One strategy was to name or label objects that she recognized in the illustrations (trees) and another was to use her mother's feedback to confirm her labeling. Her mother showed her a more sophisticated meaning-making strategy—to name the characters rather than name random items in the illustrations.

Researchers have examined many book-reading interactions between parents or teachers and young children. They have found that children use a great variety of strategies that help them construct the meaning of stories. In addition to the strategy of labeling, children ask questions about the location of characters in pictures, meanings of words, or reasons for actions (Ninio & Bruner, 1978; Yaden & McGee, 1984; Yaden, Smolkin, & Conlon, 1990). One of the most important meaning-making strategies that children use is to connect what they know about life to what is happening in stories (Cochran-Smith, 1984).

In the following book-reading interaction, Ms. Amy, the teacher, and a group of preschoolers are talking about the wordless book *The Snowman* (Briggs, 1978). In this example, Ms. Amy asked the children to identify the object used to make the snowman's nose. The children made guesses using their knowledge of objects in the real world.

Ms. Amy:	What's that he's got Ben? (points to a round, orange object [used] to form snowman's nose).
Anna and Jody:	Carrot!
Ms. Amy:	([makes] circular motion [on round object in illustration])
Bobby:	Meatball! Meatball!
Kris:	Oranges!
Ms. Amy:	Yes, Kris, I think you...That's right!
Unidentified child:	Meatball! Meatball!
Anna:	They're oranges!
Jody:	Oranges!
Unidentified child:	Tangerine!
Ms. Amy:	Well, it's kind of oval like a tangerine (makes oval shape with hands). (Cochran-Smith, 1984, pp. 185–186)

As shown in this interaction, the children made several inferences about the identity of the snowman's nose including a meatball, carrot, orange, and tangerine. This wordless book provides no textual information about the actual identity of the snowman's nose, and the illustrations only hint at shape and color. The children inferred the identity of the snowman's nose matching the clues in the illustration with what they knew.

Making inferences such as these fills in gaps of information not provided in the text or illustrations. That is, all stories have gaps or places in the text where information is not included. In order to construct a story's meaning, readers fill the gaps by making inferences (Iser, 1978; Rosenblatt, 1978). In the story *The Snowman*, the identity of the snowman's nose is a gap in the story. The children filled the gap using their real-world knowledge in conjunction with the illustration and clues from their teacher.

Supporting Children's Meaning-Making Development: Story Reader as Mediator

As shown in preceding book-reading interactions, the story readers (Kristen's mother and Ms. Amy) played critical roles in the storybook read alouds. They modified their interactions and monitored children's understandings to build bridges between children's understandings and more complete, complex meanings (Cochran-Smith, 1984).

Modifying Interactions

In the first interaction Kristen's mother modified the interaction by adjusting her reading style from reading to storytelling perhaps because she believed Kristen could understand the story better if she talked about the pictures rather than read the story. Story readers often mediate between the story content and children's understanding by modifying their reading of the text—by telling the story, interweaving words from the text with storytelling, or modifying the words of the story as they read aloud (Altwerger, Diehl-Faxon, & Dockstader-Anderson, 1985; Cochran-Smith, 1984). Oddly, parents sometimes do not change the words in the text as they share literature with their young children. Instead, they notice that their children are fascinated by the language and complex literary patterns found in quality literature and thus read the text the way it is on the page.

Kristen's mother modified the interaction in another way. She altered her facial expressions and used dramatic gestures to highlight the nature of the pig and wolf characters. She rounded her eyes to demonstrate that the wolf ought to frighten the little pig (and her daughter). The use of facial expressions and gestures are used frequently in conversation to signal certain meanings. Although these clues, called contextualization clues (Gumperz, 1977), are not in story texts, story readers often put them in the story as they read aloud, providing additional clues to a story's meaning. Kristen's mother provided many contextualization clues to the story, helping make visible the kinds of reactions that Kristen should make.

Another way that parents modify story interactions in order to mediate their children's story understanding is to stretch beyond the familiar by demonstrating more sophisticated cognitive strategies (Snow, 1983). In the first book-reading interaction, Kristen's mother confirmed Kristen's labeling objects of the trees, but also identified an important narrative element in stories—main characters—when she pointed to and named the pigs and wolf. Locating particular characters throughout a picture storybook is a more sophisticated narrative strategy than merely identifying familiar objects.

Monitoring Interactions

Parents monitor their children's story understandings and make modifications in order to help children come to more complete understandings. For example, Ms. Amy played a critical role in helping children construct story meaning when she monitored the kinds of inferences they made. She rejected the notion that the snowman's nose was a carrot (even though a carrot would make sense because carrots are used frequently in real life as snowmen's noses and because the object in the picture is orange). Ms. Amy ignored the meatball suggestion (most likely because it did not correspond to anything we would expect in real life even though meatballs are round). In this way she demonstrated to the children that they should use what they know about what makes sense in the real world to make inferences, but that the real world information must correspond to what is shown in illustrations (or said in the words).

Ms. Amy's monitoring of the children's inferences is an example of how story readers take on the role of an implied reader (Cochran-Smith, 1984). Implied readers are not real readers; they are imaginary readers who because of special knowledge, experiences, and strategies can perfectly understand the story (Chambers, 1977; Iser, 1978). That is, certain kinds of stories seem to demand certain kinds of ideal readers. According to literary critics, authors use particular syntactic or grammatical structures, specific settings and characters, and call on certain beliefs and values. Ideal readers are familiar with these kinds of characters, have these beliefs and values, and use both to fill in gaps in the text. In order to read stories successfully, real readers must take on the characteristics of and use the knowledge assumed by the implied reader (Booth, 1961).

Being an Implied Reader

Effective story readers monitor reading by making explicit the knowledge and activities of an implied reader. They orient children to the story in such a way as to point out information that an implied reader would have. They explain, for example, information about a character or setting that an implied reader would know—that a wolf would be mean and that little pigs should be afraid of him. They stop and ask questions when certain inferences should be made or make comments about and point to certain clues in the illustrations or text that are critical for anticipating upcoming events. Ms. Amy demonstrated the role of implied reader by helping the children make the kind of inferences that the implied reader would have—the snowman's nose could be a tangerine or orange, but not a meatball!

The following interaction provides another example of a teacher making explicit the particular activities used by the implied reader as she helps children carefully attend to clues about the relations between events and characters' motivations and feelings. In this interaction, Ms. King and her first graders are sharing *Me and Neesie* (Greenfield,

1975). In this story Janelle has an invisible friend, Neesie, but Janelle's mother has forbidden her to talk aloud to Neesie or talk about her as if she were real. Janelle is to begin school the next day and Neesie has rolled on Janelle's new school clothes. Janelle is very angry with Neesie and yells at her for ruining her special school outfit.

[Text in italics is read from the book. Other text is spoken in the conversation.]

King: *I said, "We're going to school tomorrow, remember?" Neesie didn't say anything. She had her head down and I leaned way over so I could see her face better. "Mama says school's going to be fun!"* Why do you think Neesie is looking sad?

Brandon: Cause she don't, um...

King: She doesn't want to do what?

Brandon: She doesn't want to go to school.

Alex: She yelled at her.

King: Who yelled at each other?

Alex: The girl, Janelle.

King: OK, so Janelle yelled at Neesie and now Neesie is sad?

Jerome: I think she don't want to go to school because the girls, they be like, "You're talking to yourself."

King: So you think Neesie would feel bad for Janelle that other kids would tease her and laugh at her 'cause they would say that she's talking to herself, is that what you're saying?

Jerome: If Neesie were here (points to the illustration of Janelle's bedroom), no one would hear her.

King: OK, so let's read on." (Reads more text about Neesie leaving Janell's room, running into the living room, and sitting on the couch behind a very old Aunt Bea who has come to visit). *Aunt Bea said, "You're pretty as ever. Soon as I sit down I want you to come over here and give me a great big hug." Nessie was still sitting. She was grinning her bad grin.* What do you think might happen next? Any guesses?

Victoria: She might kick her.

Jeffrey:	No. Maybe Neesie will hug her.
King:	But what about the bad grin? Well, let's just think about this. Neesie jumped up on the sofa and sat right behind her.
Tommy:	Gonna fall.
King:	Who's gonna fall?
Tommy:	The lady.
Victoria:	The lady is going to sit on her. "No, no, don't sit on Neesie" (in a different voice as if acting out).

In this interaction Ms. King carefully interjected questions into the reading to signal that important inferences should be made at these points in the story. She allowed the children to suggest several possible answers to her questions. They make several guesses about why Neesie might be looking sad as Janelle is preparing to go to school. The children constructed four hypotheses about the reason for the character's emotion: Neesie might not want to go to school, she might be upset because Janelle yelled at her, she might be afraid other children would make fun of Janelle, or she might be sad because she knows she will be lonely at home with no one to talk with her when Janelle is off at school. Any of these hypotheses are plausible in the story, and more importantly, they connect past story events with possible future story events. In other words, it is critical that inferences that readers make are relevant to the story as a whole rather than just within each individual story event.

Ms. King is particularly interested in having children think logically about what will happen next in the story. She takes time to review past actions and character emotions with the children in order to demonstrate how to draw inferences that make sense across the story as a whole. This draws attention to the causes and effects in relation to characters' emotions (Neesie must feel sad for a reason) and motivations (Neesie's anger and sadness at Janelle will cause her to do something that will result in Janelle getting into trouble).

Enriching Children's Interactions With Literature: The Teacher's Role

As shown in the preceding book-reading interactions, parents and teachers play important roles during storybook reading that help young children learn strategies for interacting with literature in ways that broaden and extend their literary competence. Reading literature aloud to young children in the primary grades continues to be an important start for learning more sophisticated comprehension strategies, and therefore researchers have examined ways in which teachers share books with children. They have found that teachers have a variety of storybook reading styles that provide different levels of support for children's development of meaning-making strategies (Dickinson & Smith, 1994; Martinez & Teale, 1993; McGill-Franzen & Lanford, 1994). One way that teachers' storybook reading style differs is in the amount of participation they expect from children. Some teachers encourage a high level of participation by accepting children's comments and questions; other teachers expect children to sit quietly during read alouds. Children whose teachers demand high levels of participation are more likely to achieve at higher levels in reading than children whose teachers expect silence (Heath, 1982).

Teachers also differ in the level of cognitive demand that they make on children during storybook reading interactions. Some teachers demand high levels of cognitive activity by asking children to predict and infer character motivations and actions or to recall story events and make inferences that connect story events. Other teachers engage children in lower levels of cognitive activity such as when they recite a repetitive text aloud. Not surprisingly, children learn more about constructing meaning from interacting with stories in ways that require higher cognitive levels (Snow, 1983). Two methods of sharing literature with children capitalize on high levels of participation and high levels of cognitive demand: interactive sharing and grand conversations.

Interactive Sharing

Interactive sharing is an active exchange between story readers and children. Kristen's mother, Ms. Smith, and Ms. King used interactive

sharing to support and extend the meanings children were making of literature. In interactive sharing, the story reader encourages children to participate before and during story reading by inviting predictions, reading dramatically, asking questions, providing information, relating personal responses, asking children to elaborate on and clarify their responses, and providing feedback to children's comments and questions. Children may retell story events, talk about related events from their lives or from other stories, analyze and evaluate characters and events, share personal feelings, insert themselves in the story by dramatically enacting story events, and even make up their own events or a new story (Sipe, 1996). The key to interactive sharing is that children construct meaning not just from the story text as the story is read aloud, but also through their interactions during storybook reading.

Interactive sharing does not mean that teachers interrupt reading of the story with a list of questions or that there are no times when a story should be read from beginning to end without interruptions. Rather, teachers use interactive sharing when they think children could benefit from high levels of interaction about the story's meaning. Teachers can invite children's participation by interspersing text reading with open-ended questions such as "What's going on here?", comments such as "Oh, oh, I think trouble is coming up," or pausing for children to make predictions. These activities encourage children to talk about what they perceive is happening or anticipate upcoming events.

During interactive sharing, teachers help children to extend and clarify their thinking (McGee, Courtney, & Lomax, 1994). Ms. King rephrased comments and asked questions that allowed children to make more explicit what they were thinking. Teachers can ask questions such as "What do you mean by ___?" or "What makes you think that ___?" Teachers also help children fill in important gaps in stories. Ms. King inserted two questions into her reading: "Why do you think Neesie is looking sad?" and "What do you think will happen next? Any guesses?" These questions did not directly ask children to recall information from the story, but rather to use the information to make inferences and predictions. Ms. King did not require children to get *the* correct answer to her questions. In fact, children made several different inferences and predictions to her questions. Ms. King merely made sure that the inferences and predictions were logical with the information provided in the text. When they were not, she reviewed the sequence of events and details that should have been taken into account. In other words, the focus of interactive sharing is on developing children's thinking using text and illustrations as critical information rather than on merely having children recite events from the story. Multiple inferences and predictions are encouraged and accepted.

Grand Conversations

Grand conversations, named for their resemblance to good dinner conversations rather than school question-and-answer recitations, are discussions about literature led primarily by children's comments and questions (Eeds & Wells, 1989; McGee, 1992). Grand conversations are similar to interactive sharing experiences in that children are talking actively; however, these discussions primarily take place after reading a book or portion of a book and teachers take a less directive role.

The purpose of grand conversations is to use children's responses to literature to build literary interpretations. Literary interpretations are understandings about the story, life, or one's self that are generated by

In Practice

BUILDING WALLS

There are many different ways to develop young children's narrative understandings—from modeling writing forms to reading good stories to engaging children in rich, sociodramatic play. The following exercise involves building walls that focus on the different elements of narrative.

Ask children to collect opening paragraphs from their favorite stories. Have them work in small groups to explain why the paragraphs "work." Does the paragraph introduce an intriguing character? A scary plot? An eerie setting? Next build a class story wall from butcher-block paper where each brick contains an opening narrative paragraph. Use different colors to show key narrative elements, for example, orange for paragraphs that emphasize setting or mossy green for those that show strong characters.

Once the wall is built, use it as the basis for extended discussions about "openers," such as focus (setting? character? plot?), paragraph length, use of grammatical features (number of adjectives? use of conjunctions?), and startling beginnings. Stimulate prediction-making based on the opening paragraphs, which may provide the impetus for wider reading on the part of the children.

Building story walls that show narrative elements helps children to discover the structures that support the making of a good story. What they "see" builds more than walls; it also builds meanings that strengthen story reading and writing.

Adapted from Ziebicki, S., & Grice, K. (1997). Building walls and opening doors. *Primary English, 16,* 7–9.

and connected to the story but extend beyond the literal events in the story. Literary interpretations include story understandings, but are more abstract insights into the significance of story characters and events.

Grand conversations take place primarily after reading an entire picture storybook or a large portion of a novel because the focus is on interpreting the story as a whole. In other words, constructing meaning consists of both understanding the linear presentation of story events and constructing a consistent understanding of the whole story (Riffaterre, 1978). Building consistency within a vision of the whole story involves both anticipation—having a sense of what is about to happen based on past story events—and retrospection—reevaluating past story events in light of the evolving sense of story as a whole (Iser, 1978).

The following interaction presents a portion of a grand conversation held by a group of first graders after their teacher read *Rosie's Walk* (Hutchins, 1968). The teacher initiated the conversation with an open-ended invitation to share: "What did you think about the story?" As shown in the interaction, the children began the conversation sharing parts that they liked in the story, identifying events they found amusing, and even becoming characters in the story through adding dialogue and actions (Day, 1996; Sipe, 1996).

Teacher: Now, what did you think of the story?

Aaron: It was funny. I liked it.

Nicole: It was funny when the fox got the rake, like he stepped on the bottom part and then he, he hit himself with it.

Jennifer: Yeah and then he got the stuff all over him, the sugar.

Nicole : No, I mean, yes it was funny, but it wasn't sugar. It was like a sack of flour.

Teacher: Who else?

Kevin: It was really cool with he fell in the haystack and the mice were there. Like "Yipes, what's that on me? Yipes get off, you!"

Aaron: It was funny 'cause the string got stuck on the chicken's foot, like when she walked, it made the flour in the bag spill.

As shown in this interaction, grand conversations can seem like unfocused retellings of stories with little direction or point. However, such beginnings are not uncommon and seem to allow children to review the story events in ways that are personally relevant and important for crafting more complex story understandings (McGee, 1992). The teacher played only a small role in the conversation, stepping back to allow children's responses to direct the conversation.

Grand conversations are not totally child-centered and are not directed entirely by the children's responses to the story. Instead, children are more successful at reaching high levels of story understanding when teachers encourage them to remember their thoughts and feelings as the events in the story unfold or to share their puzzlements and questions (Wiseman, Many, & Altieri, 1992). Such activities help children recall their lived experience of the story (Rosenblatt, 1978). Teachers may invite children to make associations between the story and their experiences or to other literature, describe thoughts and feelings evoked by the story, relate favorite scenes, or put themselves in a character's shoes (Wiseman, Many, & Altieri, 1992).

The following interaction presents a later portion of this same grand conversation about *Rosie's Walk*. In this part of the conversation the teacher asked an interpretive question, one that required the children to focus on the story as a whole: Does Rosie know the fox is behind her? The children explored two interpretations and used evidence from the story to support their hypotheses. Their talk about the story is much more focused and at a deeper level of understanding.

Teacher: I have a question for you. Do you think Rosie knew that the fox was following her?

Children: No, no.

Jennifer: No she never looked around. She just kept going.

Nicole: Yeah. I mean. No. I think she knew. She didn't do anything. She just ignored the fox, but she knew.

Teacher: That's interesting.

Alice: I know, I know.

Teacher: Alice?

Alice: The string on Rosie's foot, she just stepped and she didn't know and the stuff fell on the fox.

Kevin: She knew about the string. She just ignored the fox. She just kept on walking like it was a trap.

Aaron: Yeah the fox is so stupid. He was always getting in trouble and the hen knew 'cause like it was a trap.

Teacher: Chris?

Chris: She would have heard it. Rosie would have heard the flour falling on the fox. She knew. She knew.

As shown in this interaction, the children drew from events that they had recalled during the earlier part of the conversation—that Rosie had stepped on a string causing a bag of flour to fall on the fox. However, the children used this evidence in a new way—to support both hypotheses that Rosie does not know the fox is behind her and that Rosie does know about the fox. Then Chris made an important inference about the story that allowed the group to reevaluate a story event—that the flour would have made a noise falling on the fox. In other words, during this portion of the grand conversation, the children reconsidered story events in light of the story as a whole, hypothesizing about the significance of a certain event. The teacher played a more significant role by helping children focus on interpreting the story by asking only one thought-provoking question.

Conclusion

The early childhood years lay the foundation for children's continued and rich experiences with literature. Children are not born with the ability to enjoy and understand literature; they develop sophisticated strategies for understanding and interpreting literature through skillful interactions with good literature. Strategies that some parents seem to use intuitively at home with their preschoolers can be extended into the classroom where they further support children's experiences with literature. Teachers enrich children's learning when they use response-based teaching techniques such as interactive sharing and grand conversations.

An important outcome of these techniques is strengthening children's meaning-making and interpretive strategies. However, these teaching strategies also can increase children's knowledge about literature (Peterson & Eeds, 1990; Wiseman, Many, & Altieri, 1992). As children talk about literature interactively with their teachers, they develop an understanding and awareness of similarities in plot structures, images, characters, language patterns, and other literary conventions (Chambers, 1985). They notice aesthetic elements in picture-book illustrations such as line, shape, color, and borders, and they interpret illustrations' symbolic potential (Kiefer, 1995). Even preschool children notice patterns found in literature and develop intuitive understandings about literary conventions.

Interactive sharing and grand conversations are potentially powerful instructional techniques in which children's constructed understandings of literature provide the foundation for further teaching. Teachers listen to children and craft their responses in ways that move children to deeper levels of understanding and that demand logical and creative thinking.

References

Altwerger, B., Diehl-Faxon, J., & Dockstader-Anderson, K. (1985). Read aloud events as meaning construction. *Language Arts, 62*, 476–484.

Booth, W. (1961). *The rhetoric of fiction.* Chicago, IL: University of Chicago Press.

Chambers, A. (1985). *Booktalk: Occasional writing on literature and children.* New York: Harper & Row.

Chambers, A. (1977). The reader in the book: Notes from work in progress. *Signal, 23*, 64–87.

Cochran-Smith, M. (1984). *The making of a reader.* Norwood, NJ: Ablex.

Day, K. (1996). The challenge of style in reading picture books. *Children's Literature in Education, 27*, 153–166.

Dickinson, D., & Smith, M. (1994). Long-term effects of preschool teachers' book readings on low-income children's vocabulary and story comprehension. *Reading Research Quarterly, 29*, 105–122.

Dickinson, D., & Tabors, P. (1991). Early literacy: Linkages between home, school, and literacy achievement at age five. *Journal of Research in Childhood Education, 6*, 30–46.

Eeds, M. & Wells, D. (1989). Grand conversations. An exploration of meaning construction in literature study groups. *Research in the Teaching of English, 23,* 118–126.

Gumperz, J. (1977). Sociocultural knowledge in conversational inference. In M. Saville-Troike, (Ed.), *Georgetown University Roundtable on Languages and Linguistics* (pp. 191–211). Washington, DC: Georgetown University Press.

Heath, S. (1982). What no bedtime story means: Narrative skills at home and school. *Language in Society, 11,* 49–76.

Iser, W. (1978). *The act of reading: A theory of aesthetic response.* Baltimore, MD: Johns Hopkins University Press.

Kiefer, B. (1995). Responding to literature in picture books. In N.L. Roser & M.G. Martinez (Eds.), *Book talk and beyond: Children and teachers respond to literature* (pp. 191–200). Newark, DE: International Reading Association.

Martinez, M., & Teale, W. (1993). Teacher storybook reading style: A comparison of six teachers. *Research in the Teaching of English, 27,* 175–199.

McGee, L. (1992). An exploration of meaning construction in first graders' grand conversations. In C. Kinzer & D. Leu (Eds.), *Literacy research, theory, and practice: Views from many perspectives* (41st Yearbook of the National Reading Conference, pp. 177–186). Chicago, IL: National Reading Conference.

McGee, L., Courtney, L., & Lomax, R. (1994). Teachers' roles in first graders' grand conversations. In C. Kinzer & D. Leu (Eds.), *Multidimensional aspects of literacy research, theory, and practice* (43rd Yearbook of the National Reading Conference, pp. 517–526). Chicago, IL: National Reading Conference.

McGee, L., & Richgels, D. (1996). *Literacy's beginnings: Supporting young readers and writers* (2nd ed.). Boston, MA: Allyn & Bacon.

McGill-Franzen, A., & Lanford, C. (1994). Exposing the edge of the preschool curriculum: Teachers' talk about text and children's literary understandings. *Language Arts, 71,* 264–273.

Ninio, A., & Bruner, J. (1978). Antecedents of the achievements of labeling. *Journal of Child Language, 5,* 1–15.

Peterson, R., & Eeds, M. (1990). *Grand conversations: Literature groups in action.* Toronto, ON: Scholastic.

Purcell-Gates, V. (1988). Lexical and syntactic knowledge of written narrative held by well-read-to kindergartners and second graders. *Research in the Teaching of English, 22,* 128–160.

Riffaterre, M. (1978). *Semiotics of poetry.* Bloomington, IN: Indiana University Press.

Rosenblatt, L. (1978). *The reader, the text, the poem: The transactional theory of the literary work.* Carbondale, IL: Southern Illinois University Press.

Sipe, L. (1996, December). *The construction of literary understanding by young children during storybook readalouds.* Paper presented at the National Reading Conference, Charleston, SC.

Snow, C. (1983). Literacy and language: Relationships during the preschool years. *Harvard Educational Review, 53,* 165–189.

Taylor, D. (1983). *Family literacy*. Exeter, NH: Heinemann.

Taylor, D., & Dorsey-Gaines, C. (1988). *Growing up literate: Learning from inner-city families*. Portsmouth, NH: Heinemann.

Wells, G. (1986). *The meaning makers: Children learning language and using language to learn*. Portsmouth, NH: Heinemann.

White, D. (1954). *Books before five*. New York: Oxford University Press.

Wiseman, D., Many, J., & Altieri, J. (1992). Enabling complex aesthetic response: An examination of three literary discussion approaches. In C. Kinzer & D. Leu (Eds.), *Literacy research, theory, and practice: Views from many perspectives* (41st Yearbook of the National Reading Confernce, pp. 283–290). Chicago, IL: National Reading Conference.

Yaden, D., Jr., & McGee, L. (1984). Reading as a meaning-seeking activity: What children's questions reveal. In J. Niles & L. Harris (Eds.), *Changing perspectives on research in reading/language processing and instruction* (pp. 101–109). Rochester, NY: National Reading Conference.

Yaden, D., Jr., Smolkin, L., & Conlon, A. (1990). Preschoolers' questions about pictures, print convention, and story text during reading aloud at home. *Reading Research Quarterly, 24*, 188–214.

Children's Literature References

Briggs, R. (1978). *The snowman*. New York: Random.

Galdone, P. (1970). *The three little pigs*. New York: Clarion.

Greenfield, E. (1975). *Me and Neesie*. New York: Harper & Row.

Hutchins, P. (1968). *Rosie's walk*. New York: Aladdin.

CHAPTER 10

What Is the Role of Computer-Related Technology in Early Literacy?

Linda D. Labbo and Gwynne Ellen Ash

Five-year-old Kenisha and her 4-year-old brother Malcolm, who live in an inner-city neighborhood, cannot imagine a world without automatic teller machines, cordless telephones, pagers, remote controls, microwave ovens, and computers. When they go to the grocery store with their grandmother, they hear a digitized voice announcing the price of items as a cashier scans bar codes directly into a cash register. When they watch television, they see footage of space shuttle launches and hear reports of orbiting space stations. When they visit the public library, they play computer games, interact with compact disc talking books, or help a media specialist access Internet information on space shuttles.

There is little doubt that computer-related technology is revolutionizing enterprises related to business, industry, entertainment, and communication. It is estimated that by the year

2000, over 500 million people will have direct access to the wealth of information and communicative services on the Internet (Gray, 1996). Such digital services allow access to information including the most current weather reports, breaking political news, theater reviews, and airline reservations. Yet, for all the sophisticated, computer-related technology Kenisha and Malcolm encounter daily in society, when they step into their prekindergarten and kindergarten classrooms, they are likely to encounter minimal applications of computer-related educational technology.

Early childhood teachers who attend workshops at national literacy conventions, participate in graduate courses in university settings, or attend inservice staff training sessions at schools state routinely that even though they are eager to include technology as an integral part of literacy instruction, they often feel frustrated in their efforts to do so. Leu and Leu (1997) identify difficulties faced by teachers and suggest that the gap between the abundance of computer-related technology use in society and the sometimes meager use of computer-related technology in some schools may stem from many factors, including insufficient staff development, lack of developmentally appropriate software, a mismatch between available software and curricular needs, and the demands of a never-ending stream of new curricular initiatives. It is also possible that teachers who were introduced to educational technology in the 1980s grew weary of commercial software programs that focused primarily on drilling, practicing, and assessing isolated reading and writing skills; therefore, they do not see computer activities as applicable in their current classroom contexts (Reinking, Labbo, & McKenna, 1997).

Equity in access further serves to restrict integration of technological training into classroom environments. Poorer school districts, such as the one that Kenisha and Malcolm attend, have a lower computer-to-student ratio than their wealthier counterparts (U.S. Congress Office of Technology Assessment, 1995). In such districts, basic needs such as the repair of a crumbling infrastructure must take priority over the acquisition of expensive technology equipment.

Although computers have become more commonplace in some kindergarten and elementary classrooms over the last two decades (Market Data Retrieval, 1987; Morsund, 1994), many teachers report minimal use of computers for instructional purposes. Computers often are reserved for games after assigned desk work has been completed (Becker, 1993), a problematic arrangement because those children with more extensive literacy exposure consistently complete classroom assignments first, and therefore have greater access to computers. Consequently, the children who might benefit most from using a computer, those with fewer mainstream literacy experiences, are denied access. Additionally, in primary-level classrooms equipped with one computer, use frequently has been limited to copying and printing final drafts of narratives composed with traditional writing tools (pencils, pens, markers, or crayons) during writing workshop (Dickinson, 1986; Miller & Olson, 1994). This denies young children occasions to use the computer as a thought processor (Heim, 1995), a tool for thinking and figuring out how to best express their ideas for various communicative purposes. As these classroom uses of computers indicate, several educators interested in applications of technology caution that merely placing a computer in the classroom does not ensure that the teacher will have the necessary support to be able to incorporate it as an integral part of the classroom culture or that it will positively impact established instructional patterns (Becker, 1991; Miller & Olson, 1994).

The purpose of this chapter is twofold: to review briefly what we know about early literacy development and how computers might support children's learning, and to make recommendations for creating computer-enriched centers that support young children's computer-related literacy development.

Emergent Literacy and Computer-Related Instruction

In this section, we draw connections between how children develop literacy behaviors in the crucial early years in school and what technology can provide, considering how computers may support early literacy development.

Children Learn About Literacy Through Independent Explorations on the Computer

Emergent literacy is based on a constructivist perspective (Piaget, 1962). A number of researchers (see Teale & Sulzby, 1986) have investigated children's independent acquisition of knowledge about how print operates, shedding light on the crucial cognitive processes involved in literacy development. From this perspective, children act on meaningful symbols that are present within the immediate literate environment that surrounds them. Through purposeful, independent endeavors and observations, children build a knowledge base about symbols and symbol systems. Crucial to children's overall cognitive development are the symbol-making hypotheses they generate when determining how to express their ideas (Pierce, 1966). Such working hypotheses about written language include children's concepts about print (Clay, 1975, 1991), their early understandings about words (Read, 1971), their use of writing (Sulzby, 1986), and their applications of print (Downing, 1970).

The constructivist perspective helps educators understand how children's solitary ventures on the computer provide unique opportunities for learning concepts about literacy. Computer hardware and software containing linguistic, artistic, and multimedia toolboxes provide rich physical objects within an environment that fosters children's independent explorations. As young children work on the computer, they take a variety of stances toward the work they are accomplishing as it is displayed on the computer monitor, including viewing the computer as an object of play (Labbo, 1996). As with other types of exploratory play, children will examine the computer to find out how the object works (Fenson, Kagan, Kearsley, & Zelazo, 1976; Neuman & Roskos, 1991).

When children use the computer as a tool, they experience two tiers of exploration simultaneously. While examining how computer hardware works, they also may examine various symbol systems that appear on the screen as a result of their explorations. The type of software children encounter also will influence the directions they are able to explore. Software programs that are *expressive* allow children to create, discover, or represent their ideas graphically, and provide different occasions for developing insights into literacy than do *receptive* software programs. Receptive programs allow children to view, interact with, and discover the meaning of graphic symbols in the program. Examples and additional features of expressive and receptive software are given in the sections that follow (see the Figure for specific examples of expressive and receptive software).

Figure Examples of Expressive and Receptive Software

Expressive Software includes programs that allow children to create, discover, or represent their ideas graphically, and with proper support provide various occasions for developing insights into literacy.

- *Creative Writer.* (1994). Microsoft Corporation.
- *Great Beginnings.* (1993). Language Experience Series. Teacher Support Software, Inc.
- *Kidpix.* (1994). Bröderbund Software.
- *KidWorks 2.* (1994). Davidson Software.
- *Playwrite.* (1995). Sunburst.
- *Storybook Theater.* (1992). Learningways, Inc.
- *Wiggle Works.* (1994). Scholastic Beginning Literacy Skills.

Receptive Software programs allow children to view, interact with, and discover concepts about graphic symbols, print, and literacy that are presented in the program

GAMES RELATED TO LITERACY SKILLS
- *A to Zapp.* (1995). Sunburst Software.
- *Bailey's Book House.* (1995). Edmark.
- *Daisy's Castle.* (1995). Great Wave Software.
- *Reader Rabbit 1.* (1991). The Learning Company.
- *Reader Rabbit 2.* (1992). The Learning Company.
- *Reader Rabbit's Reading Development Library Level 2.* (1995). The Learning Company.
- *Kid Phonics.* (1994). Davidson & Associates.

INTERACTIVE STORYBOOKS
- *ABC by Dr. Seuss.* (1995). Living Books. Random House–Bröderbund Software.
- *Arthur's Reading Race by Marc Brown.* (1996). Living Books. Random House–Bröderbund Software.
- *Curious George Learns the Alphabet by H.A. Rey.* (1993). Queue, Inc.
- *Green Eggs and Ham by Dr. Seuss.* (1996). Living Books. Random House–Bröderbund Software.
- *Stellaluna.* (1996). Living Books. Random House–Bröderbund Software.

Children Learn About Literacy Through Computer-Related Social Interactions

Literacy learning is a sociocultural phenomenon (Vygotsky, 1934/1978). Children's interactions with literate adults and peers are crucial to their cognitive and literacy development. During routine, interactive activities, children come to use and understand how communicative symbols work. Adults in these situations serve as mediators who are in tune with the child's abilities and offer appropriate support to help the child accomplish communicative goals (Sulzby & Teale, 1991). For example, studies have shown how parents scaffold their support of children's emergent reading of books, slowly withdrawing their support as the children progress (Ninio & Bruner, 1978). Similarly, researchers who have looked closely at children's peer interactions (Dyson, 1989; Rowe, 1994) note that when young children are given time to collaborate with other children as they compose, they share literacy knowledge. In one study, for example, first graders who participated in collaborative writing workshops wrote in a variety of genres (Chapman,1994).

Computers are unique learning areas in classrooms that create opportunities for children to socially co-construct knowledge about symbol making and about literacy (Labbo, 1996; Reinking & Watkins, 1996). Studies examining effects of the introduction of computers into various areas of the curriculum on social interaction found that the number and nature of social interactions increased (Friedman, 1990; Riel, 1989; Turner & Depinto, 1992). Sharing a computer for word processing, children routinely formulated plans and reacted to drafts of writing. Computers also seem to encourage students to collaborate, share notes, write articles for school newsletters, and review books (Bruce, Michaels, & Watson-Gregeo, 1985).

Children Learn About Literacy Through Computer-Related Integrated Language Arts Experiences

Research since the mid-1980s indicates that all the language arts (listening, speaking, reading, and writing) mutually support one another (Teale & Sulzby, 1986). For example, Purcell-Gates (1988) noted that young children's early efforts at reading and writing occur in conjunction with oral language. Similarly, emergent writing and invented spelling are related to children's developing knowledge about the sounds of language (Ehri, 1994) and its structure, as are storytelling and play (Cullinan & Galda, 1998). Thus, there appears to be a close relation among various communicative modes used in processing language.

Similar relations exist among the language arts, the fine arts (for example, color, line, perspective, and balance), and the multimedia arts (for example, sound, animation, icons, and scanned images) during the process of electronic symbol making (Labbo, 1996; Labbo, Field & Watkins, 1995). Expressive software programs such as *Kid Pix 2* (Hickman, 1994) allow children to move between making symbols (Dyson, 1982; Hubbard, 1989) with either artistic tools (such as paint brush, drawing pencil, clip-art icons, or patterned designs) or with word-processing tools (such as typing with the keyboard, stamping with letter stamps, writing with a pencil tool, cutting, pasting, or erasing). Young children express ideas through various symbolic means on the computer because they respond to the world through each of their senses (Gardner, 1980). It is important for expressive software to support various modes of expression.

Children's Symbolic Expressions Employ Nonconventional but Meaningful Computer-Generated Forms

Young children routinely employ multiple conventional and nonconventional sign systems simultaneously and interchangeably in an effort to communicate meanings publicly through their use of traditional writing implements such as pencils, markers, pens, crayons, typewriters, or even alphabet stamps. Ernst (1994) observed that young children use writing and "picturing" as complementary, legitimate thinking and symbol systems. Although these forms of writing are often scribbles, letter-like forms, drawing, or strings of letters, the conceptual understanding children have constructed becomes evident as they assign meaning to the marks on the page. This assignment of meaning may occur before, during, or after children write. Children's verbalizations when making meaning with a variety of graphic symbols provide insight into their developing literacy concepts (for example, realizing that print carries meaning, recognizing left-to-right directionality, or pointing to words while rereading a work in progress).

Labbo and Ash

Multimedia software is an excellent vehicle for the development of concepts about forms and functions of symbol systems. Many of the forms children create with expressive software programs are non-conventional. For example, when young children approach the screen as "paper," they use the computer as a literacy tool to produce typographic symbolic forms. Composing processes and emergent forms of writing will depend on whether a child intends to write a narrative story, an informational expository text, or a functional text. Children's computer-generated writing may include icons "stamped" on the screen, scribbles created with a pencil tool or special-effect paint brush, random strings of keyboarded letters, carefully selected letters (stamped or keyboarded) to represent sounds heard in syllables, or copied or cut-and-pasted text (Labbo, 1996). The writing also may appear as an extension of speech that leaves a typographic visual artifact on the screen (Lemke, 1993).

Young Children Develop Computer-Related Emergent Literacy Concepts as They Engage in a Variety of Electronic Symbol-Making Experiences

The term *electronic symbol making* refers to the conceptual processes, knowledge, and strategies that young children may develop about literacy when they use classroom computers equipped with multimedia word-processing software (Labbo & Kuhn, in press). Given the proper support and opportunities to use a variety of software programs, children come to understand that computers are tools that may be used to accomplish personal and public communicative goals; to store and retrieve their own and others' work; to access symbols and symbol-making tools; to compose, print, and publish; or to play and create art. Furthermore, children learn about the processes, forms, and products of electronic symbol making. The insights they gain about such symbol making include the following: Meaning-making takes a variety of multimedia and symbolic forms, symbol-making is a recursive process, graphic symbols aid memory, procedures for meaning making rely on dependable action schemes, and the selection of appropriate symbols system is guided by communicative purpose.

Creating Computer-Related Learning Environments That Support Young Children's Literacy Development

In order to achieve the goal of creating computer-related environments that support literacy development, first we address physical features related to the design of computer centers that use both expressive and receptive software. Then we address issues related to the design and use of computer-enriched sociodramatic-play centers in the classroom.

Creating a Computer Imagination Station

Morrow and Rand (1991) remind us that the physical arrangement of the classroom learning environment is an important factor determining the overall effectiveness of teaching and learning (see also Morrow, 1990). The ways that computers are situated and organized within the classroom environment will determine the appeal and use of technology by teachers and children. The physical design of a computer center is crucial to its success in the classroom, the amount of time children spend in the center, the type of activities in which children are engaged, and the level of incorporation of the computer-center activities into the overall classroom culture (Labbo, Reinking, & McKenna, 1995). (See also Chapter 8 for further discussion on arranging the classroom to motivate literacy learning.)

Teachers need to avoid the temptation to save classroom space by placing the classroom computer or computers in an isolated corner on a small desk or a portable cart. Rather, they should consider designing the computer station as a focal point of the classroom that invites children to engage in a variety of creative and imaginative activities. Colorful displays of posters, printouts of student work, book jackets, software, and books and compact discs of books related to unit themes will invite children to remember, think about, experience, or create thematically related, computer-generated products.

Systematic observations conducted over the last 5 years in kindergarten and preschool classrooms (Labbo, 1995, 1996) have led to three recommendations about the physical design of an effective computer center related to work-surface space, user-friendly mouse pads, and helpful-hints displays.

Work-surface space. Because young children frequently feel the need to bring a variety of items with them to support their independent explorations on the computer, teachers need to place the computer on a table that has a large work surface that can accommodate various items—a favorite stuffed animal, a collection of informational resource books and artifacts, or copies of children's literature related to a unit of study. For example, in one classroom a young author often brought a favorite classroom stuffed animal to the computer as a writing pal to "listen" to her thoughts while she composed on a children's word-processing program. In the same classroom, during a thematic unit focusing on travel and forms of transportation, children brought artifacts or informational resources from other centers in the classroom (such as copies of maps, examples of airline tickets, travel booklets, or travel brochures) to support their work on the computer. Representations of maps, re-creations of information from tickets, and scenes from travel brochures appeared in the computer products they created during free-choice time in the classroom.

When enjoying a receptive software program such as a compact disc talking book many kindergarten children brought a hard-copy book version of the story with them to engage in a "screen and book read along." As children flipped through pages of the book that was placed on the table beside the computer, they would simultaneously click directional arrows that turned corresponding pages on the computer screen. By engaging in this activity, some children came to understand concepts about print such as directionality, return sweep, and the meaning-carrying function of print. In other instances, children engaged in a "screen and book echo reading" that began with them listening to a page of the story read on the screen, followed by a "rereading" or echoing of the text while tracing the print on the hard-copy version of the story. By engaging in this activity, children who were tuned in to the graphophonemic relation of sounds and letters were able to refine or expand their understanding. These findings suggest that hard copies and compact disc versions of books should be displayed together on open book shelves in the computer center for easy access.

User-friendly mouse pads. Teachers we work with suggest that early childhood educators remove the type of mouse pads that are sold in office-supply stores, those typically used by office workers. Their flat surfaces frequently are difficult for many young children to use because of the problems they present in maneuvering the mouse. Replacing mouse pads with fabric- or vinyl-covered two-inch, three-ring binders that have been taped closed allows young children to have more success with manipulating the mouse to accomplish mouse computer operations. Teachers suggest positioning the binder by sitting in front of the computer, placing the lower, closed edges of the binder at the heel of the palm, and placing the higher, ringed end of the binder on an upward incline at the fingertips.

Displays of helpful hints. Teachers can reinforce learning about both literacy and technology through the display of procedural hints and reminders about how to accomplish basic computer operations (such as how to save a file, what is the current date, or how to access software programs) on the wall where they may be seen easily by young children sitting at the computer. Helpful-hint posters might consist of a combination of pictures, icons, words, lists, or printouts of relevant computer screens. Teachers also can review and demonstrate these reference items and the actions they represent through modeling during whole-group time.

Incorporating Technology Into Sociodramatic-Play Centers

Sociodramatic play occurs when two or more children reenact stories or role play real-life situations, and can be a crucial element in young children's learning. When young children play they assimilate their experiences into an existing cognitive schema of how the world works. Educators suggest that when young children play, they refine existing cognitive concepts or even reconstruct incomplete concepts to accommodate new information (Glickman, 1979). When teachers enrich play settings with literacy props, multiple occasions arise for children to engage in literacy-related activities (Neuman & Roskos, 1991).

Several researchers have investigated the effects of including literacy props in thematic sociodramatic-play centers and have discovered that children experience an increase in literacy-related play and op-

In Practice

THE NEWS TEAM

For Mrs. Morey's second graders, the computer is more than a fascinating machine; it is an authentic literacy tool for getting things done. Either huddled around it or sitting at it, class members plan, compose, illustrate, and publish their weekly newsletter, which is circulated widely to parents and friends. Gathering the bits and pieces of classroom life, these second graders transform everyday information into newsworthy items using the tools of writing and reading as well as technology.

The children are organized into various editorial teams that work together on different sections of the newsletter. To get out the news, everyone knows what is expected of them while at the computer, and everyone has a turn at the keyboard. Throughout the process children practice their literacy skills and grapple with challenging new print concepts. They also learn to collaborate as technology users while applying their literacy understandings, skills, and creativity at the computer.

Friday, September 4   page 2

First Day Jitters   by Johanna M.

Yesterday it was the first day of school. I wasn't nervous in fact I way happy. At first I thot I was'nt going to have pals. I'm going to talk about some. Ashley is really helpful. Jacob is nice. Seth is AMAZING. Tim T. listens to every bit of GOOD information. Jennifer is OK.

portunities to develop literacy skills (Morrow, 1990; Neuman & Roskos, 1991, 1992). Additional computer-related research suggests that young children benefit in many ways when they are allowed to explore and play with the computer (Labbo, 1995). For example, children who are given time to explore the computer and software functions learn keyboard operations (how to make upper- and lowercase letters), action schemes (how to manipulate a string of computer operations within a program), and vocabulary terms (metalinguistic language that allows them to share or request specific knowledge). This knowledge base, learned through playful exploration and accompanying social interactions with peers and adults, often equips children to accomplish various communicative and personal tasks with the computer.

However, teachers may be hesitant to allow children to play with the computer because it is an expensive technological tool that they believe is more effective when placed in a writing or computer center. One way to overcome the lack of a computer or the discomfort related to placing a computer in a sociodramatic-play center is the placement of a cardboard, or make-believe computer in a sociodramatic-play center. Teachers may locate cardboard models of computers in office-supply stores where they are displayed frequently on office fur-

niture samples. Placement of a cardboard computer model will offer young children the opportunity to learn concepts related to how the computer fits into a sociodramatic, thematic setting.

For example, theme-based centers, such as a flower shop, can incorporate computers in a variety of ways. Children can learn that computers are used as a tool for writing letters, as a fax machine to receive orders from out-of-town locations, as a tool to keep an inventory of flowers, as a tool to order flowers, as a record of shoppers by zip codes, and as a place to print receipts. Similarly, if the sociodramatic-play center is set up as a post office, children may learn how the computer can function in processing and moving mail, or if center is a hospital, children may learn how the computer functions in maintaining health records and prescriptions.

Teachers can support children's play by holding informal preplay conferences with children who have signed up to play in the center. For example, before children begin to play in the center, teachers might ask them who will take what roles (for example, in the case of the florist, who will be the store manager, sales person, designer, and customer). Teachers also can initially play a role, becoming a participant and a supportive director of action (for example, "I need to buy some flowers for my parent's wedding anniversary. Please show me some of your pictures of flower arrangements, so I can decide which one I want."). In addition, the teacher can be within earshot to offer technical and literacy assistance. If children decide they need a computer-generated form or a greeting card, a teacher can be present to help them use the classroom computer to accomplish their goals and then allow the children to return to a play scenario.

The teacher also might invite children and their parents to their sociodramatic-play experiences in various ways. For example, parents may be invited to come into the flower shop during the 2-week unit and participate in the play center as a customer. Parents may use play money children have created or blank, voided checks donated from a local bank to make purchases in the center. Children then may either write or dictate, illustrate, and reread stories about their experiences in the play center. These stories may be typed by a teacher's aide or parent volunteer on the computer, displayed in a class book, and shared with parents when they visit the classroom.

Children's experiences connecting to quality children's literature during fact-finding field trips, helping to plan a play center, and playing in the literacy prop-enriched center will contribute to their growing knowledge about many components of literacy. They can playfully explore workplace functions and forms of literacy that include the computer, or they can engage in oral-language interactions that are appropriate to the play scenario. If it is possible to place a real computer in the center, children can have access to word- or art-processing programs that might allow them to incorporate the immediate application of computer operations and productions into their play. However, if this is not possible, the next best thing is the inclusion of a make-believe computer.

Conclusion

A basic assumption of this chapter is the notion that most teachers are curious and eager to include technology as an integral part of their classroom culture. Using an emergent-literacy perspective, it is evident that the type of expectations and schemata children build about computer-related literacy will depend to a large extent on the nature of the computer experiences they encounter in the classroom. For example, if children encounter only skill-and-drill electronic worksheets, they will likely consider the computer a hard task-master—one designed to control and monitor their ability to perform in test-like situations. However, if children encounter a variety of both expressive and receptive software applications and are invited to explore through play how technology is used in the world of the classroom and beyond, they are likely to view the computer as a place to wonder about ideas, to tinker with how they want to express their ideas, and to encounter new directions for their thinking.

Affordable computers and computer-related technology are likely to flood classrooms in the next several years, making technological tools even more widely accessible. Teachers in the early childhood classrooms of today have the unique opportunity to break new ground in terms of technology that may create the foundations for creative and effective classroom computer use for the future. Conceivably, the day will come when children like Kenisha and Malcolm will not be able to imagine a kindergarten classroom without well-designed computer centers, computer-enriched sociodramatic-play centers, and multiple opportunities to use both expressive and receptive software to explore and to develop literacy.

References

Becker, H. (1991). How computers are used in United States schools: Basic data from the 1989 I.E.A. computers in education survey. *Journal of Educational Computing Research, 7,* 385–406.

Becker, H.J. (1993). Decision making about computer acquisition and use in American schools. *Computers and Education, 20,* 341–352.

Bruce, B., Michaels, S., & Watson-Gregeo, K. (1985). How computers can change the writing process. *Language Arts, 62,* 143–149.

Chapman, M.L. (1994). The emergence of genres: Some findings from an examination of first-grade writing. *Written Communication, 11,* 348–380.

Clay, M. (1975). *What did I write?* Auckland, NZ: Heinemann.

Clay, M. (1991). *Becoming literate: The construction of inner control.* Portsmouth, NH: Heinemann.

Cullinan, B., & Galda, L. (1998). *Literature and the child* (4th ed.). Fort Worth, TX: Harcourt Brace.

Dickinson, D. (1986). Cooperation, collaboration, and a computer: Integrating a computer into a first-second grade writing program. *Research in the Teaching of English, 20,* 357–378.

Downing, J. (1970). Children's concepts of language in learning to read. *Educational Research, 12,* 106–112.

Dyson, A.H. (1982). Reading, writing, and language: Young children solving the written language puzzle. *Language Arts, 59,* 829–839.

Dyson, A.H. (1989). *Multiple worlds of child writers: Friends learning to write.* New York: Teachers College Press.

Ehri, L.C. (1994). Development of the ability to read words: Update. In R.B. Ruddell, M.R. Ruddell, & H. Singer (Eds.), *Theoretical models and processes of reading* (4th ed., pp. 323–358). Newark, DE: International Reading Association.

Ernst, K. (1994). *Picturing learning: Artists and writers in the classroom.* Portsmouth, NH: Heinemann.

Fenson, L., Kagan, J., Kearsley, R., & Zelazo, P. (1976). The developmental progression of manipulative play in the first two years. *Child Development, 47,* 232–236.

Friedman, B. (1990, April). *Societal issues and school practices: An ethnographic investigation of the social context of school computer use.* Paper presented at the annual meeting of the American Educational Research Association, Boston, MA.

Gardner, H. (1980). *Artful scribbles: The significance of children's drawings.* New York: Basic Books.

Glickman, C. (1979). Problem: Declining achievement scores. Solution: Let them play. *Phi Delta Kappan, 60,* 454–455.

Gray, H. (1996, August). Bringing the world to your doorstep: Bridging the communication gap. *The Mirror: Official Publication of the National Association of State Farm Agents,* 20–33.

Heim, M. (1995). *The metaphysics of virtual reality.* New York: Oxford University Press.

Hickman, C. (1994). *Kid Pix 2, Version 2.* Novato, CA: Bröderbund Software.

Hubbard, R. (1989). Inner designs. *Language Arts, 66,* 119–136.

Labbo, L.D. (1995, April). *Classroom, computer lab, and living room: Case studies of kindergartners' home and school computer-related literacy experiences.* Paper presented at the 40th Annual Convention of the International Reading Association, Anaheim, CA.

Labbo, L.D. (1996). A semiotic analysis of young children's symbol making in a classroom computer center. *Reading Research Quarterly, 31*(4), 10–32.

Labbo, L.D., Field, S.L., & Watkins, J. (1995, January). *Narrative discourse as qualitative inquiry: A whole language teacher's decision-making process.* Paper presented at the Annual Qualitative Research Conference, Athens, GA.

Labbo, L.D. & Kuhn, M. (1998). Electronic symbol making: Young children's computer related emerging concepts about literacy. In D. Reinking, L. Labbo, M. McKenna, & R. Kieffer (Eds.), *Handbook of literacy and technology: Transformations in a post-typographic world* (pp. 79–91). New York: Erlbaum.

Labbo, L.D., Reinking D., & McKenna, M. (1995). Incorporating the computer into kindergarten: A case study. In A. Hinchman, D. Leu, & C.K. Kinzer (Eds.), *Perspectives on literacy research and practice: 44th Yearbook of the National Reading Conference* (pp. 459–465). Chicago, IL: National Reading Conference.

Lemke, J. (1993, December). *Multiplying meaning: Literacy in a multimedia world.* Paper presented at the 43rd Annual Meeting of the National Reading Conference, Charleston, SC.

Leu, D.J., & Leu, D.D. (1997). *Teaching with the Internet: Lessons from the classroom.* Norwood, MA: Christopher-Gordon.

Market Data Retrieval. (1987, November/December). Computer use still growing among all schools in the U.S. *Electronic Learning, 6,* 12.

Miller, L., & Olson, J. (1994). Putting the computer in its place: A study of teaching with technology. *Journal of Curriculum Studies, 26,* 121–141.

Morrow, L.M. (1990). Preparing the classroom environment to promote literacy during play. *Early Childhood Research Quarterly, 5,* 537–554.

Morrow, L.M., & Rand, M.K. (1991). Promoting literacy during play by designing early childhood classroom environments. *The Reading Teacher, 44,* 396–402.

Morsund, D. (1994). Editors' message: Technology education in the home. *The Computing Teacher, 21*(5), 4.

Neuman, S.B., & Roskos, K. (1991). Peers as literacy informants: A description of young children's literacy conversations in play. *Early Childhood Research Quarterly, 6,* 233–248.

Neuman, S.B., & Roskos, K. (1992). Literacy objects as cultural tools: Effects on children's literacy behaviors in play. *Reading Research Quarterly, 27,* 202–225.

Ninio, A., & Bruner, J. (1978). The achievement and antecedents of labeling. *Journal of Child Language, 5,* 1–15.

Piaget, J. (1962). *Play, dreams, and imitation in childhood.* New York: W.W. Norton.

Pierce, C. (1966). *Collected papers of Charles Sanders Pierce.* Cambridge, MA: Harvard University Press.

Purcell-Gates, V. (1988). Lexical and syntactic knowledge of written narrative held by well-read-to kindergartners and second graders. *Research in the Teaching of English, 22,* 128–160.

Read, C. (1971). Pre-school children's knowledge of English phonology. *Harvard Educational Review, 41,* 1–34.

Reinking, D., Labbo, L.D., & McKenna, M. (1997). Navigating the changing landscape of literacy: Current theory and research in computer-based reading and writing. In J. Flood & D. Lapp (Eds.), *The handbook for teaching the communicative and visual arts* (pp. 77–92). New York: Macmillan.

Reinking, D., & Watkins, J. (1996). *A formative experiment investigating the use of multimedia book reviews to increase elementary students' independent reading* (Reading Research Report No. 55). Athens, GA: National Reading Research Center. (ERIC Document Reproduction Service No. ED 398570)

Riel, M. (1989). The impact of computers in classrooms. *Journal of Research on Computing in Education, 22,* 180–190.

Rowe, D.W. (1994). *Preschoolers as authors: Literacy learning in the social world of the classroom.* Cresskill, NJ: Hampton Press.

Sulzby, E. (1986). Writing and reading: Signs of oral and written language organization in the young child. In W.H. Teale & E. Sulzby (Eds.), *Emergent literacy: Writing and reading* (pp. 50–87). Norwood, NJ: Ablex.

Sulzby, E., & Teale, W.H. (1991). Emergent literacy. In R. Barr, M. Kamil, P. Mosenthal, & P.D. Pearson (Eds.), *Handbook of reading research: Volume II* (pp. 727–757). White Plains, NY: Longman.

Teale, W.H., & Sulzby, E. (Eds.). (1986). *Emergent literacy: Writing and reading.* Norwood, NJ: Ablex.

Turner, S.V., & Depinto, V.M. (1992). Students as hypermedia authors: Themes emerging from a qualitative study. *Journal of Research on Computing in Education, 25,* 187–199.

U.S. Congress Office of Technology Assessment. (1995). *Teachers and technology making the connection.* Washington, DC: U.S. Government Printing Office. (ERIC Document Reproduction Service No. ED 386155)

Vygotsky, L.S. (1978). *Mind in society: The development of higher psychological processes* (M. Cole, V. John-Steiner, S. Scribner, & E. Souberman, Eds. and Trans.). Cambridge, MA: Harvard University Press. (Original work published 1934)

CHAPTER 11

How Do We Foster Young Children's Writing Development?

Renée M. Casbergue

In an apparent celebration of her newfound mastery of written language, 6-year-old Emily brought paper and markers to the kitchen table and wrote all of the letters of the alphabet, concluding with the words of the familiar alphabet song: *now I now my abc naxst tom wan you siing with me.* As she shared her writing with her mother, singing triumphantly while running her finger under the lines of print, it was clear that Emily had truly "joined the literacy club" (Smith, 1988). She had become a writer. As is the case for most competent young writers, Emily's confident use of written language emerged from a continuing process of exploring and experimenting with print, a process that began long before she entered school.

The Beginnings of Writing

Attention to emergent writing has grown immensely since Clay (1975) first offered her detailed examination of the writing development of very young children. Many researchers have documented the reading and writing development of their own children (Baghban, 1984; Bissex, 1980; Lass, 1982); of children engaged in literacy events with their parents or primary caregivers (Beals & DeTemple, 1993; Burns & Casbergue, 1992; Dickinson & Tabors, 1991; Ferreiro & Teberosky, 1982; Heath, 1982; Hiebert, 1978; Purcell-Gates, 1994; Taylor, 1983; Taylor & Dorsey-Gaines, 1988); and of children in preschool and elementary school programs (Calkins, 1994; Dahl & Freppon, 1995; Dyson, 1983, 1993; Goodman, 1986; Holdaway, 1986).

Most of these researchers agree that children construct their own knowledge of many aspects of written language as they attempt to produce it for their own purposes. McGee and Richgels (1996) have classified children's knowledge about print into four broad categories: meaning, form, meaning-form links, and function.

Knowledge of *meaning* refers to children's developing understanding that print carries messages, and that one's own messages can be encoded intentionally. Children also know that writing can take many *forms*, and may initially believe that messages can be conveyed through scribbles, pictures, letters, or some combination of each. As they engage with print over time, children begin to recognize distinct features of letters and connected text and incorporate them into their own writing. The concept of *meaning-form links* refers to children's growing awareness that different forms of writing convey meaning in different ways. Over time, they will come to understand, for example, that a list requires a different form than a letter to a friend, that pictures function differently than print, and that in order to write specific words, they must use letters that represent the sounds in words. Children also develop knowledge about the *functions* of writing. They use writing to label pictures, to further their pretend play, to take part in family uses of print, to experiment with composition, and to join in the literate communities around them, whether at home or in the classroom (McGee & Richgels, 1996).

Issues of Balance and Continuity

Many traditional instructional programs for children assume that children should learn about each of these four aspects of writing separately. Unfortunately, this assumption often leads to an imbalance in how written language is presented to children. Many programs focus children's attention first and almost exclusively on form as letters of the alphabet are introduced and practiced until children master them (Morrow, 1989). This practice is based on the notion that children cannot begin to actually use print until they master letters, then letter-sound correspondences, and finally predetermined sets of words that can be strung together into simple sentences.

Yet there is ample evidence that even very young children actively explore all four aspects of written language simultaneously. Children's early attempts at writing illustrate that there is a natural balance in their efforts as they explore the meanings, forms, meaning-form links, and functions of language in unison, while constructing and reconstructing their own understandings of print and how to use it.

Children's changing concepts about writing reflect their movement along a continuum from very naive understandings of print to conceptual knowledge that approximates that of adults. An understanding of the full continuum of literacy learning from birth through early childhood will enable teachers to recognize children's levels of knowledge and predict what understandings they are likely to develop next, thus informing teachers' instructional choices. The following examination of writing produced by young children reveals some of the ways in which concepts about print change continuously over time and across all aspects of written language.

A Developmental Continuum

Before age 3, most children's experimentation with writing consists of random scribbling. In much the same way that infants babble purely to explore the sounds they can make and to relish their own voices, toddlers scribble to discover what happens when they put crayon or marker to paper; their efforts are as much extensions of gesturing and explorations of movement as they are an attempt to draw or write (Vygotsky, 1934/1978).

By about age 3, many children begin to recognize some functions of writing. Although their written products may look very similar to the scribbles of younger children, their expectations and intentions are quite different. Three-year-old Brandon, for example, produced what appeared to be a page full of random scribbles. When he finished, he said to his mother, "This is a letter for Santa Claus. I want this stuff." Asked to read his letter, Brandon proceeded to name all the toys he wanted for Christmas, looking at his paper and sounding very much as if he were reading.

This interaction illustrates that Brandon knew quite a bit about writing. He understood that one way to communicate what he wanted for Christmas was to write it down, exemplifying knowledge of meaning. Further, he understood that writing could be used to send a letter to someone, demonstrating his knowledge of form and function. His reading intonation suggested that he recognized that reading from print sounds different than normal speech, suggesting a beginning awareness of meaning–form links.

Like Brandon, Hannah also used scribbles to write when she was 3 years old. She sat her stuffed animals and dolls around a small table in her room and pretended that she was in a meeting taking notes. Although Hannah shared Brandon's awareness of function and meaning, her knowledge of form was somewhat different. Brandon's scribbles were spread randomly around his page, while Hannah carefully constructed lines of print made up of individual characters. These characteristics of writing suggest that Hannah used her visual knowledge of writing to produce her own forms.

Another feature of children's writing that illustrates awareness of print is their invention of letter-like forms. Daniel, another 3-year-old, used a variety of crayons on the blank inside cover of a coloring book to produce the writing shown in Figure 1 on page 202. When his mother asked what he was coloring, he replied that he was writing. She then asked what he had written; his response was, "Nothing, just letters." Nonetheless, he was not able to assign letter names to any of the characters. This interaction suggests that Daniel had a fairly strong concept of meaning and the links between meaning and form. He apparently knew that writing can communicate something and recognized that his random construction of letters did not say anything. He also demonstrated knowledge of form; his use of the word *letters*—despite the fact that few of his characters were actual letters—suggests metalinguistic knowledge about the forms that print can take.

Figure 1 Daniel's Writing of Letters

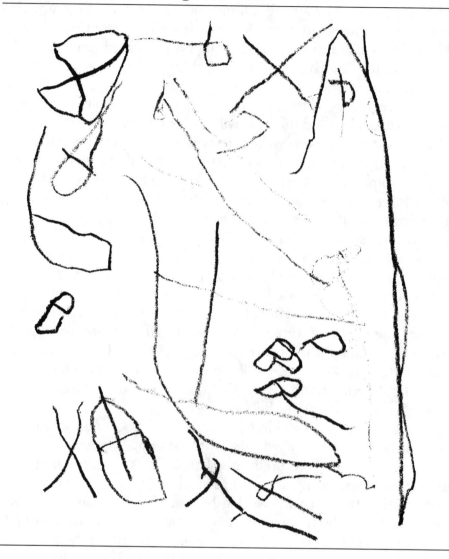

As children move along the developmental continuum toward conventional writing, their awareness of letters becomes more specific than Daniel's, and they begin to make intentional use of letter-like forms and conventional letters in their writing. Four-year-old Alonzo, enrolled in a preschool program, produced the samples presented in

Figure 2 on pages 204–205. Alonzo composed these drawings independently in the classroom art center. He then brought his writing to his teacher and told her that it was a story. She asked him to read it, and he did. Although she did not record what Alonzo said, she noted that it was cohesive and sounded like a story. Because there was no phonemic connection between the letters Alonzo used and his translation of what he wrote, he was most likely "romancing" his writing (Gardner, 1980). This occurs when children put marks on a page without intending any specific meaning in advance, and then decide what the marks mean when the piece is completed. Alonzo's goal may have been to produce something that *looked* like an acceptable story; meaning was ascribed to it only when he decided to read his story aloud to his teacher.

The teacher was surprised that Alonzo's reading intonation remained the same for both the first and second pages of his story, despite the dramatically different forms of writing that he used. This aspect of Alonzo's story is indicative of the fluidity with which children move forward and backward along the developmental writing continuum. His exclusive use of print on the first page suggests his awareness of letters in lines of written text. Yet in the same piece, Alonzo reverted to linear scribble writing to complete his story, highlighting the fact that as children discover new forms of writing, they often simply add them to their repertoire and continue to use both old and new forms.

A major leap forward on the developmental continuum occurs when children discover that print represents the sounds of words. Prior to this discovery, children are likely to determine what letters to use by employing a variety of unconventional strategies. They may decide, for example, that the word *kitten* requires fewer letters than the word *cat*, because a kitten is smaller than a cat. These strategies largely disappear once children begin to write by representing the sounds that they hear in words.

Ben's writing, shown in Figure 3 on page 206, illustrates his budding recognition that spelling is determined by the sounds of words. At the age of 5½, Ben was getting ready to run Saturday–morning errands with his father. Ben decided that they needed a list so they would not forget anything. According to Ben's list, they had to stop at the bank, pick up laundry, buy a watchband, get haircuts, and buy sunglasses. Using a very common form of early phonemic spelling, Ben

Figure 2 Alonzo's Story Using Mock Letters, Conventional Letters, and Mock Linear Writing

(continued)

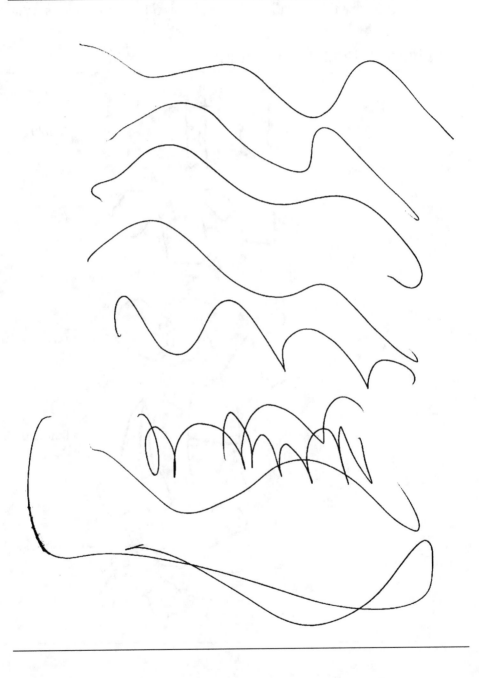

represented each word with a letter representing its initial sound. Dissatisfied, however, he went back and added a picture after each letter: a dollar bill beside the *B*, a shirt beside the *L*, a watchband next to the *W*, scissors by the *H*, and a sun beside his *S* for *sunglasses*. As he shared

Figure 3 Ben's List of Errands

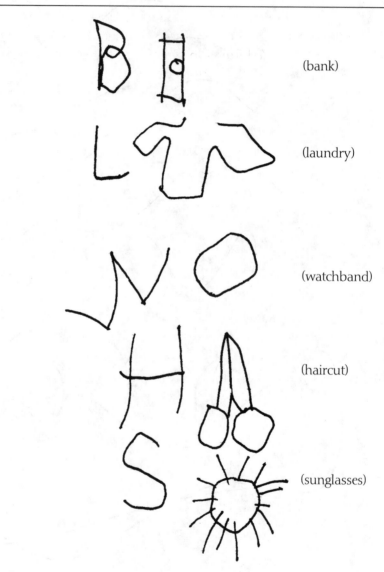

(bank)

(laundry)

(watchband)

(haircut)

(sunglasses)

the list with his father, Ben revealed that he was on the cusp of moving away from single-letter representations of words. He explained, "First I just put the words. But *B* could be bakery or something, so I put pictures." Ben had discovered a fundamental problem with using single letters to represent words—they do not provide enough information for a reader. His response to this dilemma was unconventional, but his understanding that there needs to be more to words would quickly lead him to representing more of their sounds. This development occurred in the context of meaningful writing that used an appropriate form, a list, for the clearly defined function of keeping track of errands.

Even when children discover phonemic spelling, they do not necessarily abandon other strategies. At first glance, Christine's journal entry, written toward the end of kindergarten when she had just turned 6 years old, appears to be a simple example of a child copying words from the classroom environment to fill a page of print (see Figure 4 on page 208). She apparently relied on a sign-in sheet posted inside the classroom door listing each child by first and last name. Copying environmental print is a common strategy used by many children before they develop an understanding of the connection between letters and sounds (Clay, 1975). Christine supplemented her copying by incorporating into her writing simple words that she knew how to spell. Like Alonzo, she romanced her writing when she read it aloud to her teacher. Despite the fact that Christine was primarily copying, she did show evidence of understanding the concept of word boundaries by using vertical lines to separate some, but not all, individual words. Thus, even while copying, Christine was experimenting with meaning and form.

The lack of invented spelling in the text of her journal entry implies that Christine might have had a less mature understanding of the links between meaning and form than did Ben. An examination of her picture, however, proves that Christine is more knowledgeable about meaning-form links than is evident in the text alone. After she finished writing the entry, Christine returned to her picture and labeled the objects represented in it: *Br* for birds, *flr* for flower, and *hl* for hill. Christine had discovered the connection between letters and sounds, and even understood that she needed to represent most of the sounds that she heard, resulting in semiphonemic spellings that were closer to conventional than were Ben's early phonemic spellings.

Figure 4 Christine's Journal Entry

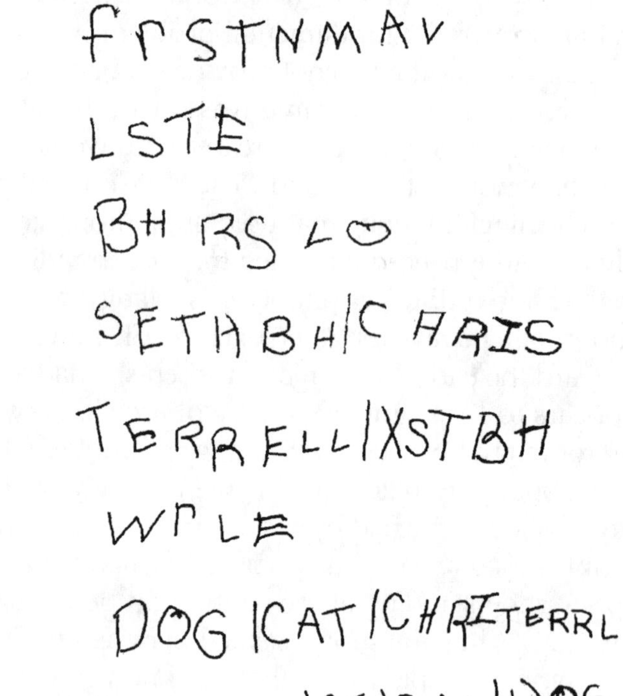

FrSTNMAV

LSTE

BH RS LO

SETH BH/C ARIS

TERRELL/XSTBH

WrLE

DOG ICAT /CHRITERRL

STSRTE ISE IC At IDOG

SUN
Br
fr   hL

Translation (as read by child)
Octopus and dinosaur. They must like each other. Queens and kings like to scream. When they scream, they scream loud. I like my dog. I had Lelia over.

That even young children begin to closely approximate conventional writing once they have experimented sufficiently with meaning, form, meaning–form links, and functions of writing is well illustrated by Jennifer's story, shown in Figure 5 on page 210. Written when she was 6½ years old and in the first grade, Jennifer's composition included a conventional title, "The Hobbit Book." Her awareness of form included recognition that periods need to go at the ends of sentences, although she showed some confusion over what constituted a sentence. Jennifer clearly understood the storytelling function of writing, and her composition included the basic elements of standard story structure. She began by establishing a setting and introducing a character, then described a conflict (the knock on the door that worried the Hobbit), and finally offered a resolution, indicating a rather sophisticated understanding of how to create meaning. The language of Jennifer's story further illustrates sophisticated knowledge of form. Her choice of words and sentence structure, most obviously in the phrase, *when a knock he heard on the door*, reveals that Jennifer was keenly aware of how written storytelling language might sound.

Jennifer's spellings demonstrate that she also was approaching the conventional end of the developmental continuum in her understanding of meaning–form links. Although many of her invented spellings were phonemic, others show that she was becoming a transitional speller. Spellings are classified as transitional when they include elements that demonstrate visual attention to the way words are often spelled or awareness of rules that govern spellings. Jennifer's inclusion of double *o*'s in the words *hobbit* and *was* are transitional, as was her use of an *idt* ending for *hobbit*.

Instructional Implications

A common thread that binds each of these examples of children's writing is the evidence of both balance and continuity in their developing knowledge of written language. In all cases, the writers demonstrated their awareness of and attention to all major categories of knowledge about print, including meaning, form, meaning–form links, and function. Equally important, the manner in which the children

Figure 5 Jennifer's Story

Jennifer

The hoobidt dook.
The hoobidt woos in the.
hase war it woos worm.
he woos hdpe in the.
hase. win a nok he hrde.
on the drop wormw it was
a man thaw. he woos hape.
wif his sdl.

The Hobbit Book
The hobbit was in the house where it was warm. He was happy in the house when
a knock he heard on the door. He was worried. It was a man, though. He was
happy with himself.

moved toward conventional writing reflected a natural and continuous refinement of personally constructed notions about writing.

The key to designing optimal instructional environments for emergent writers may be in finding ways to allow children to continue the balanced explorations with print that prompted their early development. The circumstances under which the samples of writing presented here were produced suggest some possible ways for teachers to do this.

Writing Arose From Play

Writing often emerges naturally as children incorporate it into their pretend play. Children from literacy-rich environments are likely to observe adults using writing for a variety of purposes every day. As they assume adult roles in their play, they will imitate that aspect of adult behavior. Whether taking notes at meetings as Hannah did, or creating menus and writing out bills and receipts while setting up an imaginary restaurant, children will write, using whatever forms they understand, as a way of enriching their play.

If teachers want children to continue this very natural experimentation with writing, they must do two things. First, they must allow sufficient opportunities for play in their classrooms. Although this seems obvious, many teachers feel pressured to focus children's attention on isolated skills, because mastery of skills like recognizing the letter *t* and circling pictures that start with the /t/ sound form the basis of many standardized tests that children are required to take at increasingly earlier ages (Stallman & Pearson, 1990). This practice of engaging children in isolated skills work, especially when it supplants constructive play time during the school day, interrupts the natural continuity and balance of children's earlier interactions with print. One way to restore this balance is to create equilibrium between explicit instruction and social experiences, in part by providing ample opportunities for play (Morrow, 1997).

Teachers must do more than simply provide time for play, however, if all children are to experiment with writing. It is equally important that teachers help children to link literacy and play (Neuman & Roskos, 1997). Some children, especially those who do not have many models of literate adult behavior, may not automatically incorporate writing into their play. Teachers may need to nudge these youngsters into making writing a natural part of their play.

In one classroom, the teacher was drawn to the rhythmic clanging of pots and spoons in the housekeeping area. Three little boys playing there explained with delight that they were practicing for a concert. "Can everyone come?" the teacher asked. The boys broke into huge smiles and nodded enthusiastically. The teacher then asked how everyone would know about the concert, and suggested that they might want to make a sign advertising it. The children scurried for paper and markers as she moved on to join another group in the block center. When renewed clanging again attracted her attention after a period of relative quiet, she was thrilled to see that the boys had produced not one, but three concert promotions that they had taped in strategic locations around the room. None of the signs were written conventionally, but children near each one knew that they were for the concert.

This teacher was able to steer the children toward writing as a natural outgrowth of their play. Such direct teacher involvement is not always needed, however. Another way that children can be encouraged to include writing in their free play activities is to include appropriate writing materials in all areas of the classroom. Paper, message pads, index cards, and pencils in the housekeeping area will lead many children to take phone messages, make grocery lists, and write recipes. In the block area, easy access to writing materials often leads to the creation of road signs, plaques identifying buildings, and warnings to other children not to knock down carefully constructed stacks of blocks. In any themed dramatic-play area (like a shoe store, grocery store, post office, or restaurant) strategic placement of paper and markers will encourage children to engage in the kind of writing that occurs naturally in those settings (see Christie, 1991; Neuman & Roskos, 1990; Vukelich, 1994). (See also Chapter 8 for further discussion on organizing a classroom to motivate literacy learning.)

Writing Was Done for Authentic Purposes

Just as Ben's writing was prompted by a real need to help his father organize and remember all of their errands, many children willingly engage in writing when they perceive a genuine use for their efforts.

The teacher's task is to recognize opportunities for authentic writing and help children take advantage them.

If there is something simple that needs to be communicated to parents, such as a reminder to pack lunches for a field trip, children can be encouraged to write these reminders themselves. If the children's writing is not yet readable because they are using unconventional forms, teachers can write translations of what the children say their messages are and place them beside the child's own writing.

Young writers also can engage in authentic uses of print when they are encouraged to write across all areas of the curriculum. Although many teachers still believe that expository or informational writing is beyond the capabilities of young children, there is ample evidence that many children are quite comfortable with this kind of composition even before they enter kindergarten (Casbergue, 1996; Newkirk, 1987). Children can be encouraged to try informational writing as they keep a record of their observations during science experiences, for example, as shown in Figure 6 on page 214. This writer's first-grade class was cultivating milkweed and watching caterpillars develop into monarch butterflies. Each day as they came into the classroom, chil-

Figure 6 A First Grader's Science Journal Entry

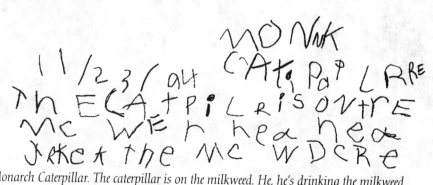

Monarch Caterpillar. The caterpillar is on the milkweed. He, he's drinking the milkweed.

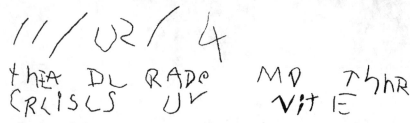

They already made their chryslis over night.

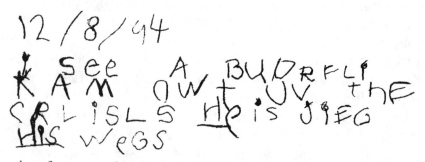

It looks like they are hanging upside down on the top.

I see a butterfly came out of the chryslis. He is drying his wings.

dren were asked to write what they saw. Ultimately, their written observations would be combined to create a classroom book on caterpillars and butterflies. Captivated by the fascinating process unfolding before their eyes and eager to publish their own book, the children proved to be keen observers and accurate recorders.

Writing Resulted From Routines That Included Literacy

Other writing samples presented here came about as children engaged in normal classroom activities designed specifically to encourage writing. Teachers can assure that all children experiment with writing by establishing classroom routines that invite children to write, by assuming they are writers, and by ascribing meaning to children's writing attempts, regardless of the forms of writing they use.

One routine that is especially effective in communicating to the youngest children that their teachers have confidence in their writing ability is the establishment of sign-in procedures (Richgels, 1995). If a teacher requires children to sign in each day as they arrive and then uses the sign-in sheet to confirm attendance, children are presented with an example of functional writing. This routine also gives them a chance to experiment with letter formation and spelling, and allows them to observe their classmates' efforts.

Another routine that serves similar purposes is to engage even the youngest children in daily journal-writing experiences. Teachers need to recognize that early attempts at writing in a journal may entail drawing or other emergent forms described earlier. Nonetheless, they should invite each child to read his or her journal entry; by "ascribing intentionality" to children's efforts, teachers can move children toward more intentional writing (McGee & Richgels, 1996). This routine reinforces children's developing understanding that writing can have meaning, and encourages children to use writing in more intentionally meaningful ways.

Writing Arose From Direct Exploration of Form

Consider Daniel's experimentation with "letters" presented in Figure 1 on page 202. Although there is much to be gained from immersing children in the complete writing process, it also is true that children do enjoy occasional focus on specific aspects of print. Professional literature abounds with examples of children initiating practice forming and manipulating letters (Calkins, 1994; Clay, 1975; McGee & Richgels, 1996; Morrow, 1989; Schickedanz, 1986). Teachers can take advantage of children's natural interest in exploring the conventions of writing by providing materials that encourage discoveries about form and by engaging children in brief sessions of explicit instruction. One way to do this is to involve children in very focused minilessons (Calkins, 1994) that serve to highlight particular features of print. Teachers can present individual letters, for example, and demonstrate how the letters are formed. They can reinforce the sounds that particular letters and letter combinations make, and then play the "I Spy" game in which children have to identify objects in the classroom that begin with a particular letter.

Teachers also can encourage children to explore various aspects of print by providing engaging, focused activities in a well-stocked writing center. Such a center should be stocked with paper of all different types and sizes, as well as a variety of writing implements to invite children to write independently. But the center also could contain a diverse collection of manipulatives that focus children's attention on form. These might include sets of magnetic letters, stencils, and letter stamps with ink pads; some children also may enjoy opportunities to trace letters in shaving cream or form letters from modeling clay. Each of these manipulatives will help familiarize children with letters and enable them to eventually incorporate conventional print into their writing.

Strategies to Address Specific Concerns

Although most children will respond to the routines described in this chapter with increased engagement in writing and clear developmental progress, some may not appear to do as well, leading teachers to question their approaches. Some common concerns, such as those that deal with children's development of form, are presented in the following section.

The children don't try to use print. They only want to scribble or draw.

In Practice

YOUNG CARTOGRAPHERS

Mr. Benson's preschoolers like to draw maps, so he had them make rather large maps of their favorite places to play in the classroom. He encouraged the children to include lots of detail and to label "the way" to their favorite play spots, so nobody would get lost trying to get there.

Evie, just 3 years old, drew a square-like shape with a red marker around the edge of the paper. Inside the space she made a few smaller shapes, which she announced were "the stove and refrigerator in the house" (housekeeping area). With a flourish she marked a scribbly tail across the paper and then paused to think. She carefully made five letter-like marks— ꙮᎪᎪᏎᎾ —and, after admiring her handiwork, shouted out, "This says house, everybody. It's where the house is."

James, 4 years old, took another approach, drawing a line diagonally across the paper straight to the blocks. He put a *B* at the beginning of the line, because that's where you start, and a large *N* at the end of the line, because that's where you stop. He heaped some shapes to look like blocks and positioned a few stick figures along the path as if they were already on their way.

As all the children worked on their maps, Mr. Benson supported their efforts to express their sense of place in a two-dimensional form. He also used this opportunity to observe the children's use of print to represent their world—their emerging knowledge of letters, word spellings, and locational terms. When the children finished, he hung their maps in the hallway for everyone to see. And later he put the maps in the different play areas they represented for the children to read and talk about as they played together.

Some children simply have not had sufficient exposure to print and may not have discovered its forms yet. Strategies like shared reading and guided reading, in which the teacher calls children's attention to the print of picture books, will begin to address this problem. Shared writing experiences, during which the teacher models writing for the children, also will help call children's attention to the forms that mature writing takes.

The children continue to use random strings of letters or copying instead of attempting invented spellings.

Children may decline to try spelling on their own because they do not have adequate awareness of the correspondence between sounds and letters. Although many children seem to discover these connections almost effortlessly, other children need to have letter-sound relations called to their attention more explicitly. Minilessons on letter–sound correspondences might be helpful to these children. Teacher modeling of how one sounds out words when writing also will help. This can be done as teachers write morning messages for children on the chalkboard, or as they take dictation from children for language-experience stories.

Other children may hesitate to begin writing using invented spellings because the task of sounding out everything they want to say is simply overwhelming. This is particularly true for children who enjoy creating long, descriptive stories to accompany their drawings. Teachers who want to acknowledge and support such children's focus on meaning, but at the same time nudge them toward more mature meaning–form links, can make use of children's drawings. While accepting the children's stories in the forms in which they are written, the teacher can encourage the children to label the items in their drawings, helping them sound out words initially. Figuring out spellings for individual words is a much more manageable task than writing connected text with invented spellings. Once children are comfortable constructing spelling for individual words, they typically will begin to apply their newfound knowledge to written text.

The children do not seem to progress beyond phonemic spelling. Will they ever become conventional spellers?

This concern is shared by most teachers at one time or another. Continued use of phonemic spellings well into the middle grades may be the one area of writing development that most concerns teachers of older children. In many cases this problem arises because instruction has failed to address the continued spelling development of children once they become fully phonemic spellers. Although it is appropriate to encourage children to sound out words when they first begin to experiment with spelling, the ability to hear sounds in words is not sufficient for conventional spelling. English spellings are determined as much by word origins and meanings as they are by sound. The best spellers are those who have a good understanding of word meanings and who have a highly developed visual sense of printed words. Although explicit study of word origins may be beyond the purview of some early childhood teachers, it is never too early to help children begin to develop a visual awareness of words.

Two simple strategies will facilitate this awareness. The first is the use of word walls. Space can be set aside in the classroom for a large display of words that children are most likely to use in their writing. A word wall can be constructed in a center set aside for theme studies to include all of the major content words related to the theme. It also can be set up in a writing center to include frequently used and misspelled words and phrases. When children ask how to spell a word that is included on a word wall, they can be directed to find the word themselves.

As a supplement, children can keep a personal word bank in their daily journals. The bank should consist of five or six words or phrases that a child will be held accountable for spelling correctly once he or she has demonstrated mastery of phonemic spelling and is ready to move on to conventional spellings. For example, a child who begins most entries with *ws upnu tom* should be supplied with the conventional spelling, *once upon a time*, and reminded to refer to it as needed. As the child begins to use these few conventional spellings consistently, they can be replaced with additional entries. This strategy will lead to rapid learning of conventional spelling for high-utility words like *is*, *was*, *are*, and *were*.

Finally, teachers can suggest visual imagery when a child who has mastered phonemic spelling asks how to spell a word. Rather then encouraging a child to "sound it out," teachers can ask, "Can you think about how it looks? What letters are in that word?" This response reinforces the use of visual as well as phonemic strategies.

Conclusions

The routines and strategies described in this chapter encompass both opportunities for encouraging free-flowing exploration of print and direct instruction regarding specific aspects of writing. Teachers of young children often are torn in their decisions about how to allocate classroom time and resources so that children's literacy learning will be optimized. On one hand, they want children to write freely and discover on their own the meanings, forms, meaning-form links, and functions of writing. At the same time, they recognize that children's development might be aided by explicit instruction.

It is suggested here that the natural tensions between discovery learning and explicit instruction represent only part of the dilemma regarding how to balance instruction. Equally important, teachers need to seek a balance within each approach in terms of the aspects of writing on which they focus children's attention. The writing samples presented here illustrate that children naturally attend to all aspects of writing as they use print for purposes that they deem meaningful. Their constructions and reconstructions of concepts about these aspects of print evolve continuously in response to their exploration of and experimentation with writing. If children's writing is to flourish, teachers must engage children in writing experiences that parallel and extend those in which they engage naturally.

References

Baghban, M. (1984). *Our daughter learns to read and write*. Newark, DE: International Reading Association.

Beals, D., & DeTemple, J. (1993). Home contributions to early language and literacy development. In D. Leu & C. Kinzer (Eds.), *Examining central issues in literacy research, theory, and practice* (42nd Yearbook of the National Reading Conference, pp. 207–215). Chicago, IL: National Reading Conference.

Bissex, G. (1980). *GNYS AT WRK: A child learns to write and read*. Cambridge, MA: Harvard University Press.

Burns, S., & Casbergue, R. (1992). Parent-child interaction in a letter-writing context. *Journal of Reading Behavior, 24*, 289–312.

Calkins, L. (1994). *The art of teaching writing*. Portsmouth, NH: Heinemann.

Casbergue, R. (1996, April). *The emergence of expository writing*. Paper presented at the 41st Annual Convention of the International Reading Association, New Orleans, LA.

Christie, J. (Ed.) (1991). *Play and early literacy development.* Albany, NY: State University of New York Press.

Clay, M. (1975). *What did I write?* Portsmouth, NH: Heinemann

Dahl, K., & Freppon, P. (1995). A comparison of innercity children's interpretations of reading and writing instruction in the early grades in skills-based and whole language classrooms. *Reading Research Quarterly, 31,* 50–75.

Dickinson, D., & Tabors, P. (1991). Early literacy: Linkages between home, school, and literacy achievement at age five. *Journal of Research in Childhood Education, 6,* 30–46.

Dyson, A. (1983). The role of oral language in early writing processes. *Research in the Teaching of English, 17,* 1–30.

Dyson, A. (1993). *The social worlds of children learning to write in an urban primary school.* New York: Teachers College Press.

Ferreiro, E., & Teberosky, A. (1982). *Literacy before schooling.* Portsmouth, NH: Heinemann.

Gardner, H. (1980). *Artful scribbles.* New York: Basic Books.

Goodman, Y. (1986). Children coming to know literacy. In W.H. Teale & E. Sulzby (Eds.), *Emergent literacy: Writing and reading* (pp. 1–14). Norwood, NJ: Ablex.

Heath, S. (1982). What no bedtime story means. *Language in Society, 11,* 49–76.

Hiebert, E. (1978). Preschool children's understanding of written language. *Child Development, 49,* 1231–1234.

Holdaway, D. (1986). The structure of natural learning as a basis for literacy instruction. In M. Sampson (Ed.), *The pursuit of literacy: Early reading and writing* (pp. 56–72). Dubuque, IA: Kendall/Hunt.

Lass, B. (1982). Portrait of my son as an early reader. *The Reading Teacher, 36,* 20–28.

Martinez, M., & Teale, W. (1987). The ins and outs of a kindergarten writing program. *The Reading Teacher, 40,* 444–451.

McGee, L., & Richgels, D. (1996). *Literacy's beginnings: Supporting young readers and writers.* Needham Heights, MA: Allyn & Bacon.

Morrow, L.M. (1989). *Literacy development in the early years: Helping children read and write.* Englewood Cliffs, NJ: Prentice Hall.

Morrow, L.M. (1997, May). *Designing and using literacy center learning: Balancing social experiences and explicit instruction.* Paper presented at the 42nd Annual Convention of the International Reading Association, Atlanta, GA.

Neuman, S., & Roskos, K. (1990). Play, print, and purpose: Enriching play environments for literacy development. *The Reading Teacher, 44,* 214–221.

Neuman, S., & Roskos, K. (1997). Literacy knowledge in practice: Contexts of participation for young writers and readers. *Reading Research Quarterly, 32,* 10–32.

Newkirk, T. (1987). The non-narrative writing of young children. *Research in the Teaching of English, 21,* 121–144.

Purcell-Gates, V. (1994). *Relationships between parental literacy skills and functional uses of print and children's ability to learn literacy skills* (Final Report X257A). Washington, DC: National Institute for Literacy.

Richgels, D. (1995). Invented spelling ability and printed word learning in kinder-garten. *Reading Research Quarterly, 30,* 96–109.

Schickedanz, J. (1986). *More than the ABCs.* Washington, DC: National Association for the Education of Young Children.

Smith, F. (1988). *Joining the literacy club.* Portsmouth, NH: Heinemann.

Stallman, A., & Pearson, P.D. (1990). Formal measures of early literacy. In L.M. Morrow & J. Smith (Eds.), *Assessment for instruction in early literacy* (pp. 7–44). Englewood Cliffs, NJ: Prentice Hall.

Taylor, D. (1983). *Family literacy.* Portsmouth, NH: Heinemann.

Taylor, D., & Dorsey-Gaines, C. (1988). *Growing up literate: Learning from inner-city families.* Portsmouth, NH: Heinemann.

Vukelich, C. (1994). Effects of play interventions on young children's reading of environmental print. *Early Childhood Research Quarterly, 9,* 153–170.

Vygotsky, L.S. (1978). *Mind in society: The development of higher psychological processes* (M. Cole, V. John-Steiner, S. Scribner, & E. Souberman, Eds. and Trans.). Cambridge, MA: Harvard University Press. (Original work published in 1934)

CHAPTER 12

How Do We Assess Young Children's Literacy Learning?

Terry Salinger

Assessment is one of the most controversial topics in education, and the assessment of young children, especially their progress in acquiring literacy, is among the most contentious issues of all. Traditionally, standardized tests were considered the most objective of all measures of academic growth, but the value of paper and pencil tests, especially for young learners, has been questioned severely (Kamii, 1990; Meisels, 1987; National Association for the Education of Young Children & National Association of Early Childhood Specialists in State Departments of Education, 1992; see also *Young Children*, July 1993). Criticisms have been voiced for many reasons, not the least of which is that most young children are not good test takers, especially when tests are administered by strangers or require children to complete unfamiliar and confusing tasks, sit quietly for long periods of time, or make marks in the right place on an answer grid. Tests and testing situations do not give children opportunities to show what they know and can do. It is also true that young children grow and learn almost daily, so any single test score may be highly inaccurate at a later point in time. Further, single measurements of ability cannot accommodate the range of development that is considered normal at any given age.

Recognizing the potential errors inherent in basing placement, curriculum, or other decisions on standardized-test data, early childhood educators, researchers, and theorists have looked for alternative methods of measuring learning and growth. They have wanted assessments that are based in the classroom, not developed by external agents, and that are "congruent with and relevant to the goals, objectives, and content of [early childhood] program[s]." These assessments should use "an array of tools and a variety of processes" and rely "on procedures that reflect the ongoing life of the classroom...[and] on performance during real, not contrived, activities [such as] real reading and writing." Assessment should "demonstrate children's overall strengths and progress and be a collaborative process involving children and teachers, teachers and parents, school and community." These lofty goals for assessment are among those put forth by the National Association for the Education of Young Children (Bredekamp & Rosegrant, 1995, p. 17). The roots of these goals lie in sound early childhood educational theory and practice.

Constructs From Early Childhood Education

In early childhood classrooms, three important constructs interact: development, instruction, and observation. Understanding these constructs and their interaction is the starting point for good early childhood assessment because quality assessment derives from teachers' beliefs, their sense of best practice, and their professional knowledge base. This chapter first discusses these constructs and their interaction, then offers ways that understanding this interaction can provide teachers with methods for classroom-based assessment that are both practical and theoretically sound.

Development is how children grow and learn, and what they can do and understand. It is complicated because although educators and other professionals have some benchmarks or expectations for "normal" development by certain ages (Bredekamp & Rosegrant, 1995), no two children develop in exactly the same way. Yet, recognizing the routine patterns of development along with the unexpected nuances of children's progress toward competence is an essential element of assessment. Indeed, "[e]valuation in school should mean assessing development. Unfortunately, evaluation has frequently come to mean reducing definitions of people to scores, numbers, or labels" (Whitmore & Goodman, 1995, p. 162). In contrast to this reductionist approach, teachers who interact with their students daily can tell, with high degrees of reliability and validity, what students know and can do; they also realize how to refine instruction to help their students grow. Often, teachers only store this kind of information in their minds, even though it should be recorded briefly in some useful format as part of the overall assessment procedures (Lamme & Hysmith, 1991).

When we consider children's literacy learning, we see how involved the construct of development can be. Learning to read and write is a complex process, and children differ across the many dimensions that contribute to literacy acquisition. They acquire language and social competence at different rates, they value literacy in different ways, and they approach literacy instruction with varying amounts of background knowledge about how print functions as a communicative mode (McGill-Franzen, 1992). These are all reasons why standardized paper and pencil tests are such inadequate measures of young children's learning.

Although teachers and researchers recognize individual differences, they know that the ability to read and write is not inborn like hair color or complexion. This is where instruction becomes so important. Children must *learn* to be literate. There is no one best way to teach children to read and write, but literacy learning, like other aspects of human development, follows general patterns (Whitmore & Goodman, 1995). Drawing from what they know about children, informed teachers recognize these patterns and use them as indicators of growth to guide both their instructional decisions and their reporting about students' progress. Further, teachers who provide rich and challenging experiences to help children learn create opportunities for what Chittenden (1991) has termed a rich "database for literacy assessment" (p. 28).

Observation is the third important construct in early childhood education. Early childhood teachers are constantly observing their students, engaging in behaviors called "kidwatching." According to Goodman (1971, 1985; Whitmore & Goodman, 1995)

> [K]idwatching means observing children, with a knowledgeable head, and focusing on children's strengths; it leads to designing open-ended tools to assist with recording evaluative information.... Kidwatching answers the question, How does what children say and do show us what they know about oral and written language? (Whitmore & Goodman, 1995, p. 163)

Learning to be a good observer of young children is the first step toward becoming an assessment expert.

Kidwatching teachers often focus primarily on the processes students use to make sense of literacy learning, but assessment also requires looking closely at students' products. Work samples of all kinds complement teachers' observations and provide exemplars of the different developmental stages through which young learners pass. Work samples are important assessment documentation, not because they are right or wrong, but because they offer concrete evidence of what students are doing and thinking. For example, writing samples collected over several months demonstrate a child's progress through stages of invented spelling, suggest the extent to which the child is gaining control of the letter-sound correspondences necessary for reading, and reflect the child's experiential base. Analyzing the samples helps teachers determine the new challenges the child can handle and any reteaching that will be beneficial.

Getting Started as an Assessment Expert

Accepting the challenge of becoming an assessment expert necessitates thinking deeply about what goes on in one's classroom and what students' behaviors and work show about their progress. Specific questions can guide teachers' development as assessment experts:

- What are the signs of quality literacy development for children at this age?

- Where and when can evidence be gathered to demonstrate each child's progress?

- To whom and for what purposes will results be communicated?

Although they may not realize it, most skilled teachers already assume what have been called "assessment stances" (Chittenden, 1991). For example, they *keep track* of what students are doing in relatively informal ways, and they also *check up* through more structured and focused activities, with the specific goal of accumulating documentation about students' progress. These two assessment stances—keeping track and checking up—involve both formal and informal methods as teachers observe students, analyze work samples, engage in impromptu conversations, hold conferences, or listen to children read. Although relatively informal, they yield information that helps teachers understand their students thoroughly enough to plan helpful instruction and interventions (Omalza, Aihara, & Stephens, 1997).

Finding out, the third assessment stance, involves interpretation of accumulated data. To gather these kind of data, teachers often assign specific tasks, such as reading from a graded series of books or writing on a particular topic. Data that result are often quite sophisticated, especially after teachers have interpreted student work and compared it against standards for what usually is accomplished by a particular developmental level. The important factor is the depth and intensity of teachers' analysis. Data developed at this level complement more informal information gathered as part of keeping-track and checking-up activities to create a full and valid picture of students' accomplishments. Recognizing the extent to which teachers already engage in assessment activities and searching out additional opportunities to gather assessment data are first steps toward becoming an assessment expert.

The Right Classroom Environment for Assessment

Two contextual factors make it possible for teachers to become assessment experts, and fortunately both are within each teacher's control. The first is the classroom itself, which must be full of opportunities for students to explore and use literacy in purposeful ways. For example, story time can yield information about children's understanding of story structure, the relation of illustrations and print, and listening comprehension skills. Daily journal writing documents growth in invented spelling and various expressive skills. Informal settings, such as the block, dramatic-play, or art areas, furnish information about children's oral language competence and inclination to incorporate literacy into their play activities (see Neuman & Roskos, 1990, 1997). To illustrate, the grocery list in Figure 1 was developed during dramatic play in a housekeeping center. It provides evidence that the kindergarten child who created the list understands the function of print. It further shows that the child has a good grasp of initial, medial, and final consonant sounds and of phonemic awareness. The rendering for *bologna* is three-syllables long—*bu-lo-e*—and is impressive evidence of the child's ability to segment words. The handwriting, although all upper case, is strong. All these pieces of assessment data are valuable in determining an appropriate instructional program for this kindergarten student.

The second contextual factor is organization, which can pose real challenges for teachers who want to assume assessment responsibilities. Classroom-based assessment activities generate large quantities of

Figure 1 Grocery List Prepared by Kindergartner

notes and student work that must be dated, stored, collated, evaluated, and synthesized into a usable form (Salinger & Chittenden, 1994). Folders, filing cabinets, bins for papers, and notebooks are some of many devices that can help teachers and students handle the notes and work samples that soon accumulate. Periodic culling of this accumulation also helps; for example, all but the most significant of students' work can be sent home regularly.

Organization also includes finding time to engage in assessment activities. In addition to recognizing the many routine contexts they have for assessment, teachers need to schedule times periodically to step back and check on how students go about the business of learning to read and write. It is also important that teachers have "the patience to stand back and watch and listen, and trust that in response to [their] patience, children will in fact reveal what they know, what they are struggling with, and what they want to learn next" (Siu-Runyan, 1990, p. 102). Later, surrounded by their own notes and students' work, teachers can determine what all the data mean and reflect on what course the data suggest their instruction should take.

Assessment Procedures and Strategies

Classroom-based assessment opportunities, like literacy learning in general, involve considerable social and verbal interaction. They must be real-life, authentic classroom contexts that allow teachers to view what goes on as young literacy learners engage in purposeful tasks. They invite teachers to use three kinds of assessment strategies: observation of students' working, conferencing with or interviewing students, and administering some sort of informal instrument or using a standardized task. These different approaches to assessment—observing, interviewing and conferencing, and posing specific tasks—are discussed next.

Observations

Observation for assessment purposes involves more than merely scanning the classroom and observing behavior. Teachers search for answers to specific questions, detect many attributes of students' individual working styles, and form records of what individual students or the whole class can do. These records will vary in form and specificity according to the purpose of the observation. In deciding what to note and what degree of detail to include, teachers need to ask themselves a complex two–part question: what *aspects* of literacy do they want to see occurring and what specific kinds of *behaviors* will constitute evidence that these are occurring? A third question validates observations as an assessment tool: What do these literacy behaviors mean in terms of *students' progress* toward competence as readers and writers?

For illustrative purposes, suppose that a teacher wants to gather information during reading workshop. Walking around the room, looking over children's shoulders, crouching beside them, or merely scanning the classroom, the teacher looks for those students who understand the required procedures for the workshop period. Because he is interested not just in whether students can read independently but also in how they go about accomplishing this task, a simple checklist would not be an appropriate recording device. Observation charts such as those shown in Figure 2 allow teachers to record brief narrative notes that show the range of behaviors students demonstrate. (For numerous other useful forms, see Chittenden & Courtney, 1989; Salinger, 1996.) As the teacher observes, he makes notes about what he sees. Reviewing these notes later, the teacher gains insight into behaviors of individuals and into the dynamics of the entire class. Patterns emerge from this analysis, contribute to overall instructional planning, and point to further instruction that must be offered to individuals. In his review and analysis, the teacher uses his knowledge of the individual students, of child development, and of best practices in literacy instruction to draw conclusions such as the following:

- Two children seemed to wander around the room for about 5 minutes before settling down; they need to be monitored and reminded about appropriate procedures so that their transition to independent reading can be accomplished more efficiently and with less interruption to others.
- One child becomes distracted easily, puts her book down readily, and daydreams. She too needs to be monitored and reminded of the task-at-hand; she also may need to be encouraged to

Figure 2 Sample Recording Forms for Observations and Conferences

Version 1: For use with individual student

Directions: This can be used to record observations about individual children or to make summary notes after literacy conferences.

Student _____

Date	Reading Behaviors	Writing Behaviors	Oral Language Behaviors	Spontaneous Uses of Literacy

Version 2: For use with small group or whole class

Directions: This record is best limited to a single observation or observations conducted over a short period of time. Brief narrative notes are recorded about each child observed.

Date(s) of observation _____

Reading _____ Writing _____ Oral language _____ Other focus _____(Check one)

Name _____	Name _____	Name _____
Name _____	Name _____	Name _____

read different, possibly more challenging or motivating books that will hold her attention more effectively.

- Another child appears to finish one book before going back to the library area to get another. His posture and general stance as he reads is relaxed; he smiles and chuckles to himself in obvious satisfaction. It might be a good idea to make sure that he is challenging himself enough to foster growth.

- Two other children seem to read the same kinds of books each workshop period; it's time to check their list of books read and nudge them into other topics and genres, without sacrificing their strong interest for recreational reading.

- Two children talk productively and enthusiastically with each other about their reading and sometimes become loud enough to disturb others. It's time to talk to them about consideration for their neighbors and suggest that they do their sharing in a quiet corner of the room and in softer voices.

Later still, when he is preparing for parent conferences, the teacher can use these forms again. Data on such charts situate individual children within a larger learning community, and the teacher can easily share a copy of one of his record-keeping charts (with individual names obscured) with parents so that they can see how their child functions within the class, interacts with others, understands and follows procedures, and in general orchestrates literacy learning. This demonstration of classroom life and the assessment approach helps parents recognize the complexity of learning to read and write.

Interviews and Conferences

The idea of conducting interviews and conferences with students may sound formal, but the close bond between teacher and learners ensures that the time is friendly and productive. Interviews with young children do not need to take long or be held too often, but they should be structured around a predetermined set of questions that can yield information about how students are learning.

The key to productive interviews is the questions teachers ask. Questions may target numerous aspects of literacy learning and students' work or their attitudes toward school in general. Asking all children in a class the same or similar questions gives teachers a useful but nonjudgmental class-wide comparison. Answers will differ from child to child because of their distinct language styles and abilities to reflect on their work and articulate their learning strategies, but teachers will factor into their interpretation of responses both their knowledge of child development and their familiarity with each of their students. The following sets of questions can be starting points for developing interview protocols to find out about students' literacy development (Salinger, 1996).

- To find out about reading attitudes: Do you like to read? What do you like to read about? When do you like to read? Do you ever read at home? What do you read there? Does someone read to you?
- To find out about reading behaviors: How do you select books you read? What kinds of books do you like? What do you do if you don't know a word in what you are reading? What do you do if you don't understand what you read?
- To find out about writing attitudes: Do you like to write? What do you like to write? When do you like to write? Do you ever write at home? What do you write there?
- To find out about writing behaviors: How do you think of the topics you write about? What do you do if you can't think of a topic? When you can't think of how to spell a word, what do you do? What would you say to help someone who is just learning to write?

Answers to interview questions reveal much about students' experiences with literacy and about their attitudes, attributions, and strategies. Responses to questions that ask for self-assessment (for example, Do you think you are a good reader or writer?) can be particularly revealing. Discrepancies between students' assessment of their competence and teachers' assessment must be dealt with directly and immediately, but tactfully. If students are to become truly engaged in their learning and if they are to be able to evaluate their own progress, they must become realistic about their own skills and strategies. Interviews give teachers opportunities to keep track of these aspects of students' literacy development.

In the purest sense, there are two kinds of conferences: assessment and teaching. In the pragmatic world of the classroom, the two overlap. Conferences provide the ideal "teachable moment" because both teachers and students are focusing on something the student has read or a piece of writing the student is working on. As discussion ensues, teachable moments become evaluative moments, because "[t]he teachable or evaluative moment is a growth point, a window of spontaneous insight for both [the] student and [the teacher]" (Morrissey, 1989, p. 87).

Unlike interviews, teachers do not frame the conference with predetermined questions. Instead, teacher and students engage in a discussion. Students know they are responsible for coming to a scheduled conference prepared to talk about work they are doing. For example a child might come to a conference with the following story, the second draft of a piece that she has been working on all week:

> We got a new puppy...and her name is Sadie and she is gray and has big ears and blue eyes and she likes to run around in the house and outside...and she's only 12 weeks old and I give her puppy chow three times a day.

After the child reads the story aloud, the teacher should encourage her to think about what she has heard and what she has written to help her recognize that she needs to eliminate some of the *ands* if her story is to flow smoothly. The teacher also might query the young writer about descriptive words and help her understand that the story would be improved by adding more detail about the new puppy and about how the child feels about her pet. While still conferencing with the teacher, the child might begin editing her piece so the teacher can see her actually applying her strategies to begin a new draft of the piece. In addition to helping the child with these aspects of writing, the teacher might suggest an extension, perhaps in the form of an ongoing diary about her puppy's first 6 months. This project would take advantage of the child's enthusiasm for her pet and give her opportunities to develop a theme in depth. This project also can produce an excellent longitudinal record of her progress, as well as a meaningful record of the pet's early experiences.

Conferences give teachers opportunities to check up on their students by talking with them about their reading and writing; they also allow teachers to provide one-on-one instruction tailored to an individual's needs. Further, conferences give students opportunities to participate in self-evaluation, an important and often-neglected component of early childhood assessment (Bredekamp & Rosegrant, 1995).

Standardized Activities

The final category of assessment activities accumulates documentation in more standardized ways. These activities are considered "standardized" or systematic, in that each follows certain procedures, but they are still so similar to typical classroom activities that students do not perceive them as artificial or contrived. Some of these activities involve students as record keepers, and some are administered by the teacher in standardized ways. Data or work samples collected through these means must be analyzed in depth to find out how students are doing.

The range of standardized assessment activities will vary according to grade level, students' literacy accomplishments, and teachers' needs for accountability. They are classroom based but suitable for sharing with others to document the progress of individuals or of a whole class. Products of these activities lend themselves extremely well for inclusion in a portfolio.

It is important to assess two aspects of young learners' reading: strategies for identifying words and strategies for making sense of what they read. Running records and story retellings are appropriate mechanisms for this kind of assessment.

Running records. Taking running records (Clay, 1993) can be labor intensive. However, it is time well spent because running records make visible the strategies students use to identify unfamiliar words and generally guide their reading. Teachers often keep a set of graded books separate from the classroom library to use for running records; these books are unfamiliar to the students so that no one has the advantage of already knowing a book when he or she reads it to the teacher. As part of their regular assessment schedule, teachers should set aside time to collect running records. Here is a simplified version of how this assessment method works:

- The teacher selects a book that seems appropriate, hard enough to be challenging but still within the student's range. The teacher has the text of the book typed on a sheet of paper.

- As the student reads, the teacher marks any deviations, omissions, repeated words, prompts, or requests for help that can provide insight into how the student has negotiated the text. The teacher will analyze this script later to find out what the student knows and has done.

- Finally, the teacher may ask the student some questions about the story to gauge comprehension or response or guide the student through reflection about the story.

Analysis of "miscues" or deviations from text as shown in an individual running record can be especially revealing of what students know about phonics, semantics, and the use of context to aid in reading (Goodman, Watson, & Burke, 1987). For example, a child who miscues consistently on medial vowel sounds differs in his or her decoding strategies from the child who attends primarily to context for help in decoding unfamiliar words. Analysis of running records kept on students over several months provides glimpses into their reading development that may reveal problems or misconceptions before they become habituated. Teachers have documentation for seeking intervention services, such as Reading Recovery or other pull-out programs, or for changing instructional strategies. Additionally, they have concrete evidence of students' reading behavior to share with parents during conferences. See Figure 3 for two retellings collected one month apart from a competent first-grade reader. Note how in December she depended more on picture clues than on graphophonemic information (for example, *elephant* and *clown*); note also the reversal of *P* and *B* in January. In the retellings the circled *P* indicates a teacher prompt, and *SC* indicates an unprompted self-correction.

Story retellings. Story retellings give information about students' comprehension abilities (Morrow, 1988). The approach is even valid for prereaders who retell a story the teacher has read to them. Here is how this approach works, with variations noted to accommodate students' progress:

Figure 3 Two Running Records

Group A

<u>In My Bed</u>
(Rigby- Literacy 2000)

Name_____

Date *Dec 4, 94*

Known _____ Unknown ✓

In My Bed *our rabbit* Ⓣ

There's ~~a~~ room in my bed

for my rabbit.

There's room in my bed

for my dog.

There's room in my bed

for my teddy. *bear* (looked at picture)

There's room in my bed

for my cat.

~~There's room in my bed~~ *elephant* ← ⓈⒸ (looked at picture and visual)

for my ~~clown.~~

There's room in my bed

for my elephant. But...

there's no room

in my bed for me!

(60 words)

Group B

<u>Too Big For Me</u>
(Story Box)

Name_____

Date *Jan 5*

Known _____ Unknown ✓

Too big for me

Up up up

Up up, up *came* ~~came~~ little spider,

to see ~~what~~ *Want* Ⓣ he could see. Ⓟ Look at picture

"What a big fly," he said.

"Too big *pig* for me to catch." *C-a-t*

"What a *pig* big bee.

he said. Ⓟ

"Too big *pig* for me to catch." Ⓟ Ⓟ Does that make sense?

"What a big butterfly,"

he said.

"Too big for me to catch."

"What a big, big bird,"

he said.

"He will catch me!"

Down, down, down I go. *Bird/Go* Ⓟ Does that make sense?

"He ~~is~~ way to big for me." *His* Ⓢ Ⓒ

(77 words)

- The teacher may read a story to an individual or small group or may ask children to read a story silently.

- Very soon after listening or reading, the teacher listens to individual children retell the story. The teacher notes what the child includes in an unprompted retelling and may give brief prompts such as, "Well, what did the main character do then?" or "Why do you think that happened?"

- The teacher notes what the student says, listening for the presence of at least a beginning, middle, and end to the story, and recording the extent to which more accomplished readers cite details of characterization, locale, plot development, and other elements of the story.

- Alternately, students may be asked to draw or write their retelling. This is an efficient way to collect retellings from more than one student at a time. For beginning readers, teachers may fold a piece of paper into thirds and ask the listeners or readers to draw something about the beginning, middle, and end and write or dictate a brief sentence about what has happened. More advanced readers can fill out a story map for writing their summary in their own words.

Teacher records. Teacher notes about oral, written, or drawn retellings can be analyzed to determine students' comprehension strategies. Information about the parts of the stories they attend to, their perceptions of connections between character and plot, and their sense of story structure are revealed by their retellings. Over time, a portrait of their active use of comprehension strategies emerges.

Both story retellings and running records are examples of the "finding out" level of classroom-based assessment because teachers must analyze and interpret the data that result. Analysis of running records and retellings collected at several different times shows students' development in terms of real behaviors. Teachers can see the growth of reading strategies and also can identify weaknesses or misconceptions that need attention before they become habituated.

Additional information can be discovered by having children record the books they read over time. At first, students may simply record titles, perhaps accompanied by a smiling or frowning face as a kind of "review" of the book; later they may write one or two sentences in review or summary. Lists of books are more than mere catalogs. They show how widely students' interests range and can be good starting points for reading conferences. Teachers might, for example, suggest that students explore different authors or different genres because analysis of the reading lists suggests too narrow a selection of books for independent reading.

Writing assessment. Writing can be assessed through standardized activities as well. Teachers can periodically ask all students to write about the same topic and collect these samples for analysis. It is essential that these topics are relevant and authentic, not contrived and artificial (Salinger, 1996), although sometimes results can be surprising. Figure 4 on page 240 shows a first grader's response to the request that class members write their reactions to *Charlotte's Web* (White, 1952). At the time, the student was a reluctant reader who often refused to participate in any oral reading; he did, however, love to write for many purposes. His rendition of *Charlotte's Web* shows clearly that he had comprehended the book his teacher had read and also reflects his confidence in his own ability to extend the basic story in new directions. This demonstration of writing competence, creativity, and confidence suggests to the teacher that writing should move this child into higher levels of literacy.

Student-selected writing samples are appropriate for analysis too. These, like lists of books read, can be discussed during conferences and then kept in a separate folder for analysis. Before students are asked to select pieces, however, teachers need to spend time helping them understand the criteria for determining appropriateness. Minilessons, small-group instruction, writers' workshops, author's-chair sessions, and one-on-one conferences are all good vehicles for helping students understand how to evaluate their own and others' writing. Student-selected writing samples are most valuable when explanatory notes are attached. Sticky notes can be used for students to record the rationale for their selections.

Writing samples of both types illustrate students' progress in learning to use print to communicate. They show how students construct their messages in terms of style, tone, awareness of audience, and also

Figure 4 Writing Sample in Response to *Charlotte's Web*

there was a spidveaud the nam was svlit the spidve and svlit was al. wase a lam; and then two Bugs cama nd one avv the Bugs sid my nawi is niche and the avv Bug. Sid my nam is Johre So they wit foudinre and thet isthe En

in terms of the mechanical aspects of composition such as spelling, punctuation, and word choice. Looking at writing samples across time helps teachers see patterns of development and areas that may need direct instruction, individually, in a small-group minilesson, or contextualized within a student-teacher conference.

Teachers can think of many other standardized assessment activities to gather documentation about students—art samples, especially those that accompany writing or are in response to reading; individual goals set by students; spelling "tests"; audiotapes of students reading graded material; and even sight-word lists. But one unusual piece can offer a unique perspective: a self-evaluation reflection chart. Even young children can be encouraged to reflect on their own growth and engage in self-evaluation. They can think about the quantity and quality of their work, and their interests and attitudes toward reading and writing. Even more than teacher-administered interest inventories, self-evaluation provides glimpses of how students think about themselves as learners. In one school system (Salinger, 1996), even kindergarten students engage in reflection and self-evaluation periodically throughout the year. They are guided in this process by the simple form shown in Figure 5. The quality of their thinking sharpens as they engage in this process until they are able to write extended analyses at the end of second grade when all students compose an essay called "On Becoming Eight: Reflections on Learning to Read and Write."

It should be clear that classroom–based assessment produces a lot of material: notes on observations, interviews, and conferences; student work samples; results of standardized activities; and other evidence of both student process and product. Many teachers have begun to keep these accumulated materials in a portfolio that spans at least a year's worth of growth and development. Numerous books and articles have described portfolio assessment of literacy (Glazer & Brown, 1993; Graves & Sunstein, 1992; Salinger, 1996; Tierney, Carter, & Desai, 1991), so this chapter will not detail the theory and methodology of bringing together and analyzing the accumulated documentation of students' learning.

Let us merely assume that teachers do collect varied information about their students' growth, development, and learning, and they engage periodically in a systematic attempt to find out what all the

Figure 5 Sample Chart to Help Students Reflect on Their Work

Name _____   Date _____

	What Have I Learned?	What Do I Need To Do Better?
Math		
Reading		
Writing		

documentation suggests about each child. What they find will help them better support students' learning, but it also should provide them with information that can be shared with parents, administrators, and others for accountability purposes.

Reporting and Issues of Accountability

The process of documenting student growth changes dramatically when reading and writing are perceived as integrated processes, when aspects of the literacy curriculum meld into one another, and when teachers invest in developing methods for classroom-based assessments. An essential part of this process is assigning scores or levels to the accumulated documentation; this is what pushes the collection of student work and teacher notes into the realm of assessment. Johnston (1990) referred to this accumulation of student work and teacher notes as an "accountability audit" (p. 27), documenting the methods, the data, and the interpretations of student work. Making evaluative judgments about accumulations of work is a serious undertaking, especially if the rating will be communicated outside the classroom to administrators or parents and used for accountability purposes.

To bring objectivity to this weighty task, teachers often compare their students' work against sets of anchors or standards that describe in terms of behavior what students can do at different levels of competency. The best sets of anchors are the ones that teachers develop themselves from their own understanding of theory and their beliefs about literacy learning. For example, teachers in one New Jersey district developed a six-point emergent literacy scale that they use as the rubric against which they evaluate the contents of their students' portfolios (Bridgeman, Chittenden, & Cline, 1995; Salinger & Chittenden, 1994; Suskin, 1996). Teachers in this district had spent time together discussing their own beliefs, their instructional practices, and the theoretical underpinning of the their vision of sound early literacy instruction. They developed their descriptive scale by looking at student work and standardized task data, and they revised the scale five times before considering it workable and reliable enough for district accountability purposes.

Other teachers may take a different route to evaluation. For example, Au (1994) writes that she and colleagues at the Kamehameha Elementary Education Program in Hawaii included motivation to read and higher-level thinking as outcome measures in their portfolio because standardized tests overlook these important goals. Morrissey (1989) offers another example. She developed a form on which to track writing growth. She listed attributes of writing quality and writing conventions and used a coding system in her monthly evaluation of students' progress. She assigned *NE* when she saw no evidence of the attribute, *D* when the attribute was developing, and *C* when students demonstrated control of the target attribute. She also developed a method for evaluating spelling "by documenting the percentage of invented spelling and conventional spelling in each piece [and noting] changes in both the high frequency and low frequency words over time" (p. 89).

The common theme in these examples is that the teachers have combined their beliefs and their knowledge to form a tool they can use to evaluate students. Rather than adopting someone else's system or rubric, they have worked to create their own. Sources such as the developmental sequence offered by Whitmore and Goodman (1995)

would, of course, be invaluable references in crafting a scale, but it is primarily the teachers' own knowledge that should inform these assessment rubrics. When teachers undertake this process together, they provide a reliability check on one another, essentially by calibrating one another's assessments. They debate among themselves the markers of progress and the sequence in which various literacy skills and strategies develop, pooling their knowledge and experience and drawing from their understanding of theory and of real children. Together they look at enough evidence to reach consensus about the accuracy of their interpretations. Other examples of teachers working together to develop assessment systems can be found in Valencia, Hiebert, and Afflerbach (1993).

No matter how carefully a group of teachers works to develop a rubric for evaluating students' progress and no matter how theoretically sound their assessment approach may be, they still must communicate to a broader audience. Their assessment data must be reduced to a useful and comprehensible form, but a mere checklist fails to express the integrative nature of learning. Narrative reports are one alternative, but because these often require teachers to write extensive amounts of information about students, they are impractical except with small classes. Variations of the narrative detail of the Primary Language Record (Barrs, Ellis, Hester, & Thomas, 1989) are being developed but are still too extensive for many purposes (Falk, 1998). The Primary Language Record is a comprehensive assessment system that combines teachers' notes on students and on their conversations with parents concerning students' progress and teachers' analysis of multiple forms of student work.

A good compromise between the extensiveness of narratives and the brevity of most checklists is an external reporting format that offers a standardized and developmentally appropriate explanation of the range of achievement appropriate for any level and a brief teacher-written summary of each child's progress in relation to that standard. The explanation should be in straightforward language that communicates to audiences not familiar with the jargon of literacy learning. Additionally, explanations should be couched in terms of development, stating in unequivocal terms that most students move along a normal continuum and do so at their own pace and in their own styles. For

In Practice

CELEBRATIONS

A formal tribute to a job well-done, celebrations are designed to allow us to share what has been learned in projects and activities with others. Celebrations are public displays, highlighting children's efforts and achievements. They honor child-centered explorations and creative endeavors, and encourage connections between home and school, inviting parents and caregivers to share in children's learning activities.

Try to think of different forms of celebrations. For example, creating a videotape of children's learning activities is sure to bring parents together. Or, inviting other classrooms to see and learn more about a special project is a way to bring attention to children's learning. Consider the following options:

- Invite parents to a bagel breakfast or a morning tea to celebrate children's published works. It is often easier for parents to participate in early-morning activities before work.

- Invite members from the community to join in celebrating young children's efforts—the local fire chief, a police officer, and other local workers are important figures to young children and are likely to be a very responsive audience.

- Invite senior citizens from the community; they tend to be highly appreciative audiences.

example, a reporting form might explain the development of spelling competency, from beginning invented spelling to mastery of traditional spelling strategies. Perhaps it might illustrate this progression with authentic sample sentences typical of each stage. Teachers then could state where a child can be placed on this continuum and support this placement with samples of the child's work. A sampling of the kinds of material students can read at different stages is valuable too in that it illustrates the progression from simple sentences, easy vocabulary, and basic concepts to more complex, interesting, and challenging text. The developmental sequence offered by Whitmore & Goodman (1995) can provide many ideas for teachers for categories to include on reporting forms that encapsulate the developmental range of literacy behaviors.

The keys to successful use of narrative reporting forms are to use plain language in describing the behaviors and to anchor them with real examples of student work. Successful parent conferences employ similar strategies: straightforward discussion of what students know and can do, equally plain discussion of areas that need improvement, and real examples of work the child has produced. In the case of reading, sharing with parents a tape recording of a child's efforts to negotiate text and explaining the strategies the child is trying to use is a powerful way to document a child's progress.

The benefits of this kind of reporting are many. First and most practically, narratives anchored with student work acknowledge the complexity of the any classroom-based assessment system. They reduce the accumulated notes and work samples to a form that communicates concisely but does not sacrifice the richness of the assessment data to the convenience of a mere series of checkmarks.

Second, this kind of reporting reflects the theoretical underpinnings of good early childhood literacy instruction. It clearly demonstrates the value of focusing on development over time, rather than putting forth a deceptively simple list of isolated skills and strategies. It shows the complexity of literacy learning and suggests the integrated nature of the many components of text production and comprehension that children must learn to orchestrate as they acquire literacy. Finally, its use of real examples of student work contextualizes any score or rating developed by analyses of students' work in terms that many audiences can understand.

One Caveat

A word of caution must be raised in conclusion. Acceptance of classroom-based assessment has validated informed practice and placed teachers at the center of decision making. Rich, contextualized data such as work samples and audiotapes make parent conferences more meaningful and offer important dimensions to consider in making decisions about intervention and many other special services. But reliance solely on classroom-based assessment data for important decision making such as removal from a regular school setting or retention in a grade can be as dangerous as reliance solely on a single standardized test score. It is crucial that important decisions be made only on the basis of data that have been "triangulated," that is, verified by reference to multiple sources and multiple evaluators (Cambourne, Turbill, & Dal Santo, 1994). Further, data must show that every effort has been made to capture the nuances of developmental changes over time and in different contexts. Accomplishing these goals may necessitate a combination of instruments and evaluative measures.

When early childhood teachers assume the role of assessment expert, they add to their already vast responsibilities some of the most rewarding and most important work that they can ever do. They are proclaiming their knowledge of child development, learning theory, and instructional practice, and they are accepting responsibility communicating about their students' learning and growth. As assessment experts, teachers grow in their ability to plan and implement instruction that is sensitive both to students' needs and also to the accountability needs of the schools and districts in which they teach.

References

Au, K.H. (1994). Portfolio assessment: Experiences at the Kamehameha Elementary Education Program. In S.W. Valencia, E.H. Hiebert, & P.P. Afflerbach (Eds.), *Authentic reading assessment: Practices and possiblities* (pp. 103–126). Newark, DE: International Reading Association.

Barrs, M., Ellis, S., Hester, H., & Thomas, A. (1989). *Primary language record.* London: ILEA/Centre for Language in Primary Education.

Bredekamp, S., & Rosegrant, T. (Eds.). (1995). *Reaching potentials: Transforming early childhood curriculum and assessment, Vol. 2.* Washington, DC: National Association for the Education of Young Children.

Bridgeman, B., Chittenden, E., & Cline, F. (1997). *Characteristics of a portfolio scale for rating early literacy.* Princeton, NJ: Educational Testing Service.

Cambourne, B., Turnbill, J., & Dal Santo, D. (1994). Yes, but how do we make assessment and evaluation "scientific"? In B. Cambourne & J. Turbill (Eds.), *Responsive evaluation: Making valid judgments about student literacy* (pp. 104–112). Portsmouth, NH: Heinemann.

Chittenden, E. (1991). Authentic assessment, evaluation, and documentation of students performance. In V. Perrone (Ed.), *Expanding student assessment* (pp. 22–31). Alexandria, VA: Association for Supervision and Curriculum Development.

Chittenden, E., & Courtney, R. (1989). Assessment of young children's reading: Documentation as an alternative to testing. In D.S. Strickland & L.M. Morrow (Eds.), *Emerging literacy: Young children learn to read and write* (pp. 24–28). Newark, DE: International Reading Association.

Clay, M. (1993). *An observation survey of early literacy achievement.* Portsmouth, NH: Heinemann.

Falk, B. (1998). Using direct evidence to assess student progress: How the Primary Language Record supports teaching and learning. In C. Harrison & T. Salinger (Eds.), *International perspectives on reading assessment.* London: Routledge.

Glazer, S.M., & Brown, C.S. (1993). *Portfolios and beyond: Collaborative assessment in reading and writing.* Norwood, MA: Christopher-Gordon.

Goodman, Y.M. (1971). Kidwatching: An alternative to testing. *National Elementary Principal, 57*(4), 41–45.

Goodman, Y.M. (1985). Kidwatching: Observing children in the classroom. In A. Jagger & M.T. Smith-Burke (Eds.), *Observing the language learner* (pp. 9–18). Newark, DE: International Reading Association.

Goodman, Y.M., Watson, D., & Burke, C. (1987). *Reading miscue inventory.* Katonah, NY: Richard C. Owen.

Graves, D., & Sunstein, B. (1992). *Portfolio portraits.* Portsmouth, NH: Heinemann.

Johnston, P. (1990). Constructive evaluation and the improvement of teaching and learning. *Teachers College Record, 91,* 1–42.

Kamii, C. (Ed.). (1990). *Achievement testing in the early grades: The games grown-ups play.* Washington, DC: National Association for the Education of Young Children.

Lamme, L.L., & Hysmith, C. (1991). One school's adventure into portfolio assessment. *Language Arts, 68,* 629–640.

McGill-Franzen, A. (1992). Early literacy: What does "developmentally appropriate" mean? *The Reading Teacher, 46,* 56–58.

Meisels, S. (1987). Uses and abuse of developmental screening and school readiness testing. *Young Children, 42,* 4–5, 34–40.

Morrissey, M. (1989). When shut up is a sign of growth. In K. Goodman, Y.M. Goodman, & W. Hood (Eds.), *The whole language evaluation book* (85–97). Portsmouth, NH: Heinemann.

Morrow, L.M. (1988). Retelling stories as a diagnostic tool. In S.M. Glazer, L.W. Searfoss, & L. Gentile (Eds.), *Reexamining reading diagnosis*, (pp. 128–149). Newark, DE: International Reading Association.

National Association for the Education of Young Children (NAEYC) and National Association of Early Childhood Specialists in State Departments of Education (NAECS/SDE). (1992). Guidelines of appropriate curriculum content and assessment in programs serving children ages 3 through 8. In S. Bredekamp & T. Rosegrant (Eds.), *Reading potentials: Appropriate curriculum and assessment for young children, Vol. 1* (pp. 9–27). Washington, DC: National Association for the Education of Young Children.

Neuman, S.B., & Roskos, K. (1990). Play, print and purpose: Enriching play environments for literacy development. *The Reading Teacher, 44,* 214–221.

Neuman, S.B., & Roskos, K. (1997). Literacy knowledge in practice: Contexts of participation for young writers and readers. *Reading Research Quarterly, 32,* 10–32.

Omalza, S., Aihara, K., & Stephens, D. (1997). Engaged in learning through the HT process. *Primary Voices K–6, 5,* 4–17.

Salinger, T.S. (1996). *Literacy for young children.* Columbus, OH: Merrill/Prentice Hall.

Salinger, T.S., & Chittenden, E. (1994). Analysis of an early literacy portfolio. *Language Arts, 71,* 446–452.

Siu-Runyan, Y. (1991). Learning from students: An important aspect of classroom organization. *Language Arts, 68,* 100–107

Suskin, S. (1996). *The South Brunswick Early Literacy Portfolio: Bridging the gap between classroom assessment and district accountability.* Unpublished manuscript.

Tierney, R.J., Carter, M.A., & Desai, L.E. (1991). *Portfolio assessment in the reading-writing classroom.* Norwood, MA: Christopher Gordon.

Whitmore, K.F., & Goodman, Y.M. (1995). Transforming curriculum in language and literacy. In S. Bredekamp & T. Rosegrant (Eds.), *Reaching potentials: Transforming early childhood curriculum and assessment, Vol. 2* (pp. 145–166). Washington, DC: National Association for the Education of Young Children.

Valencia, S.W., Hiebert, E.H., & Afflerbach, P.P. (Eds.). (1993). *Authentic reading assessment: Practices and possibilities.* Newark, DE: International Reading Association.

Children's Literature Reference

White, E.B. (1952). *Charlotte's web.* New York: Harper.

CHAPTER 13

How Do Practicing Teachers Grow and Learn as Professionals?

Kathleen A. Roskos and Carol Vukelich

What makes the difference in the literacy achievement of young children is their teachers. All budding writers and readers deserve teachers who possess the knowledge, skill, and personal qualities—like patience, curiosity, caring, and imagination—that make literacy attainable and personally meaningful in their young lives.

However, the human qualities that excellent early literacy teaching demands often are not discussed and even less often nurtured. Traditionally, teachers' professional development has concentrated on transmitting knowledge and skills, not on promoting teachers' intellectual and personal abilities to deal with the perplexing problems of their practice. Too frequently teachers are *told* about writers' workshop, literacy in play, literacy portfolios, parent-involvement strategies, but rarely are they afforded opportunities to critique and debate these ideas, to question and deliberate about them, or to adapt and generate new knowledge in relation to them. Professional development, unfortunately, is generally something done *to* teachers, not *with* them. The professional development provided early literacy teachers is no exception.

In the recent round of educational reforms, however, many recognize the inadequacies of inservice training of teachers and call for the reform of professional development itself (Sykes, 1996). They argue for approaches that engage teachers in studying their own teaching, collaborating with colleagues, learning about their own learning, and participating actively in their professional community (Ball, 1996; Little, 1993). A new vision of professional development is emerging—one that sees teachers as learners, shapers, promoters, and critics of their own teaching. Excellence in early literacy instruction for all children can benefit from this more enlightened view of teachers' professional education. In fact, we would argue that if the ideas so artfully described in the preceding chapters are to live in teachers' literacy practices, then teacher development and learning must be at the heart of our effort.

This chapter, therefore, is about ourselves as developing professionals, as learners, and as members of a broad-based professional community. It focuses on who we are, how we learn, and ways we can grow professionally and intellectually. We start by considering teacher development and learning in a general way. We then use this information to explore two models of professional development as contexts for learning, thus closing a book on best practices in early literacy by placing the matter where it rightly belongs—in the hands of intelligent teachers.

The Teacher as a Developing Professional

Compared to our knowledge of children's development, we know very little about adults' development in the years following adolescence. Certainly adults continue to grow cognitively, personally, morally, and ethically, but the processes and benchmarks of this development are not well-articulated. Erickson (1975), for example, described three comprehensive psychosocial tasks for adults: early adulthood as intimacy versus isolation, adulthood as generativity versus stagnation, and old age as integrity versus despair. Links between these turning points in adult-hood and teacher development have been observed. There is evidence, for example, that the isolation and routine of classroom contexts may stifle adults' generativity. Teachers stagnate or "get in a rut," which ulti-mately may arrest the growth process. However, these observations are tentative at best, because the theories of adulthood phases are just that—theories. They offer descriptions of what adult development might look like, but are far from explaining how it happens.

Teachers' Concerns

Closer to the topic of professional development, we know some of how teachers develop as professionals across their teaching careers. This development, some argue, can be summarized in what teachers are concerned about (Fuller, 1969; Hall & Rutherford, 1990). During the preservice years, aspiring teachers tend to express few concerns about anything, and are quite confident that they can handle any classroom if given the opportunity. In the early phases of teaching, however, be-ginners become less confident, showing increasing concerns about themselves and their instructional effectiveness as they grapple with the realities and uncertainties of daily teaching. With experience and greater control of basic instructional routines, teachers' concerns shift to their students and to what extent they impact their students' achievement and the broader educational arenas of school and school district. Development, in short, progresses from innocence to self-awareness, and finally to another perspective in which students' needs and interests take precedence.

Teachers' Career Phases

Approaching development from a different angle, others have fo-cused on the career phases of teachers. Three phases often are men-tioned among teachers themselves (Burden, 1990). *Survival* characterizes the first year of teaching as beginners struggle to cope with the com-plex and exhausting work of teaching. For the next 5 years, there seems to be a period of *competency building* as teachers fine-tune what works for them while at the same time searching for new instructional techniques to add to their repertoires. Past the 5-year mark, teachers enter a cycle of *stability* during which they adopt a more student-centered focus and refine their personal teaching style.

But surely there is more to a teaching career than three broad phases of development, as some have rightly observed. Offering a more thorough description of career development, Fessler and Christensen (1992) identified eight levels in a teacher's career cycle: preservice, induction, competency building, enthusiastic and growing, career frustration, stable and stagnant, career wind-down, and career exit. Although clearly evident, these phases of occupational progression are not set in stone. Each level is influenced by personal experiences, such as family and personal crises, and also organizational features, such as school culture, management, and social expectations. Yet each represents a distinct set of experiences and attitudes; each new level is qualitatively different and more complex than the former. Teachers mature and grow cognitively as they progress through these career levels. Generally, the first four levels are times of high motivation, high productivity, generativity, and active participation in the profession. The remaining four can be frustrating times as teachers begin to question their worth and the value of teaching; teaching itself may become less satisfying and disillusionment may set in. However, the erosion of commitment and decline of enthusiasm seen in later years of teaching can be prevented through professional development and through the assumption of new roles, such as serving as a mentor. What it means to be a teacher is highly influenced by where teachers work and the people they work with, as well as their individual personal qualities. Well-timed professional opportunities and educational activities can make a difference in a teacher's career development, steering it toward fuller, healthier, and happier ends.

Teachers' Cognition

To complete this discussion of teachers' development, we turn lastly to knowledge of teachers' cognition, that is their reflecting, knowing, and problem solving. How knowledgeable teachers are and how well they think and reason has a bearing on student achievement. Smarter teachers, in fact, produce smarter students (Kennedy, 1991). Yet, how teachers' pedagogical knowledge and beliefs develop to higher order levels of thinking is not well-understood despite two decades of research on teacher cognition (Kagan, 1990). From information-processing research, we do know that teachers' thinking reflects less complex to greater amounts of cognitive complexity. This has been observed clearly in teachers' lesson planning (Borko & Livingston, 1989; Roskos, 1996). Beginning teachers mentally go about creating instructional plans quite differently from experienced, successful teachers. Beginners tend to seek a quick solution in the form of a concrete plan whereas experts devote more mental energy to the process of planning itself. As a result, experienced teachers devise more comprehensive and complete plans that often work, while novices often produce incomplete plans that require considerable adjustment during instructional episodes, sometimes with disastrous results. A closer evaluation of teachers' planning reveals the more elaborated cognitions and superior pedagogical reasoning of experts, but it does not shed light on how these abilities develop in adult teachers.

For this, we need to turn to a constructivist perspective, which assumes that all humans progress through stages of cognition as they build meaning from experience. The process of growth involves passing through a sequence of stages that is hierarchical and invariant. Individuals who are in more complex stages are understood to be more adequate in the use of problem-solving strategies, more flexible in modes of thought and action, and more efficient in resolving moral conflicts and ethical dilemmas. Do teachers' pedagogical knowledge and beliefs reflect this kind of growth? King and Kitchener's (1994) classic work on adults' reflective judgment strongly suggests that this may be the case. Their results indicate that adults do exhibit stage and sequence growth in reflective judgment from authority-based concrete thought to some self-reflection to true reflective judgment. The growth process is slow but sure, with no regressions and no skipping of stages. Similarly, teachers' thinking may follow a stage and sequence path that moves them conceptually toward more abstract, principled, and interdependent forms of pedagogical thinking.

As recent research supports the stage-growth theory of teacher development, it also raises important questions about the relation between a teacher's level of cognitive development and his or her teaching behavior. We cannot help but wonder—is a higher level of cognitive development better?

There is considerable research evidence that indicates that teachers who process experience at higher stages of development are more competent, effective, and efficient (Feiman-Nemser & Remillard, 1996). They exhibit many personal qualities that contribute to a healthy learning environment, for example, greater empathy with students' needs and concerns. They are excellent mentor teachers, providing sensitive yet highly accurate feedback to beginners under their charge. And they are open to change, generally adopting or adapting innovative methods that enhance the quality of their instruction. On the other hand, teachers who process experience at lower stages of cognitive development perform at increasing levels of incompetence when faced with complex tasks. They are less flexible, more judgmental, often negative, and resistant to change in teaching methods. This observation, of course, leads to the even more important question of how to stimulate and support teachers' growth to higher levels, which we will discuss shortly. Before addressing this topic, however, it is important to summarize what teachers' development implies for professional education.

Implications for Professional Education

Two broad patterns emerge from the (albeit slim) evidence. One is the more obvious pattern that teachers' concerns, interests, thinking, and attitudes are different at different times in the course of their career. Teachers mature professionally, and as they do their pedagogical ideas and understandings change. The other, less easily detected pattern, is that teachers' cognition develops through a sequence of stages—a growth process that may continue across the entire span of their careers. Pedagogical growth is not merely a matter of aging; it is shaped and influenced by a host of environmental factors. Where teachers work, their peers, and their learning opportunities make a difference in their development and thinking as professional educators.

Together, these patterns suggest strongly that the one-size-fits-all approach to professional development will not suffice. Like the developing writers and readers they teach, teachers are developing professionals and thinkers who differ from one another in important and significant ways. To acknowledge and build on these differences, teachers need many and varied professional learning opportunities that challenge their intellect and beliefs. Although a one-day workshop on a single topic may benefit some teachers some of the time, this approach alone cannot provide all teachers excellent professional education. This is not to say, of course, that one-day workshops should be abandoned. Some offer teachers valuable information and training that enlarge their understandings and sharpen their technical skills. To be most productive, however, workshops should be integrated into a well-conceived set of professional education experiences that offer a variety of learning opportunities—some more practical, some more theoretical, but all contributing to teachers' developing pedagogical knowledge and commitment.

The Teacher as a Learner

Startling new images of teaching and learning are on the horizon. Schools, many educators argue, need to become places that support meaningful student *and* teacher learning (for example, National Commission on Teaching and America's Future, 1996). Schools need to be places where both students and teachers can become users of knowledge, skilled problem-solvers, collaborators, and self-assessors—places that expect teachers and students to be researchers; to use the skills of inquiry, examination, and reflection; and to contribute to a learning community. Schools must be intellectually exciting places that enable students and teachers to use their minds effectively and to learn for understanding.

Changing views of what schools should be and do have deep implications for what teachers need to know and learn, for they change the nature of teaching from technical to intellectual work (McLaughlin & Talbert, 1993). Teachers are given considerable responsibility to make professional judgments based on a deep understanding of content and pedagogical knowledge. To develop inquiring, knowledgeable students, teachers must be knowledgeable and open to divergent views. Moreover they need to create learning conditions that inspire and challenge their students to engage in the difficult intellectual work that real inquiry entails. Such "adventurous" instruction is demanding because it asks both teachers and students to exert more mental effort, to take risks, and to tolerate uncertainties about knowledge and procedure (Cohen, 1988). It also has implications for how teachers learn and where their learning occurs. To relinquish old practices and take on complex new ones that promote conceptual understanding takes time. It involves a deep knowledge of what is to be taught, considerable trial and error, lots of support and encouragement, and a willingness to adapt to existing classroom realities. A large amount of self-confidence and tremendous patience also help, because teaching for understanding can be stressful and at times very frustrating as the teacher strives to advance the learning of all students.

How teachers learn and achieve more ambitious teaching practices, however, is a problem yet to be untangled. Research and practice since the mid-1980s have revealed some ideas that move us toward a better understanding of teacher learning and the conditions that support it (Ball, 1996). We know, for example, that teachers' prior beliefs and experience exert a powerful influence on what they learn from professional-development experiences. Their personal and professional histories are lenses through which they interpret new information. We know, too, that the depth of a teacher's subject-matter knowledge is very important. When teachers lack knowledge as a resource, they are reluctant to take instructional risks and cannot fully exploit the learning potential of learning tasks and class discussions. It is also increasingly clear that the contexts in which teachers work impact their learning. Settings in which professional development occurs may facilitate or impede teachers' understandings and skills. Environmental features such as time to learn, opportunity to discuss ideas with one's peers, models, on-site coaching, and action research seem to encourage learning and trigger teachers' conceptual development (Miller, 1995; Roskos & Bain, in press). In many respects what we need to know about teacher learning is no different from what we have come to understand about all human learning: It needs to be active, sensitive to context, and a function of what is already known from experience.

These broad insights, however, do not specify how teachers may learn to reach higher levels of complexity in their instructional decision making. How do teachers learn to get better as practitioners of pedagogy?

This exposes what we do not know about teacher learning, although some researchers have forged paths into this unknown territory.

Tharp and Gallimore (1988), for example, propose that teachers learn higher order teaching skills through a four-stage process. Assisted by more capable others, in Stage 1 a teacher develops an awareness of the capacity to be acquired, for example, responsive questioning to aid text comprehension. Through conversation, modeling, and other forms of assistance, he or she learns to see the activity as the expert does and to comprehend its full meaning in terms of performance. This is not an easy or quick process as the beginner is often confused and filled with self-doubt. Much assistance and many interactions are required to clarify how the activity is to be done before the beginner masters the intricacies of skilled performance. In Stage 2 responsibility shifts from assistance by others to self-assistance. Now the voice of expert is acquired gradually by the teacher in a variety of forms from

feedback and checklists to self-talk, self-questioning, and even self-scolding. By Stage 3, self-assistance or help from others is no longer needed as the activity becomes internalized and nearly automatic. Viewed by others, the performance seems effortless. The teacher even wonders why he or she struggled as his or her confidence and comfort grow and he or she enjoys doing the activity. However, the capacity to do something is not fixed; it is subject to disruption by environmental changes, individual stress, or forgetfulness. In Stage 4 what is lost is found again through self-regulating behaviors, such as posting reminders or talking to oneself until automaticity in the performance is regained. For most practicing teachers, regrettably, involvement in this kind of learning apprenticeship is rare. Few professional development programs can offer the kind of in-depth, situated form of assistance that underlies highly skilled, precise teaching performance.

Au and Carroll's (1997) recent work with the KEEP Demonstration Classroom Project in Hawaii also offers some interesting insights on teacher learning. In their efforts to implement a whole-literacy curriculum, they observed "how easy it is to underestimate the teacher expertise needed to make a constructivist approach work" (p. 218). Not only the will to adopt new practices, but also the necessary skills in constructivist teaching appeared critical to full, productive implementation. Teachers expressed concern with glittering generalities, such as "community of learners," which they felt lacked specificity as to exactly how holistic instructional goals might be achieved in daily practice. They found two tools especially helpful in guiding their teaching work toward the actual achievement of learning communities. One was a classroom implementation checklist, which identified concrete program features that should be present in their classrooms, such as a place for collaborative writing activity. Over time, the implementation checklist served as the source for ongoing dialogue among the teachers and the basis for inservice activities geared to their specific learning needs.

Another crucial tool was a set of grade-appropriate benchmarks that were used to track student achievement, for example, "corrects spelling during the editing process." Like guideposts, these benchmarks helped to keep the teachers' attention focused on program goals while simultaneously helping them keep track of individual students' progress in relation to these goals. They also supported more deliberate, careful lesson planning that in turn led to more focused and consistent instruction. In addition, the benchmarks were made known to the students, thus creating a shared vision of literacy learning between the teachers and the children. In sum, the implementation checklist and the set of benchmarks were practical tools that helped to organize the teachers' "seeing" and brought into sharper focus what a whole-language curriculum should actually look like in day-to-day instruction.

What these examples show about teacher learning is the progressive expansion of understanding as the critical features of what must be done to effectively carry out a practice are explicated and elaborated over time. Learning is guided and supported by many human interactions, much talk, and practical tools, as the teacher builds a relevant, accurate representation that he or she can work from in his or her own situation.

These examples also reveal that we do not know nearly enough about how to create and sustain the conditions for this kind of learning, much less understand the processes of adults' acquisition of teaching knowledge and skill. How does professional development, for example, shift from simply transmitting information and tips to seriously helping teachers reconstruct the intricacies of their teaching practices? What does this demand from teachers and teacher educators, not only cognitively, but also in terms of personal qualities? What are the systemic and contextual resources that facilitate or inhibit teachers' learning aimed at higher order teaching skills? So far answers to these questions have come only in scattered ways. Yet at the same time they suggest profound changes in the structure and processes of professional development that offer all educators opportunities to learn and grow.

Returning to our purpose, what do we gain from the emerging insights on teacher learning that inform professional development endeavors? Our brief excursion into teachers' development indicated that a one-size-fits-all approach is not sufficient, because teachers are at different places cognitively and progressively in their careers. In our exploration of teacher learning, we discover the complex nature of adults' achieving higher levels of skilled performance. Getting better at teaching is not an independent act; it depends on a host of factors, ranging from access to excellent mediation, such as more-capable teachers and dialogue with peers, to external supports, such as a culture of inquiry

Roskos and Vukelich

In Practice

INSTRUCTIONAL TUNING CLINICS

Teachers at Hopkins Elementary School know the value of talking about teaching. Together with teacher educators they regularly hold Instructional Tuning Clinics for preservice and experienced teachers. Clinics provide an opportunity for individuals to "fine-tune" their lesson design and hone their teaching strategies. Prospective and practicing teachers make an appointment to come to the clinic, which includes a panel of educators (classroom and university teachers). At the clinic, the individual describes a lesson or unit to be taught or one already conducted. The educator panel probes it, then critiques it, weaving in reactions from experience, theory, and the moment. After listening, the presenter comments on feedback, poses new questions, and explores dilemmas. "We have discovered that learning occurs on both sides of the table," one panelist remarked. "To share our work, to draw on others' expertise, to talk—therein lies the power of this experience."

Instructional Tuning Clinic Session

- Introductions   10 minutes
- Teacher presentation   20 minutes
- Clarifying questions from panel   5 minutes
- Examining student work   15 minutes
- Developing feedback contributions   3 minutes
- Providing warm and cool feedback to teacher   15 minutes
- Reflection aloud by teacher   15 minutes
- Debrief (open discussion)   10 minutes

and practical tools to guide teaching actions to higher levels of performance. To be significant and worthwhile, it seems clear that professional development cannot be superficial or faddish. Instead, it must demand a lot from teachers, if they are to use their minds well, and from the professional community, if it is to provide learning experiences that help teachers rebuild their practices around the ambitious goals of educational reform.

We recognize, for example, that professional development geared to teacher learning needs to be long range in scope, ongoing, intellectually challenging, and situated in the real work of teaching (Little, 1993; Sparks & Hirsch, 1997). It seems particularly powerful and productive when local educators (school and university) work together to establish strong school-wide professional communities that share a clear sense of purpose for all students' learning. The members collaborate with one another, take collective responsibility for maintaining professional standards, and express a sense of moral responsibility about their practice and its meaning for children and their families. Such communities are sustained by cultural conditions that instill a dedication to inquiry and innovation and foster supportive leadership, and also by structural conditions that create interdependent work structures, small-scale activity settings for learning, and considerable autonomy to plan and do around local needs (Louis, Marks, & Kruse, 1996). Professional communities like these, of course, do not just happen. They arise and grow from hard work, fueled by an ethos of trust, respect, and sharing of expertise and power.

Professional Development Models With Promise

Changing visions of literacy teaching and learning reveal the fundamental mismatch between the growing complexity of teachers' work and their opportunities for professional growth. Helping all students meet more challenging expectations stretches the capacities of individual teachers. Literacy reform asks not only that teachers gain additional understanding and skills, but also that they alter the literacy goals they hold for their students and change the way they see themselves as members of the literacy profession. Building capacity in both of these responsibilities is more than a matter of imparting information; it requires professional activities that help develop a strong sense of professional identity, motivation, and the willingness to undertake the hard work that changes in daily practice demand. In recent years new models for professional development that seem to enhance teachers' expertise and sense of professional self have emerged.

In the remainder of the chapter, we discuss two professional-education models that appear to increase teacher learning, strengthen motivation, and develop teachers' professional leadership: teacher networks and action research. Certainly not panaceas for all teachers' growth and development, these models do, however, give evidence of substantive teacher change and also offer suggestions as to the design of professional development that creates learning contexts for educators.

Teacher Networks

Teacher networks are groups of individuals that function as a learning community. They have a common purpose driven by a clear focus on certain subject-matter areas, teaching methods, or approaches. Collaborative networks among teachers can be formed within a single school building or by teachers with a shared goal of interacting with others to improve their professional practice. Such networks require more of teachers than an agreement to participate and to cooperate; true collaborative networks require a commitment to inquiry into one's teaching practices, a willingness to share and talk about what is troubling in that practice, and a goal of critical discourse aimed at improving teaching and learning. Motivation and attitude are at the very core of group membership and participation.

Teacher literature includes many descriptions of networks and many testimonials documenting teachers' perceptions of the power of networks to improve teaching practices and consequently students' learning. In addition, there is a burgeoning database including information about how to develop networks that improve teachers' knowledge, motivation, and sense of empowerment (Firestone & Pennell, 1997). There also is a smaller, but steadily growing database that documents the effects of networks on student achievement outcomes (Fine, 1994).

One of the best-known literacy networks among literacy educators is likely the National Writing Project. Each summer, groups of teachers come together for a 4- to 5-week institute with the twofold aim of teaching one another about writing and about the teaching of writing. Collectively each community of scholars develops the curriculum, the issues, and the questions to guide their study during the institute. All members of the learning community write, all discuss and analyze research, and all share descriptions of their classroom practices for scrutiny by their peers. Through these experiences, teachers share and reshape their beliefs about the teaching of writing and take charge of their own professional development. After the summer institutes, teachers continue to meet—on Saturdays, after school, and in one another's classrooms—to support one another, to continue to critique one another's practices, to raise new questions, to initiate research projects, and to share. Through their reading, writing, and talking, teachers form professional communities that become learning contexts for engaging in collaborative analyses and the interpretation of teaching work. Shared inquiry helps teachers to see their writing instruction with new eyes as it happens in their classrooms and to revise their practices in ways that ultimately improve their students' writing achievement.

We learn two valuable lessons from the National Writing Project pertinent to teachers' professional development and learning. The first is that changing one's practice takes time. "One-shot workshops" will not do, because teachers need time to immerse themselves in the types of writing experiences they have long desired for their students, but too often failed to fully realize with them. They need time to witness and try the activities they might do and to practice strategies to a stage of self-assistance as discussed earlier. They need time to connect the new meanings they are constructing about pedagogy to the specifics and uncertainties of daily practice.

The second lesson is that changing one's practice is not easy. Setting higher standards, for example, does not automatically produce change in daily teaching practices. The bridge from "what should be" to "what is" must be built through consistent, sustained effort every day. This requires abundant support—not only in the form of instructional tools, but also in the form of social and emotional resources—so as not to lose heart. Ongoing assistance and feedback also are critical so that teachers' adaptations to practice align with new goals and lead to improvement in student learning.

Still, networks as learning contexts are no guarantee that teachers will develop and advance their expertise to higher levels of teaching performance. Thoughtful design of networks is key if their learning potential is to be realized. Successful, productive networks share several common features (Lieberman & McLaughlin, 1992).

- They focus on a single subject area or teaching method, thus giving participants a common purpose and identity.

- They offer participants a range of learning opportunities. Activities like workshops, leadership institutes, seminars, and conferences offer teachers flexibility and self-selection opportunities. Moreover, care is taken to ensure that although some procedural knowledge may be imparted, the focus is on conceptual knowledge. The goal is deep understanding that allows adaptation to local instructional realities.

- They provide a support community for teachers to discuss teaching problems with one another. There is an emphasis on building of community and fostering feelings of belonging and respect for one another's work. Teachers are encouraged to put their ideas on the table, to admit what they do not know and share what they do, to express reservations, and expose their passions.

- They create new possibilities for career enhancement outside the administrative hierarchy, offering opportunities to work with peers, to assume leadership roles, and to practice leadership skills.

Within the context of such carefully crafted learning communities, teachers gain support for the careful, critical examination of their practices. As with many groups formed under the National Writing Project umbrella, the focus of instructional scrutiny might be literacy teaching practices. Such networks have the potential to unleash even veteran teachers' intellectual energies and to rekindle their commitment to their teaching work. Together teachers begin and continue to pursue the difficult, slow process of change.

Action Research

The teacher-as-researcher, or action-research movement, exemplifies for many the kind of critical inquiry stance needed to respond adequately to the literacy reform agenda. In this model, teachers cast their "wonderings" gathered from their real-world observations and dilemmas into scientific investigations. The purpose is to inquire about one's own practice in systematic ways during the course of daily teaching with the twofold goal of understanding the basis for teaching actions and directing one's own professional growth. Central to the action-research model is the development of the practitioner as a professional person; its focus is on the individual teacher's learning.

Wells (1994) suggests action research should answer three questions for the inquiring practitioner: Has my inquiry deepened my understanding of the teaching-learning relation? Has it provided a more explicit, principled basis for my practice? Has it resulted in meaningful learning experiences for my students? In answering these questions, the teacher's research activity and professional development become linked inextricably as problems are researched in light of one's own actions. The individual teacher identifies a problem, seeks and tests solutions, evaluates the effectiveness of applications, and reflects on the efficacy of results for his or her practice in terms of professional growth and student learning.

Several assumptions undergird serious action research. First, teachers become engaged in action research to solve immediate and pressing problems evident in their teaching. The classroom becomes their laboratory for testing hypotheses and procedures. Because behavior is influenced heavily by the context in which it occurs, it makes sense to study the teaching-learning relation in the classroom setting. From experience we know that every group of children is different. Each class is a mix of backgrounds, personalities, abilities, interests, strengths, and limitations. Each teacher has a particular teaching style or personal theory based on beliefs, past experiences, knowledge, and skills. Together, a particular teacher and a particular group of students in a particular location constitute the learning community, which is the focus of an individual teacher's concerns and research. The problems to be solved or questions to be answered are those evident in this community during this year. As participants in this community, teacher–researchers become ethnographers, using a range of descriptive techniques (for example, field notes, dialogue journals, photography, videotape recordings, checklists, rating scales, questionnaires, interviews, shadowing, and group discussion) to capture experience. Assuming this stance toward the teaching–learning relation, teachers become not only inquirers into their own practice, but also learners as they seek to understand how their actions are interpreted by students.

Second, action research employs a methodology that is systematic, evaluative, and scientific. Indeed, some may argue that effective teachers have always monitored their practice and used their observations to correct their actions, but this is not action research. Teachers have long attempted to keep abreast of developments in their field and to use their new knowledge to improve their teaching, but this also is not action research. Many teachers work unconsciously on their classroom's day-to-day problems and incidentally discover solutions, yet still this is not action research.

Action research requires making systematic observations and identifying what is happening during instructional events, planning for adaptations or changes in light of these observations, implementing plans and carefully monitoring what occurs, and evaluating and reflecting on the success and shortcomings of the intervention. Throughout the intellectual work of research intersects with the teacher's personal theories as these inform and are informed by the research cycle. In connecting practical and scientific knowledge in these ways the teacher cultivates a reflective stance that is the hallmark of the teacher-researcher. Reflection, in turn, is the engine of change, sparking the deliberation of underlying assumptions and teaching actions in light of new evidence.

Gianotti's (1994) experiences as a teacher–researcher illustrate the power of action research and the reflection it engenders for individual growth and change. She wrote the following:

> I believe one of the strongest aspects of doing classroom research is reflection. In the course of [a project on talk during Writing Workshop], I was engaged in deliberate reflection in action and, at later times, reflection on action. It is reflection that leads to understanding, growth, and change. (p. 57)

Gianotti uses Schön's (1987) two kinds of reflection to describe her teaching behaviors: Reflection *in* action occurred while she was teaching, when the aim was to generate new theories and conjectures; reflection *on* action occurred when she behaved like a critic of her own performance. She thought about features of her teaching actions after they occurred that prompted her to behave differently in subsequent instructional episodes. However, Gianotti discovered that reflection alone was insufficient for a comprehensive exploration of her inquiry. Reading the work of others and sharing her work with colleagues also proved to be important. Other ideas and perspectives helped her to understand her data and to connect her experiences with those of other teachers outside her immediate situation. Sharing her ideas with her colleagues and listening to their responses also offered a new slant on her data and helped her to remain open to alternative explanations.

Action research as a means of professional development is very different from traditional approaches. Instructional change is not externally imposed; teacher-researchers personally choose to change themselves. Professional development is not done to the teacher, but rather is initiated by the teacher. In this respect action research is a model with astounding potential, for it goes to the heart of what it means to be a professional person—one who sees himself or herself capable of initiating changes that contribute to the profession as a whole. It is the teacher's self-chosen inquiries that influence the professional community and create the overall complexion of instructional practice. Individual inquiry, therefore, drives the profession's progress and change.

Conclusion

We have made significant progress in our exploration of professional development in a rapidly developing new age of what it means to teach and learn. As is the case in most professions, we know some of how professional educators develop and learn, which has led to improvements in professional-development opportunities. Teacher networks and action research are two newer models that seem to advance teachers' expertise more appropriately and substantively than earlier staff-development approaches. Both capitalize on the intellectual resources teachers bring to their own professional education, harnessing this potential in the pursuit of practical solutions to real teaching problems through collaboration and inquiry. Both position the practitioner more centrally in the design and implementation of professional education. Both hold promise for supporting teachers' efforts to change their classroom practices in ways consistent with new literacy reform. These are excellent trends, because they forge new and stronger connections between pedagogical theory and practice, between teacher educators and teachers, and among members of the educational professional community.

As in other professions, we have much to learn about how teachers develop and grow intellectually in their understanding of pedagogy and their ability to wield technical skill well in the uncertain world of classroom instruction. How teachers become expert at what they do, for example, involves cognitive and social processes yet to be explained. As practicing teachers and students of literacy pedagogy ourselves, we nonetheless are quite certain of two things: New discoveries and insights about these topics will be made, and these will spring not only from the careful work of educational researchers, but also from the thoughtful inquiries of teachers teaching literacy everyday.

References

Au, K., & Carroll, J. (1997). Improving literacy achievement through a constructivist approach: The KEEP demonstration classroom project. *The Elementary School Journal, 97*, 203–221.

Ball, D. (1996). Teacher learning and the mathematics reforms: What we think we know and what we need to learn. *Phi Delta Kappan, 77*(7), 500–508.

Borko, H., & Livingston, C. (1989). Cognition and improvisation: Differences in mathematics instruction by expert and novice teachers. *American Educational Research Journal, 26*, 473–498.

Burden, P. (1990). Teacher development. In R. Houston (Ed.), *Handbook of research on teacher education* (pp. 311–328). New York: Macmillan.

Cohen, D. (1988). Teaching practice, plus que ça change.... In P.W. Jackson (Ed.), *Contributing to educational change: Perspectives on research and practice* (pp. 27–84). Berkeley, CA: McCutchan.

Erickson, E. (1975). *Life history and the historical moment.* New York: Norton.

Feiman-Nemser, S., & Remillard, J. (1996). Perspectives on learning to teach. In F. Murrary (Ed.), *The teacher educator's handbook* (pp. 63–91). San Francisco, CA: Jossey-Bass.

Fessler, R., & Christensen, J.C. (1992). *The teacher career cycle: Understanding and guiding the professional development of teachers.* Boston, MA: Allyn & Bacon.

Fine, M. (1994). Chartering urban school reform. In M. Fine (Ed.), *Chartering urban school reform* (pp. 5–30). New York: Teachers College Press.

Firestone, W.A., & Pennell, J.R. (1997). Designing state-sponsored teacher networks: A comparison of two cases. *American Educational Research Journal, 34,* 237–266.

Fuller, F. (1969). Concerns of teachers: A developmental conceptualization. *American Educational Research Journal, 6*(2), 207–226.

Hall, G., & Rutherford, K. (1990). *A preliminary review of research related to stages of concern.* Paper presented at the annual meeting of the American Educational Research Association, Boston, MA.

Gianotti, M.A. (1994). Moving between worlds: Talk during writing workshop. In G. Wells (Ed.), *Changing schools from within: Creating communities of inquiry* (pp. 37–60). Portsmouth, NH: Heinemann.

Kagan, D. (1990). Teacher cognition. *Review of Educational Research, 60*(3), 419–470.

Kennedy, M. (1991). *An agenda for research on teacher learning* (technical report). East Lansing, MI: Michigan State University.

King, P., & Kitchener, K. (1994). *Developing reflective judgment: Understanding and promoting intellectual growth and critical thinking in adolescents and adults.* San Francisco, CA: Jossey-Bass.

Lieberman, A., & McLaughlin, M.W. (1992). Networks for educational change: Powerful and problematic. *Phi Delta Kappan, 73,* 673–677.

Little, J.W. (1993). Teachers' professional development in a climate of education reform. *Educational Evaluation and Policy Analysis, 15,* 129–152.

Louis, K., Marks, H., & Kruse, S. (1996). Teachers' professional community in restructured schools. *American Educational Research Journal, 33*(4), 757–800.

McLaughlin, M., & Talbert, J. (1993). Introduction: New visions of teaching. In D. Cohen, M. McLaughlin, & J. Talbert (Eds.), *Teaching for understanding* (pp. 1–12). San Francisco, CA: Jossey-Bass.

Miller, E. (1995). The old model of staff development survives in a world where everything else has changed. *The Harvard Education Newsletter, 11*(1), 1–3.

National Commission on Teaching and America's Future. (1996). *What matters most: Teaching for America's future.* Woodbridge, VA: Author.

Roskos, K. (1996). When two heads are better than one: Beginning teachers' planning processes in an integrated instruction planning task. *Journal of Teacher Education, 47*(2), 120–129.

Roskos, K., & Bain, R. (in press). Professional development as intellectual activity: Features of the learning environment and evidence of teachers' intellectual engagement. *The Teacher Educator.*

Schön, D. (1987). *Educating the reflective practitioner.* San Francisco, CA: Jossey-Bass.

Sparks, D., & Hirsch, S. (1997). *A new vision of staff development.* Alexandria, VA: Association for Supervision and Curriculum Development.

Sykes, G. (1996). Reform of and as professional development. *Phi Delta Kappan, 77,* 464–467.

Tharp, R., & Gallimore, R. (1988). *Rousing minds to life.* New York: Cambridge University Press.

Wells, G. (1994). Teacher research and education change. In G. Wells (Ed.), *Changing schools from within: Creating communities of inquiry* (pp. 1–36). Portsmouth, NH: Heinemann.

Afterword

The chapters in this book testify to our great progress in understanding and teaching literacy in early childhood. It was not that long ago when ideas of reading readiness, the separation of writing and reading development, and skill-specific reading instruction in the primary grades prevailed. Learning to read and write was a first-grade matter and achieving success depended to a large extent on one's individual abilities. Few professionals observed, much less understood, the continuities in early writing and reading development or the literacy processes woven into the fabric of young children's everyday lives.

Research and thought in the mid-1980s, however, changed this, opening our eyes to the emergence of literacy before school, its integration into the broader language systems of listening and speaking, and the powerful social forces that shaped these processes. Literacy, as Holdaway (1979) pointed out, is a cultural, social, and personal matter. It starts at the beginnings of life and develops through myriads of social and physical interactions, more or less formal, that bring each child into the literacy community.

What this expanded view of literacy acquisition means for parents, teachers, and early childhood educators is still a stimulating and productive topic of conversation. It has produced an explosion of information and resources related to early literacy learning in a short period of time. Books on early literacy research and development fill our bookshelves alongside the best children's literature and newer technologies that bring writing and reading increasingly under young children's control (much to their delight). It is indeed remarkable how far we have come in such a short amount of time—even more so if we distill the best from what we have gained and strive to make it the norm for all children in our educational care. That is the hope presented in the chapters of this book: the best for all children.

In the end, children's successful achievement of literacy rests on us achieving the best literacy education for all children. Each chapter takes up this challenge and offers possibilities for practice rooted in scientific evidence. Each attempts to apply broad principles to the contexts of real children and teachers and their literacy learning work. Each grapples with the "rub between theory and practice" (Miller & Silvernail, 1994, p. 29), recognizing that good literacy teaching is complex, not simply a matter of simplistic formulas or "cookie-cutter" routines. Steered by the set of instructional guidelines presented in Chapter 1, the contributing authors bring forth the critical specifics of literacy teaching and learning in today's early childhood classroom—designing the environment, planning appropriate lessons, evaluating children's work, and collaborating with parents. The final chapter situates these different pedagogical content knowledges in the broader framework of teacher learning that supports young children's literacy learning. Only through regular, collegial exchange where teachers study, and share knowledge and debate it can the best literacy practices be refined and spread.

Collectively, these 13 chapters help to consolidate what we know about excellent and effective literacy instruction in the critical early period of writing and reading learning. When we started this project, we sensed we were at a crossroads in early literacy education. It seemed a time to pause and take stock, to let go of some old ideas (even dearly held ones) and to embrace new ones, to specify and detail newly discovered regions of emerging literacy, and to put to good use what we had come to know. This book reflects this stance, looking ahead even as we look back to acknowledge what we have gained. We truly appreciate the expertise and commitment of our colleagues who so willingly participated in the goals of this book. Their professional work in homes, communities, and schools helped us all to more clearly see where we are, what we know, and how we might better teach the next generations of writers and readers.

S.B.N

K.A.R

References

Holdaway, D. (1979). *The foundations of literacy*. Portsmouth, NH: Heinemann.

Miller, L., & Silvernail, D.L. (1994). Wells Junior High School: Evolution of a professional development school. In L. Darling–Hammond (Ed.), *Professional development schools: Schools for developing a profession* (pp. 28–53). New York: Teachers College Press.

Learning Resources for Young Writers and Readers

Compiled by Lisa Lenhart

This appendix includes a collection of literacy resources for parents, caregivers, and teachers that appeals to and expands the interests of very young children. The appendix describes more than 150 resources and is divided into the following six sections: Books, Magazines, Software, Toys, Videos, and Web sites.

* By any title denotes favorites.

Books

1. Activity Books

My Favorite Nursery Rhymes
POCKETS OF LEARNING
> Each page is interactive, accompanying a rhyme. For example, on the Humpty Dumpty page, Humpty not only falls off the wall, his three Velcro™ pieces come off. Children can enjoy putting Humpty back together again and again.

My Quiet Book
ALMA'S DESIGNS
> One in a series, this hands-on book allows children the opportunity to zip, tie, button, snap, buckle, and more.

* Snuggle Time
DISCOVERY TOYS

> Every page of this book is a touchable surprise. Fabrics, sounds, and a little interactive bear reward baby's investigation with a sensory experience.

2. ABC Books

* ABC
WILLIAM WEGMAN. HYPERION

> This ABC book features photographs of dogs posed as letters.

Alef-Bet: A Hebrew Alphabet Book
MICHELLE EDWARDS

> As they go about their day–to–day activities, three children (the eldest in a wheel chair) and their parents demonstrate letters and words in Hebrew.

* Alligators All Around
MAURICE SENDAK. HARPER TROPHY

> These gators are on the go, whether they are juggling jellybeans or bursting balloons.

* Alpha Bugs
DAVID A. CARTER. LITTLE SIMON

> There's a different bug for each of the letters, which pop up in surprising places.

* The Alphabet Sticker Book
ROBIN PAGE. HOUGHTON MIFFLIN

> Readers take part in the story by placing stickers of objects on the pages of the book.

* The Butterfly Alphabet
KJELL B. SANDVED. SCHOLASTIC

> Through stunning full-color close-up photographs, Sandved shows the shape of each letter of the alphabet literally written by nature on the bodies and wings of butterflies and moths.

* Chicka Chicka Boom Boom
BILL MARTIN JR AND JOHN ARCHAMBAULT. SIMON & SCHUSTER

> All the letters of the alphabet race up the coconut tree. Children love this book with its rhyming, repetitive text.

Eating the Alphabet
LOIS EHLERT

> This alphabet book uses fruits and vegetables to introduce the ABCs.

The Handmade Alphabet
DIAL BOOKS
> This unique ABC book uses the manual alphabet symbol for each letter of the alphabet.

The Icky Book Alphabet
JERRY PALLOTTA
> Pallotta puts a twist on the alphabet book by using insects.

Jambo Means Hello: Swahili Alphabet Book
MURIEL FEELINGS. ILLUSTRATED BY TOM FEELINGS.
> Letters of the alphabet are presented by words of the Swahili language. A brief explanation of the word includes cultural information of east African countries.

3. Concept Books

Animal Families
SNAPSHOTS
> Colorful and up-to-date, this is a first book on animal classification.

Color Farm and Color Zoo
LOIS EHLERT. HARPERFESTIVAL
> Babies are introduced to colors, shapes, and animals in these colorful books. As the child turns the page, different colors and shapes combine to form new animals.

My First Look at Colors
RANDOM PUBLISHING
> Brightly multicolored objects are the focal point of this color book.

Push Pull Empty Full
TANA HOBAN
> Photographs of children playing introduce the concept of opposites.

Getting Dressed
DESSIE AND CHEVELLE MOORE
> This beautifully illustrated book shows a young child dressing himself.

Early Words
RICHARD SCARRY
> This classic book labels objects for young readers.

Red, Blue, Yellow Shoe
TANA HOBAN
> Colorful, everyday objects are photographed to reinforce color words.

Kitty In and Out
NORMAN GORBATY
> Shows a playful kitty going in, out, over, under, around, and through things.

Baby's Clothes
NEIL RICKLIN
> Introduces the words for familiar articles of clothing such as hat, bib, and shoes.

All About Baby
SNAPSHOT PUBLISHING
> This colorful board book shows babies doing all sorts of things babies do.

Soft as a Kitten
AUDEAN HOHNSON
> This classic touch-and-feel book allows children to explore their five senses.

What Do Babies Do?
DEBBY SLIER
> A delightful book with photos of babies crawling, walking, and clapping.

Over, Under and Through
TANA HOBAN
> This book features photographs of children demonstrating concept words.

I Read Signs
TANA HOBAN
> Excellent in its use of environmental print. Children will easily recognize signs such as STOP and EXIT and feel like readers.

My First Books
DORLING KINDERSLEY
> These outstanding books explore basic concepts in colorful illustrations and language-rich text. Titles include: *My First Book of Time*, *The Lifesize Animal Opposites Book*, *The Lifesize Animal Counting Book*, *My First Number Book*, and *Things That Go*.

The Lifesize Animal Opposites Book
LEE DAVIS
> Chicks, crocodiles, and toucans teach young readers about opposites in this giant book that features a colorful combination of fold-out pages, rhymes, and lifesize animal photographs.

The Lifesize Animal Counting Book
DORLING KINDERSLEY

Striking lifesize photographs of puppies, cats, a baby gorilla, insects, and more, are sure to grab the attention of the youngest children and entice them into counting.

Counting Cranes
MARY BETH OWENS

It is not the counting that is important in this book, but what is being counted: whooping cranes. Children learn about the beautiful endangered bird in delicate paintings and lyrical language that captures the crane's life and life cycle.

Counting on Calico
PHYLLIS LIMBACHER TILDES

Calico, a long-haired calico cat, is the star of this counting book. A clever mouse leads readers from one beautifully crafted page to another and offers them not just an opportunity to count cats and kittens but also to learn all about them.

Sense Suspense: A Guessing Game for the Five Senses
BRUCE MCMILLAN

Can it be seen, touched, smelled, tasted, or heard? Children will have fun figuring out which senses they are most likely to use as two youngsters take them on a sunny Caribbean sense-adventure that features appealing color photographs and a Spanish/English text.

Lunch
DENISE FLEMING

A hungry little gray mouse eats one colorful fruit or vegetable after another, covering himself with their delicious stains. Colors are clear, the text is short and bold, and the whole book is a delightful and fun way to introduce young children to colors.

Dinosaur Roar!
PAUL AND HENRIETTA STRICKLAND

All kinds of dinosaurs, every shape, size, color, and personality, roar through pages of this fun-filled book of opposites. The brief rhyming text and bright, humorous illustrations captivate and engage children in exploring these fascinating creatures.

Dry or Wet?
BRUCE MCMILLAN

Designed as a wordless concept book depicting wet and dry, this is a stunning celebration of multiracial children. Using paired color photographs to illustrate the concepts, the photographer has captured the innocence, joy, and earnestness of children.

Look and Learn Books

ISTAR SCHWAGER

This series of early learning books teaches basic skills through the use of bright, full-color photographs of children, objects, animals, and toys. Titles in the series include, *What's Different, Counting, Sorting*, and *Matching*.

4. Informational Books

First Discovery Books

JEUNESSE, DE BOURGOING, DELAFOSSE & PRUNIER

This wonderful set of informational books have transparent overlays that allow the child to discover how nature works. Titles include *Colors, The River, Dinosaurs, The Egg, The Earth and Sky, Fruit, Weather*, and *The Ladybug*.

My Five Senses

ALIKI

Outstanding children's book that discovers the nature of the five senses in easy-to-understand language.

What Will the Weather Be?

LYNDA DEWITT

A good first informational book on weather.

Stopwatch Books

STOPWATCH

These wonderful, close-up, full-color photos explain the stages of development, and are accompanied by simple text. Some titles in the series include: *Butterfly and Caterpillar, Tadpole and Frog, Apple Tree*, and *Chicken and Egg*.

I Want To Be an Astronaut

BYRON BARTON

Through dynamic pictures with bold colors and simple lines, a reader can imagine what it would be like to be in a space shuttle. The simple text and pictures show the crew eating, sleeping, floating in space, building a space factory, and finally returning to earth.

Dinosaurs, Dinosaurs

BYRON BARTON

The world of long ago comes to life through the vivid colors, simple shapes, and brief descriptive text that give even the youngest child a vision of what the world may have looked like when dinosaurs roamed the earth.

Tool Box
GAIL GIBBONS

Tools frequently found in a tool box are drawn clearly and accurately. Grouped together by use, such as tools that scrape, grip, saw, or cut, the individual tools are identified. This is a very brief and basic introduction to the fascinating world of tools used to build and fix things.

My New Kitten
JOANNA COLE. ILLUSTRATED BY MARGARET MILLER

A young girl enjoys visiting her Aunt Bonnie and her aunt's cat, Cleo. She is delighted when Cleo has kittens and she is allowed to pick one for her very own. Beautiful color photographs illustrate the miracle of birth and the early weeks of a kitten's life.

Fish Faces
NORBERT WU

A few words on each page describe the unusual fish faces and bodies found in beautiful full-color photographs. Children will be entranced by the variety of fish and their colors and expressions.

Circus
LOIS EHLERT

Bold, brilliantly colored cut-out shapes simply but dramatically illustrate scenes from the circus. The brief text will remind old-time circus fans of the ringmaster's patter while it acts as an introduction to the circus for young children.

A Country Far Away
NIGEL GRAY. ILLUSTRATED BY PHILIPPE DUPASQUIER

Two boys, one in Africa and one in Britain, help at home, have fun with their friends, and celebrate the birth of a sister, all in very different but similar ways. The brief text and the pictures show how much children around the world have in common.

5. Predictable Books

Predictable books can be in a number of forms. Some can be identified by characteristics such as repetitive language patterns, story patterns, rhyming phrases, or cumulative sequences of events. The following is a sample of a few tried and true titles.

* The Napping House
AUDREY WOOD. ILLUSTRATED BY DON WOOD

> A cumulative tale that is perfect for reading aloud, its illustrations move from drowsy blue tones to a final burst of brilliant color.

Drummer Hoff
BARBARA EMBERLEY. ILLUSTRATED BY ED EMBERLEY

> "Private Parridge brought the carriage" begins the cumulative, rhyming text that leads to "Drummer Hoff fired it off" and a big "Kahbahbloom." The woodcut illustrations show vibrantly colored, old-fashioned military figures.

King Bidgood's in the Bathtub
AUDREY WOOD

> When the court is concerned because the king refuses to get out of the bathtub, only the young page knows what to do. Illustrations reminiscent of an opera stage setting show off the full glory of the court scenes.

I Know an Old Lady
G. BRAIN KARAS

> The illustrations are just the right match for the zany lyrics of the classic children's song about an old lady's appetite for things such as spiders, goats, and horses.

Five Little Monkeys Jumping on the Bed
RETOLD BY EILEEN CHRISTELOW

> Five little monkeys get ready for bed and say goodnight to their mama. Suddenly the bed is rocking as the old nursery rhyme breaks forth and bounces the monkeys all over the bed.

* Brown Bear, Brown Bear, What Do You See?
BILL MARTIN JR. ILLUSTRATED BY ERIC CARLE

> In repetitive, rhythmic verse, each animal in turn is asked the question with some surprising answers. Big, bold illustrations on double-page spreads show a purple cat, a blue horse, and even a mother who sees beautiful children looking at her.

A Dark Dark Tale
RUTH BROWN

> Suspense mounts in this tale that begins on a dark, dark moor in a dark, dark wood with a dark, dark house. The scenes are dark and murky with mystery, leading to a punch line.

Millions of Cats
WANDA GAG
> The very old man and woman decide that a sweet little cat is just what they need, and the man goes off in search of one. When he finds "hundreds of cats, thousands of cats, millions and billions and trillions of cats," he cannot decide which one he wants.

Teeny Tiny
RETOLD BY JILL BENNETT. ILLUSTRATED BY TOMIE DE PAOLA
> A teeny tiny woman stars in a teeny tiny story that is a teeny tiny bit scary for teeny tiny children. Endearing animals are with the teeny tiny woman throughout her ordeal.

The Little Engine That Could
RETOLD BY WATTY PIPER. ILLUSTRATED BY GEORGE AND DORIS HAUMAN
> A happy little train breaks down while carrying gifts to the children. His optimism, the repetitive rhythmic text, and colorful animated toys encourage and cheer him has he goes over the top.

Mr. Gumpy's Outing
JOHN BURNINGHAM
> Mr. Gumpy says the children, their pets, and the farm animals can all go out on his boat. Once on the river, they misbehave and the boat tips, throwing them all into the water. The whimsical pictures have an active, childlike look.

Goodnight Moon
MARGARET WISE BROWN. ILLUSTRATED BY CLEMENT HURD
> A little rabbit says goodnight to each and every thing in his room before he finally falls asleep. Illustrations become progressively darker with each turned page as the rhyme invites sleep.

The Three Billy Goats Gruff
PAUL GALDONE
> "Trip trap, trip trap" signals the approach of three famous billy goats. The artwork draws the reader into the midst of the story by staring into the eyes of the goat and by getting a troll's-eye-view of the bridge.

* The Wheels on the Bus
MARYANN KOVALSKI
> After a hard day of shopping, a grandmother and her two grandchildren decide to sing as they wait for the bus. The full-color pictures are guaranteed to encourage participation from readers and listeners.

* Where's Spot?
ERIC HILL

A mother dog searches the house for her puppy. The reader must lift flaps to peer into and behind objects where all sorts of animals do silly things in strange places. At last, even Spot is found.

* If You Give a Mouse a Cookie
LAURA JOFFE NUMEROFF. ILLUSTRATED BY FELICIA BOND

The consequences of giving a cookie to an energetic mouse runs a young boy ragged as he scrambles to fill the cycle of requests. What fun to have a mouse like this around the house!

6. Storybooks

* Something From Nothing
PHOEBE GILMAN

When Joseph is a baby, his grandfather makes him a wonderful blanket. As Joseph grows and the blanket becomes tattered, his grandfather transforms it into smaller items until all that is left is a button. Family love warms the hearts of all in this retelling of a traditional Jewish folktale.

Stone Soup
RETOLD BY MARCIA BROWN

An inhospitable town learns a lesson in cooperation. Orange and brown pictures portray peasant life in a long ago French village.

* When I Am Old With You
ANGELA JOHNSON. ILLUSTRATED BY DAVID SOMAN

A small child, not yet understanding the cycle of life, tells Granddaddy all the things that they will do when the child is old with them.

* Flossie and the Fox
PATRICIA M. MCKISSACK. ILLUSTRATED BY RACHEL ISADORA

In the rich language of the rural South, a story is spun of a little girl who out-smarts a fox. The glow of sun filtering through the leafy woods on every page adds to the story.

Ira Sleeps Over
BERNARD WABER

Ira is excited about spending the night with Reggie until his big sister starts taunting him about his teddy bear.

Caps for Sale
ESPHYR SLOBODKINA

> Before taking his nap, the peddler checks his own cap, then the gray, brown, blue, and red caps. When he wakes up, his caps have been taken by monkeys.

Where the Wild Things Are
MAURICE SENDAK

> Sent to bed without any supper, Max travels "in and out of weeks and almost over a year to where the wild things are." Taming them with a special trick, Max suddenly feels lonely and longs to be at home.

Make Way for Ducklings
ROBERT MCCLOSKEY

> Having hatched her ducklings and taught them to march nicely in single file, Mrs. Mallard decides to take them straight through Boston's busy streets to their new home in the Public Garden and pond.

The Snowy Day
EZRA JACK KEATS

> Peter has fun on a snow-covered day making tracks and snow angels, building a snowman, and even trying to save some of the icy stuff for later. Collage pictures capture the wonder of a small child's trudge through the new snow.

Mike Mulligan and His Steamshovel
VIRGINIA LEE BURTON

> Mike Mulligan and his steamshovel, Mary Anne, find themselves out of work because of new technology. Finally the two find happiness in the basement of Popperville's new city hall. Drama, loyalty, and personification of the steamshovel are matched in text, illustration, and design.

It Takes a Village
JANE COWEN-FLETCHER

> Yemi feels very grown up when she has the responsibility of looking after little brother Kokou on market day in her small village. Only when he wanders away does she become aware that all of the village people are looking for him too.

* In Coal Country
JUDITH HENDERSHOT. ILLUSTRATED BY THOMAS B. ALLEN

> Beautiful charcoal and pastel scenes of a Depression-era coal mining town work with a gentle, reminiscent text to create a memorable look at family life. Although Papa and Mama work hard, the entire family remembers times of great joy.

*Amazing Grace

MARY HOFFMAN. ILLUSTRATED BY CAROLINE BIRCH

Grace loves hearing and acting out stories more than anything else. When her teacher announces that the class will be putting on the play *Peter Pan*, Grace says that she wants to be Peter. Classmates say she cannot be Peter because she is a girl and because she is black, but Grace uses her spirit and talents to win them over.

Magazines

*Babybug

CARUS PUBLISHING COMPANY
315 FIFTH STREET
PERU, IL 61354

A baby's very first magazine. This one is similar to a board book and is geared for the younger "reader."

Bear Essential News for Kids

2406 S 24TH STREET
PHOENIX, AZ 85034

Educational and entertaining. Features creative writing by children. Appropriate for prekindergarten to Grade 7.

Chickadee Magazine

SUITE 304, 56 THE ESPLANADE
TORONTO, ONTARIO, M5E 1A7

Science publication that educates and entertains. Appropriate for ages 4–9.

Cricket: The Magazine for Children

CARUS PUBLISHING COMPANY
315 FIFTH STREET
PERU, IL 61354

Imagination in reading is encouraged through children's literature and art from around the world. Appropriate for ages 6–12.

Highlights for Children

2300 WEST FIFTH AVENUE
PO BOX 269
COLUMBUS, OH 43216

Short stories, poems, drawings, and questions are accepted from readers. Appropriate for ages 2–12.

Humpty Dumpty's Magazine
PO Box 10003
Des Moines, IA 50340

This magazines encourages good health. It publishes reader's articles, stories, and poems. Appropriate for ages 4–6.

Jack and Jill
PO Box 10003
Des Moines, IA 50340

Combines short stories with humor and adventure. Accepts stories, poems, and artwork from children. Appropriate for ages 6–8.

* Ladybug
Carus Publishing Company
315 Fifth Street
Peru, IL 61354

Stories, poems, cartoons, and songs for the very young. Appropriate for ages 2 and up.

Pennywhistle Press
Gannett Publishing
PO Box 500-P
Washington, DC 20044

A national publication newspaper supplement that encourages readers to respond to news, sports, and entertainment. Appropriate for ages 4–14.

Reflections
PO Box 368
Duncan Falls, OH 43734

This poetry magazine includes children's original writing, as well as interviews with authors and poets. Appropriate for ages 4–18.

Science Weekly
Subscription Department
2141 Industrial Parkway
Silver Spring, MD 20904

Combines writing with reading, problem solving, math, and technology. Appropriate for Grades K–8.

Sesame Street Magazine
PO Box 52000
Boulder, CO 80322

Colorful issues filled with stories, games, and projects for children ages 2–6.

* Skipping Stones: A Multi-Ethnic Children's Forum
80574 HAZELTON ROAD
COTTAGE GROVE, OR 97424
> Readers from diverse cultures and backgrounds have an opportunity to share experiences. Appropriate for children of all ages.

U*S* Kids
FIELD PUBLICATIONS 4343 EQUITY DRIVE
PO BOX 16630
COLUMBUS, OH 43216
> True stories, news, natural science, fiction, and activities are included. Appropriate for ages 5–10.

Zoobooks
3590 KETTNER BLVD.
SAN DIEGO, CA 92101
> This magazine includes artwork, animal facts, and photos of wildlife.

Software

What Is a Belly Button?
THE LEARNING COMPANY
AGES 3–7
> Children can discover answers to questions about their bodies such as Why do we have different skin colors? and Why don't haircuts hurt? There are four choices on this main menu: Have the story read to you, play inside the story, play games, or find answers to questions. The story follows a day in the life of a little girl who asks questions that are answered by her friend, Baxter the Bear.

* Paint, Write and Play!
THE LEARNING COMPANY
GRADES K–2
> Paint, Write & Play! encourages young children to develop their vocabulary and basic writing skills. Spoken help is offered for emerging readers. Children write simple stories and paint colorful pictures. Includes a pick-and-click word list to let early writers add words to their stories without typing, and picture word lists help them identify the meanings of new words. Text-to-speech capability lets students hear their stories read aloud.

* Storybook Weaver and Storybook Weaver Deluxe
GRADES K–6

Allows children to weave stories from their own imaginations. It provides everything a child needs to create an original story. Builds writing and storytelling skills in users of varying abilities. Has a text-to-speech feature that reads the story aloud. Builds writing skills and develops vocabulary and story sequencing. Books can be printed out to share with family and friends.

* Reader Rabbit 1
THE LEARNING COMPANY
GRADES K–1

Helps young students build fundamental reading skills using over 200 phonetic consonant-vowel-consonant words. Builds letter-pattern recognition, consonant and vowel recognition, word recognition, and vocabulary development.

* Reader Rabbit and Friends Let's Start Learning
THE LEARNING COMPANY
GRADES PRESCHOOL–K

Preschoolers enter an interactive play world where they discover and develop letter and number skills, shapes and patterns, and matching and sorting. Offers four challenge levels within each activity and encourages multisensory learning through sight, sound, and movement. In the ABC Diner, Reader Rabbit serves up a progressive meal of skills from matching letters, to recognizing letters and their sounds, to identifying first-letter sounds.

* Reader Rabbit's Interactive Reading Journey 1
THE LEARNING COMPANY
GRADES K–1

Students take an exciting journey through 20 imaginative Letter Lands, stopping at Skill Houses along the way to develop skills that will help them read 40 stories. The program systematically combines three components—word recognition, phonics, and progressively challenging stories. Develops word recognition, letter knowledge, phonemic awareness, and reading comprehension.

Big Anthony's Mix-up Magic
MECC
GRADES K–4

Students can read Tomie de Paola's *Strega Nona Meets Her Match* themselves, hear it read by the author, or jump right in and join the main character, Anthony, in any of nine activities. Strega Nona encourages storytelling and reading comprehension, as well as word recognition. Promotes reading for learning and enjoyment.

The Art Lesson
MECC
GRADES K–4

Based on Tomie de Paola's book, *The Art Lesson* allows children to read the book themselves and explore pages in dozens of ways. Illustrations and text are colorful and noisy. Fourteen art activities allow children to create right along with de Paola. Through video clips, children explore his studio, hear him tell about his childhood, and learn about his life as a famous author and illustrator.

SnapDragon
MECC
GRADES PRESCHOOL–1

Children join a dragon and a teddy bear as they explore the concepts of classification and grouping. A variety of settings are provided to allow children to play with many objects.

At Home With Stickybear
OPTIMUM RESOURCE
AGES 1–5

This program encourages children to discover the alphabet, numbers, shapes, and colors, as well as other preschool skills. Children can play games in Bumper's bedroom or help him clean it up.

* Stickybear's Early Learning Activities
OPTIMUM RESOURCE
AGES 2–6

Introduces preschoolers to the alphabet, counting, shapes, opposites, and colors. Has lively animation and sound effects. This is a best seller.

JumpStart Preschool
KNOWLEDGE ADVENTURE
AGES 2–6

JumpStart titles show teachers how each child is advancing in the JumpStart curriculum. JumpStart Preschool introduces children to letters, numbers, shapes, and colors. Over 40 areas include reading readiness, memory development, numeral recognition, and auditory discrimination. There are frequent rewards and interactivity designed to keep young children engaged.

* Chicka Chicka Boom Boom
DAVIDSON
GRADES PRESCHOOL–2

This award-winning rhyming alphabet book includes hundreds of things to see, hear, and do while following A through Z up the coconut tree. It is narrated by Ray Charles and comes with the book as well as a teacher's manual in the school version.

Reading Blaster Journal
DAVIDSON
GRADES PRESCHOOL–2

Reading blaster shows children how to sound out vowels and consonants; match pictures, sounds, and animations with written words; identify word families; match prepositions and simple verbs; and form sentences.

* Mixed Up Mother Goose Deluxe
DAVIDSON
GRADES PRESCHOOL–1

Eighteen of Mother Goose's favorite characters have lost an object from their rhyme, and she asks the game player for help in finding these objects. Students will become familiar with the nursery rhymes, improve memory skills, and match speech to print.

* Build a Book With Roberto
DAVIDSON
GRADES PRESCHOOL–K

Preschoolers can create more than 100 original stories about a hippo. It can be viewed on screen or printed as a read-along book. Masks and puppets also can be printed to extend the story. Encourages story structure, sentence formation, and cause and effect.

Davidson's Kid Phonics 1
DAVIDSON
GRADES PRESCHOOL–2

If you're looking for a phonics program, this is one of the most popular. A cast of characters introduce students to letter sounds in a "rousing, rhyming, fill-in-the-blank game."

The Adventures of Peter Rabbit and Benjamin Bunny
MINDSCAPE
AGES 3–7

This software contains 2 stories, 13 illustrated nursery rhymes, and 6 magical activity areas. Reinforces word recognition, memory, vocabulary development, and problem solving.

Jo-Jo's Reading Series
MINDPLAY
GRADES PRESCHOOL AND UP

This is a series consisting of five programs (Circus, Castle, River, Ranch, and Rocket) targeted at developing reading skills. The movements on the screen visually represent the meaning of the words and sentences.

* Bailey's Book House
EDMARK
GRADES PRESCHOOL–2

> Bailey is a cat whose job it is to inspire young readers to learn letters, words, rhyming, and storytelling. The compact disc version also exposes children to adjectives and sentence structure.

* Curious George Learns the Alphabet
QUEUE
GRADES PRESCHOOL–3

> Curious George teaches children about letters and words on this music-filled compact disc. Children can listen to narration and hear George Chatter as H.A. Rey's book comes to life. Children are able to create and print out their very own alphabet books.

Fun Around the House
QUEUE
GRADES PRESCHOOL–2

> Over 250 words are introduced, each with a picture in an appropriate setting, and in a picture dictionary. There is also a creative writing section that encourages users to create their own stories.

Madeline: European Adventure
CREATIVE WONDERS
AGES 5 AND UP

> In this story, Madeline is in pursuit of a thief who stole a genie's magic lamp. Her adventures take her through France, Italy, Switzerland, and Turkey, where players search for clues while matching and sequencing. The book also has games that teach French and Spanish vocabulary words. Fans of the Madeline books will have fun with this software.

Children's Treasury of Stories, Nursery Rhymes and Songs
QUEUE
GRADES PRESCHOOL–3

> Nursery rhymes and classic songs are presented with music and graphics. In addition, this software features over 6 hours of narrated stories. *The Spectacular Velveteen Publisher* allows children to write, illustrate, and print stories, posters, and reports based on the characters in the stories.

Tales From Long Ago and Far Away I
QUEUE
GRADES K–4

> Features fables, myths, and legends from European, Asian, African, and Native American cultures. Includes a publishing program that allows children to write, illustrate, and print out their own stories.

Kidwriter Golden Edition
SPINNAKER/SPRINGBOARD
GRADES K–4

Children can create and print out their own storybooks using word and picture stories, while learning the fundamentals of word processing.

Alphabet Zoo
SPINNAKER/SPRINGBOARD
GRADES PRESCHOOL–3

This program strengthens letter-recognition skills. It teaches sound-symbol relations and helps sharpen vocabulary and spelling skills.

* Kindercomp Golden Edition
SPINNAKER/SPRINGBOARD
GRADES PRESCHOOL–3

This software contains eight games for young children. The alphabet, upper- and lowercase letters, spelling, counting, number sequence, and simple addition are all reinforced.

Multisensory Kindergarten
ORANGE CHERRY
GRADES PRESCHOOL–2

Children can explore a schoolroom where they can discover many activities that reinforces basic skills such as sequencing, alphabet, classification of colors and shapes, and days of the week.

* Stickybear's Reading Room
OPTIMUM RESOURCE
AGES 4–8

This award-winning software builds reading skills through the use of hundreds of pictures and words and thousands of sentences. It also has a record and playback option.

Stickybear's Reading Fun Pack
OPTIMUM RESOURCE
AGES 3–6

Users are guided through four activities that address both auditory and visual discrimination. It contains hundreds of high frequency words from beginning consonant sounds to nonsoundable sight words.

* Living Books
BRODERBUND
GRADES PRESCHOOL AND UP

Stellaluna, The Tortoise and the Hare, Just Grandma and Me, Green Eggs and Ham, and *Dr. Seuss's ABC* are just some of the titles available from the Living Books collection. Each compact disc comes with a paperback version of the book, cross-curricular activities for each program, thematic unit suggestions, teacher suggestions, and reproducible images from the books. Many interactive activities are hidden within the pages of the books.

Magic Tales
DAVIDSON
GRADES PRESCHOOL–3

Based on traditional folk tales from around the world, each *Magic Tale* contains dozens of original songs and surprises on every page of the story. Children can read the story at their own pace or follow along with the highlighted words.

A Story About Me
PHILIPS
AGES 3–7

With *A Story About Me*, children are the stars of animated interactive stories. Children's photos become an integral part of the adventure.

Playskool Puzzles
HASBRO INTERACTIVE
GRADES PRESCHOOL–K

Playskool Puzzles puts a fun spin on letters and pattern recognition. A fun compact disc for emergent readers.

Stanley's Sticker Stories
EDMARK
GRADES PRESCHOOL–2

Students build stories that come to life on screen or make alphabet books, write letters, and more. Strengthens prereading skills.

The Gigglebone Gang World Tour
HEADBONE INTERACTIVE
AGES 3–8

Children join talking animals for fun in far off lands such as India, Australia, Ghana, China, and Egypt. A tiger tells the folk tales of each country; a raccoon challenges children to matching games about landmarks, customs, and languages; and a pig relates interesting and incredible information about each country.

Toys

Memory
MILTON BRADLEY

Children learn to recognize, match, and sort in this classic game that develops memory skills.

The Very Hungry Caterpillar Matching Game

A twist on the classic memory game. A new butterfly is created every time you play.

Boggle Jr. Letters
PARKER BROTHERS

For ages 3–6, there are different levels of play in these matching and spelling games. Children learn and practice word recognition and letter skills.

* Phonics Traveler
LEAPFROG

An electronic, interactive phonics game that uses talking flash cards and alphabet letters for children to touch, hear, and see.

Big Talk

Big Talk builds vocabulary skills. It contains more than 2,000 words with sound effects and animal noises. No reading is required for this language development program.

Reading Safari

Three different built-in modes teach, reinforce, and sharpen beginning reading skills. Heavy emphasis is placed on phonic instruction.

* Placemats
VARIOUS MANUFACTURERS

Placemats that feature letters, numbers, shapes, and colors allow for informal conversations between parents and children at mealtime.

Learning/Counting/Puzzle Map Squares
VARIOUS MANUFACTURERS

These indoor, interlocking play mats are made of soft foam. Numbers and letters can be taken out for manipulation. Pieces lock together, making it fun to spell familiar names and words in the carpet.

* Alphabet Sorting Tray
CHILDCRAFT

This wooden tray, with printed letter compartments, develops letter recognition and sequencing. Also encourages word and sentence building. Comes with letter, word, and picture cards.

Alphabet Land
LIL LEARNER

No reading is required in this letter recognition game. Children learn to identify letters as they travel through this playland.

* Magnetic Letters
VARIOUS MANUFACTURERS

Fun on magnetic boards or the refrigerator, these manipulatives encourage letter recognition, spelling, and vocabulary skills.

Easels
STEP 2

This bigger than average easel allows a lot of room for children to draw and write. A large paper clip holds paper for painting. The game folds flat for easy storage.

* Alpha Build Deluxe Set
PLAYSKOOL

This set includes 68 colorful shapes that encourage children to build letters, numbers, and shapes. It comes with an easy to follow play mat.

A B Seas Alphabet Fishing Game
DISCOVERY TOYS

In this undersea-themed game, children "fish" to find the letters (both upper and lowercase) that match their playing cards. It's a fun way to work on letter recognition.

Kids' Schoolhouse
TODAY'S KIDS

Children learn different subjects with this two-sided activity center. It comes with letters, numbers, a clock, and a minilocker to store pieces. There's a pull-out desk and a bristle board for playing with the letters and numbers.

StoryTime Cards Kit
STORYTIME CREATIONS

Young storytellers weave tall tales with these picture cards, some of which they draw themselves.

Junior Computer Plus
TEAM CONCEPTS

This lightweight laptop computer teaches basic skill concepts in reading and math.

Playful Patterns
DISCOVERY TOYS

Puzzle building helps build the visual and perceptual skills. This 132-piece set of foam shapes comes with 34 progressively challenging design cards that encourage children to problem solve and create their own designs.

Secret Square
UNIVERSITY GAMES

> For children ages 4 and up, this game of logic and deductive reasoning helps players guess which of 25 pictures covers the hidden chip.

Curiosity Cubes
DISCOVERY TOYS

> This set of four colorful nesting boxes allows toddlers to learn about placement concepts, such as *in* and *out*. As they grow, they can identify shapes, colors, and letters as they problem-solve to match the shapes.

Geo Safari, Jr.
EDUCATIONAL INSIGHTS

> This electronic learning game comes with cards that are inserted into it. Children can learn about sight words and phonic sounds, as well as the names of different animals.

Letter Cards
IDEAL SCHOOL SUPPLY COMPANY

> This set of 52 cards has both upper- and lowercase letters printed on them. Children can become familiar with the letters of the alphabet, match letter cards, and spell simple words.

* Plastic Alphabet Stamps
EDUCATIONAL INSIGHTS

> These big, bold letter stamps allow preschoolers to play with letters. Leads to recognition and encourages spelling.

Little Smart Touch 'N Turn Book
V-TECH

> Babies 6 months and up will enjoy this interactive book featuring a friendly bookworm. With electronic sound effects, this book has large, shaped buttons for the smallest fingers.

Talk and Learn Alphabet Center
EZ TECH

> This carry-along electronic center reinforces numbers and the ABCs. Children can also spell simple words.

Sesame Street Talking Numbers
SESAME STREET

> Big Bird responds positively when numbers are placed in the right spot. This toy comes with 10 individual blocks for manipulative play.

Videos

Stories for the Very Young
More Stories for the Very Young
CHILDREN'S CIRCLE

> This series of home videos brings classic children's books to life. Some of the titles include *The Little Red Hen, Corduroy, Blueberries for Sal, The Napping House,* and *Petunia.*

Toddlers at Work
BMG VIDEO

> Young children get the opportunity to see and imitate other toddlers as they try to perform simple tasks: dressing, washing, brushing teeth, and bed making.

The Very Hungry Caterpillar
ERIC CARLE
WALT DISNEY HOME VIDEO

> Five of Eric Carle's storybooks are animated in this video anthology. It includes *The Very Hungry Caterpillar, The Very Quiet Cricket, The Mixed-Up Chameleon, I See a Song,* and *Papa, Please Get the Moon for Me.*

* Reading Rainbow
PBS VIDEO

> Hosted by LaVar Burton, this series features excellent children's literature. Each video features a book with real experiences to enhance the text. For example, *The Sign Painter's Dream* by Roger Roth takes a look at the role signs play in our everyday lives. Burton goes behind the scenes of an advertising agency and a sign company. Books for further reading are always reviewed. Some other titles include *Imogene's Antlers* by David Small, *Mama Don't Allow* by Thatcher Hurd, and *Tar Beach* by Faith Ringgold.

* My Sesame Street Home Video
RANDOM HOUSE HOME VIDEO

> Children can learn many basic skills from Big Bird, Ernie, Elmo, and the whole Sesame Street Gang in these introductory videos. Through music, animation, and comedy children learn about letters and numbers, explore foreign countries, and listen to stories. Some titles include
>> The Alphabet Game
>> Getting Ready to Read
>> Learning About Numbers
>> I'm Glad I'm Me
>> Big Bird's Story Time
>> Bedtime Stories and Songs

Getting Ready For School
Learning To Add and Subtract
Big Bird in Japan
Big Bird in China

Number Concepts
BATTERIES CHARGED!

Charger and Zip, two animated batteries, lead the way on an educational journey to explore preschool fundamentals. Number concepts such as counting and writing numerals are introduced.

Web Sites for Young Children

There are hundreds and hundreds of Web sites available for children to explore. The following is a sampling to get the young Web surfer started.

Public Broadcasting System
HTTP://WWW.PBS.ORG

This Web site features popular PBS shows. On Marc Brown's *Arthur*, which is based on a book series, children are able to select the series' theme song and to sing along with the text as it appears on the screen. This is a good exercise in speech-to-print match for the early reader.

The Big Busy House
HTTP://WWW.HARPERCHILDRENS.COM

This is a Web site for all of HarperCollins's children's books.

Planet Troll
HTTP://WWW.TROLL.COM

Among other fun things for youngsters, this Web site has news for children, comics, and a dictionary, as well as parent and teacher information.

Nikolai's Web Site
HTTP://WWW.NIKOLAI.COM/NNN.HTM

At this site you'll find stories, crafts, and activities. Check out the ABCDs of learning, too!

The White House
HTTP://WWW.WHITEHOUSE.GOV

When you click on the White House for Kids button at this site (hosted by Socks the cat), you can learn about White House children from Tad Lincoln to Chelsea Clinton.

* The Children's Literature Home Page
HTTP://WWW.UCALGARY.CA/~DKBROWN/INDEX.HTML

A great guide to children's literature resources on the Internet, it includes awards lists from Canada, the United States, and beyond. Links lead to information about authors and fictional characters, electronic children's books, children's literature discussion groups, and resources for parents and teachers.

The Internet Public Library
HTTP://IPL.ORG

In the Youth Division, young people can Ask the Author questions about his or her life and writing. Very famous children's books' authors appear here. You also can discuss books with Bookie the Bookworm, attend a Story Hour, enter a Writing Contest, and more.

Jumping Off Points

Here are some selected homepages that are starting points onto the Internet.

Kids On The Web
HTTP://WWW.ZEN.ORG:80/BRENDAN/KIDS.HTML

This is an ongoing list of Web sites that offers information for and about children. It includes many fun sites to play with and some information about education and schools.

* Kid Sites
HTTP://DB.COCHRAN.COM/DB_HTML:THEOPAGE.DB

This is a listing of many, many Web sites for children. Each site is rated on a scale of 1 to 5.

Yahoo
HTTP://WWW.YAHOO.COM

This is one of the best known search engines on the World Wide Web. There is a simple search menu that lets you search for items by category, or you can do a key-word search if you know what subject you're looking for. This is perhaps the best place to start looking.

* Yahooligans
HTTP://WWW.YAHOOLIGANS.COM

Created by the popular search engine, Yahoo, this lists sites just for children. This is a great starting place.

Author Index

Note: An *f* following an index entry indicates that the citation may be found in a figure.

Bruner, J., 164, 178, 185, 197
Bryant, P., 30, 36, 50, 54, 123, 141, 142
Bryk, A., 33, 36
Burden, P., 252, 269
Burke, C., 236, 248
Burke, J., 9, 19, 122, 123, 141, 143
Burns, S., 199, 220
Byrd, J., 99, 101, 119

C

Calculator, S.N., 78, 96
Calkins, L., 199, 216, 220
Cambourne, B., 247, 248
Carroll, J., 259, 269
Carter, M.A., 241, 249
Casbergue, R., 199, 213, 220
Cavrasco, R., 119
Cazden, C., 104, 119, 154, 160
Chall, J., 72, 73
Chambers, A., 167, 177
Chapman, M.L., 185, 195
Chard, C., 16, 19
Chittenden, E., 225, 227, 229, 230, 242, 248, 249
Chomsky, C., 49, 54
Christensen, J.C., 253, 270
Christie, J., 212, 221
Clark, F.L., 100, 119
Clay, M., 47, 54, 183, 195, 198, 207, 216, 221, 235, 248
Cline, F., 242, 248
Cochran-Smith, M., 162, 164, 165, 167, 177
Cohen, D., 257, 269
Cohen, L.B., 25, 25f, 26, 28, 36
Coleman, P.P., 77, 96

Collier, V., 63, 73
Commins, N., 57, 62, 65, 75
Conlon, A., 164, 179
Connell, R.W., 57, 73
Consalvi, J., 58, 74
Content, A., 33, 36
Couillard, E.L., 99, 119
Courtney, L., 172, 178
Courtney, R., 230, 248
Crawford, J., 58, 74
Crawford, L., 122, 141
Csikszentimihalyi, M., 146, 160
Cullinan, B., 186, 195
Cummins, J., 61, 64, 74
Cunningham, P.M., 87, 88, 96
Cushner, K., 99, 119

D

Dahl, K., 51, 52, 55, 199, 221
Dal Santo, D., 247, 248
Day, K., 174, 177
Delgado-Gaitan, C., 58, 72, 74
Depinto, V.M., 185, 197
Desai, L.E., 241, 249
DeTemple, J., 199, 220
Dewey, J., 152, 160
Dickinson, D., 162, 170, 177, 182, 195, 199, 221
Diehl-Faxon, J., 165, 177
Dixon, C., 68, 74
Dockstader-Anderson, K., 165, 177
Dorsey-Gaines, C., 75, 120, 122, 142, 162, 179, 199, 222
Downing, J., 78, 96, 183, 195
Dyson, A., 10, 19, 74, 185, 186, 195, 199, 221

E

Edelsky, C., 69, 74
Edwards, P.A., 134, 136, 141
Eeds, M., 172, 177, 178
Ehri, L., 41, 44, 50, 55, 186, 195
Eilers, R.E., 33, 36
Eimas, P.D., 28, 36
Elkonin, E.G., 34, 36
Ellis, S., 244, 247
Enright, D.S., 57, 74
Erickson, E., 251, 269
Erickson, F., 102, 119
Erickson, H.L., 160
Erickson, K.A., 96, 97
Ernst, K., 186, 195
Evans, H.M., 33, 37

F

Falk, B., 244, 248
Falvey, M.A., 78, 96
Fantz, R., 25, 36
Farquhar, C., 9, 19, 122, 123, 141, 143
Feiman-Nemser, S., 255, 270
Fenson, L., 183, 195
Fernandez-Fein, S., 32, 36
Ferreiro, E., 41, 42, 55, 199, 221
Fessler, R., 253, 270
Field, S.L., 186, 196
Field, T., 148, 160
Fine, M., 263, 270
Firestone, W.A., 263, 270
Fisher, B., 31
Flippo, K.F., 77, 96
Flores, B., 69, 74
Ford, M.E., 146, 160
Forman, E., 154, 160

Forsyth, A.G., 32, 37
Forsyth, P., 32, 37
Foster, M., 100, 119
Freeman, D., 65, 72, 74
Freeman, Y., 65, 72, 74
Freppon, P., 52, 55, 199, 221
Friedberg, J.B., 138, 142
Friedman, B., 185, 195
Froebel, F., 148, 160
Fuller, F., 252, 270

G

Galda, L., 186, 195
Gallimore, R., 258, 271
Garcia, E., 57, 58, 69, 74
Gardner, H., 186, 195, 221
Gianotti, M.A., 267, 270
Gibson, E.J., 35, 36
Giroux, H., 99, 119
Glazer, S.M., 241, 248
Glickman, C., 190, 196
Glynn, T., 136, 141
Golan, S., 117, 120
Goldenberg, C.N., 72, 74
Goldsmith, E., 136, 141
Gonzales, R., 104, 119
Gonzalez, N., 119
Goodman, Y.M., 122, 141, 199, 221, 225, 226, 236, 243, 245, 248, 249
Goswami, U., 123
Gough, P., 50, 55
Graves, D., 241, 248
Gray, H., 181, 196
Green, C., 136, 141
Griffith, P., 50, 55
Gumperz, J., 166, 178

H

Haight, W., 33, 36
Hall, G., 252, 270
Hall, N., 122, 123, 141
Handel, R., 136, 141
Hannon, P., 122, 123, 129, 132, 138, 140, 142
Harris, J., 85, 96
Hart, B., 32, 36
Hayman, W.C., 104, 119
Heath, S., 19, 102, 119, 122, 142, 170, 178, 199, 221
Heim, M., 182, 196
Henderson, E., 40, 55
Henn, H., 122, 141
Henry, A., 101, 119
Herring, G., 122, 141
Hester, H., 244, 247
Hickman, C., 186, 196
Hiebert, E., 199, 221, 244, 249
Hirsch, S., 262, 271
Hoffland, S.C., 99, 119
Hoien, T., 30, 36
Holdaway, D., 199, 221, 272, 274
Hollins, E.R., 104, 119
Hubbard, R., 186, 196
Huber, T., 100, 119
Hudleson, S., 69, 74
Hulme, C., 30, 33, 36
Huttenlocher, J., 33, 36
Hysmith, C., 225, 248

I

Igoa, C., 58, 74
Inge, K.J., 77, 96
Inhelder, B., 155, 161
Iser, W., 165, 167, 174, 178

J

James, S., 122, 142
Janisch, C., 58, 74
Jensen, J.M., 107, 119
Johnson, D.W., 154, 160
Johnson, N., 148, 160
Johnson, R.T., 154, 160
Johnston, P., 242, 248
Jordan, C., 13, 19
Jorgensen, C.M., 78, 96
Juel, C., 50, 55

K

Kagan, D., 254, 270
Kagan, J., 183, 195
Kalman, S.L., 77, 96
Kamii, C., 223, 248
Karpova, S., 41, 55
Katims, D., 77, 96
Katz, L., 16, 19
Kearsley, R., 183, 195
Kennedy, M., 253, 270
Kiefer, B., 177, 178
King, J.E., 104, 119
King, P., 254, 270
Kitchener, K., 254, 270
Kline, F.M., 100, 119
Knapp, M.S., 104, 120
Kolinsky, R., 33, 36
Koppenhaver, D.A., 77, 96, 97
Krashen, S., 62, 75
Kruse, S., 262, 270
Kuhn, M., 187, 196

L

Labbo, L.D., 181, 183, 185, 186, 187, 188, 192, 196, 197
Ladson-Billings, G., 101, 120
Lamme, L.L., 225, 248
Lanford, C., 170, 178
Lass, B., 199, 221
Leavell, A.G., 85, 96
Lee, M.S., 99, 119
Leichter, H.J., 105, 120
Lemke, J., 187, 196
Leu, D.D., 181, 196
Leu, D.J., 181, 196
Lieberman, A., 265, 270
Lightfoot, S.L., 120
Lindfors, J., 66, 75
Lindsay, G., 136, 143
Little, J.W., 251, 262, 270
Livingston, C., 254, 269
Locke, J.L., 138, 142
Lomax, R., 172, 178
Louis, K., 262
Lundberg, L., 30, 36
Lundenberg, M.A., 99, 119
Lyons, T., 33, 36
Lyunch, M.P., 33, 36

M

Maclean, M., 123, 142
Maehr, M.L., 144, 160
Maldonado-Guzman, A.A., 119
Mandler, J., 148, 160
Many, J., 175, 177, 179
Market Data Retrieval, 181, 196
Marks, H., 262, 270
Martinez, M., 170, 178, 221
Mason, J.M., 102, 119, 138, 142

McClelland, A., 99, 119
McCloskey, M., 57, 74
McCombs, B.L., 146, 160
McCormick, C.E., 138, 142
McGee, L., 44, 50, 55, 164, 172, 175, 178, 179, 199, 215, 216, 221
McGill-Franzen, A., 170, 178, 225, 248
McKenna, M., 181, 188, 196, 197
McLane, J.B., 7, 12, 19
McLaughlin, B., 57, 58, 74
McLaughlin, M., 256, 265, 270
McNamee, G., 7, 12, 19
McNaughton, S., 136, 141
Meek, M., 123, 142
Mehan, H., 58, 75
Meisels, S., 223, 248
Metzger, D., 115, 120
Michaels, S., 185, 195
Miller, E., 257, 270
Miller, L., 182, 196, 273, 274
Miramontes, O., 57, 62, 63, 65, 68, 75
Mohatt, G., 102, 119
Moll, L.C., 119
Montes, J., 58, 74
Montessori, M., 148, 149, 160
Moore, G., 148, 160
Moore, M., 138, 143
Morais, J., 33, 36
Morris, D., 42, 55
Morrissey, M., 234, 243, 248
Morrow, L.M., 1, 4, 6, 15, 19, 87, 96, 145, 147, 148, 150f, 151, 152f, 160, 161, 188, 192, 196, 200, 211, 216, 221, 236, 249
Morsund, D., 181, 196

N

Nadeau, A., 57, 62, 75
Nance, J., 97
Nation, K., 30, 33, 36
National Association for the Education of Young Children (NAEYC), 223, 249
National Association of Early Childhood Specialists in State Departments of Education (NAECS/SDE), 223, 249
National Commission on Teaching and America's Future, 256, 270
Nessel, D., 68, 74
Neuman, S.B., 8, 10, 15, 16, 19, 39, 51, 55, 57, 75, 136, 138, 142, 147, 148, 161, 183, 190, 192, 196, 197, 211, 212, 221, 228, 249
Newkirk, T., 213, 221
Nieto, S., 99, 120
Ninio, A., 164, 178, 185, 197
Nutbrown, C., 122, 132, 138, 142

O

Oldfather, P., 146, 161
Oller, D.K., 33, 36
Olson, J., 182, 196
Omalza, S., 227, 249
Ovando, C., 63, 75

P

Pasta, D., 58, 75
Pearson, P.D., 211, 222
Pennell, J.R., 263, 270

Perez, B., 66, 72, 75
Peterson, R., 177, 178
Peyton, J., 69, 75
Piaget, J., 155, 161, 182, 197
Pierce, C., 183, 197
Pinker, S., 40, 55
Plewis, I., 9, 19, 122, 123, 141, 143
Polakow, V., 13, 19
Poremba, K., 44, 55
Potter, G., 106, 120
Purcell-Gates, V., 44, 50, 51, 55, 162, 178, 185, 197, 199, 221

Q

Quinn, P.C., 28, 36

R

Ramey, D., 58, 75
Ramirez, J., 58, 75
Rand, M., 148, 161, 188, 196
Read, C., 33, 36, 49, 55, 183, 197
Reed, L., 69, 75
Reinking, D., 181, 185, 188, 196, 197
Remillard, J., 255, 270
Rendon, P., 119
Reyes, M. de la Luz, 69, 75
Richgels, D., 44, 49, 52, 55, 178, 199, 215, 216, 221, 222
Riel, M., 185, 197
Riffaterre, M., 174, 178
Rigg, P., 68, 75
Risley, T.R., 32, 36
Rivera, A., 119
Roberts, B., 41, 55
Roller, C.M., 97

Rosegrant, T., 224, 235, 247
Rosenblatt, L., 165, 175, 178
Roskos, K., 8, 10, 15, 19, 39, 51, 55, 57, 75, 147, 148, 161, 183, 190, 192, 196, 197, 211, 212, 221, 228, 249, 254, 257, 270
Rosner, J., 33, 36
Rossi, R., 57, 75
Rowe, D.W., 185, 197
Rusk, R., 148, 161
Rutherford, K., 252, 270
Ryback, D., 128, 142

S

Safford, P., 99, 119
Salinger, T.S., 229, 230, 233, 239, 240, 241, 242, 249
Saracho, O., 74
Schickedanz, D., 32, 37
Schickedanz, J., 32, 33, 37, 149, 161, 216, 222
Schon, D., 268, 271
Schumm, J.S., 85, 96
Scotland, J., 148, 161
Segel, E., 138, 142
Seltzer, M., 33, 36
Seymour, P.H.K., 33, 37
Shaver, D., 117, 120
Shuy, R., 69, 75
Silvernail, D.L., 273, 274
Sipe, L., 171, 174, 178
Siu-Runyan, Y., 229, 249
Skinner, E., 161
Sloane, J., 138, 143
Smith, F., 198, 222
Smith, M., 170, 177
Smolkin, L., 164, 179

Snow, C., 72, 73, 123, 142, 166, 170, 178
Sparks, D., 262, 271
Spodek, B., 74
Staats, W., 128, 142
Stallman, A., 211, 222
Stanovich, K., 30, 36, 44, 50, 55
Staton, J., 69, 75
Steffens, M.L., 33, 36
Stephens, D., 227, 249
Stokes, S.J., 106, 119
Strauss, M.S., 26, 36
Strickland, D.S., 1, 4, 6, 15, 19
Stringfield, S., 57, 75
Sulzby, E., 1, 4, 6, 7, 19, 123, 142, 182, 183, 185, 197
Sunstein, B., 241, 248
Suskin, S., 242, 249
Swinson, J., 138, 142
Sykes, G., 251, 271

T

Tabors, P., 162, 177, 199, 221
Talbert, J., 256, 270
Taylor, D., 75, 120, 122, 132, 142, 162, 179, 199, 222
Teale, W.H., 1, 4, 6, 7, 19, 123, 142, 170, 178, 182, 185, 197, 221
Teberosky, A., 41, 42, 55, 199, 221
Tenery, M.F., 119
Tharp, R., 258, 271
Thomas, A., 244, 247
Tierney, R.J., 241, 249
Tizard, B., 9, 19, 122, 123, 141, 143
Toomey, D., 138, 143
Topping, K., 136, 143
Torres-Guzman, M., 66, 72, 75

Tough, J., 62, 75
Treiman, R., 50, 55
Turnbill, J., 247, 248
Turner, J.C., 146, 161
Turner, S.V., 185, 197

U

Urbano, R., 33, 36
U.S. Congress Office of Technology Assessment, 181, 197

V

Valencia, S.W., 244, 249
Vaughn, S., 85, 96
Vukelich, C., 212, 222
Vygotsky, L.S., 107, 120, 185, 197, 200, 222

W

Wade, B., 136, 138, 143
Wagner, M., 117, 120
Watkins, J., 185, 186, 196, 197
Watson, D., 236, 248
Watson-Gregeo, K., 185, 195

Weinberger, J., 122, 123, 132, 142, 143
Wells, D., 172, 178
Wells, G., 122, 123, 143, 162, 179, 266, 271
White, D., 179
Whitehurst, G.J., 30, 32, 37, 136, 141
Whitmore, K.F., 225, 226, 243, 245, 249
Wiseman, D., 175, 177, 179
Wittrock, M.C., 144, 161
Wong-Fillmore, L., 59, 75, 76
Woolverton, S., 104, 120

Y

Yaden, D., Jr., 164, 179
Yoder, D.E., 77, 96, 97
Young Children, 223
Younger, B.A., 25, 25f, 28, 36
Yuen, S., 58, 75

Z

Zelazo, P., 183, 195

Children's Literature Authors

Subject Index

Note: An *f* following an index entry indicates that the citation may be found in a figure, an *n* that it may be found in a footnote.

A

B

BALANCE ISSUES, 199–200

BEARS (TOPIC): language experience with, 68, 69f

BEN (STUDENT): list of errands, 203–207, 206f

BEST PRACTICES, 14–18; guidelines for, 7–14

BIG BOOK OF BOOKMARKS, 157

BLOCK CENTER: materials and activities for, 153

BOOK CLUBS: for parents, 103

BOOK PAGES: turning, 89

BOOKMARKS: Big Book of Bookmarks, 157

BOOK-READING INTERACTIONS: examples, 163–164, 168–169; modifying, 165–166; monitoring, 166–167

BOOKS: ABC, 276; activity, 275–276; concept, 277–280; homemade, 47f; informational, 280–281; interactive storybooks, 184f; parent favorites, 103; predictable, 281–284; storybooks, 284–286; for young writers and readers, 275–286

BUILDING WALLS, 173

C

CAREER PHASES, 252–253

CARTOGRAPHERS, 217

CASE EXAMPLE, 108–115

CELEBRATIONS, 245; options, 245

CHARACTERS: understanding, 163–165

CHILDREN: English as a Second Language students, 58; interactions with literature, 170–176; interactions with parents, 139f; symbolic expressions, 186–187; Web sites for, 299–300. *See also* Students; Young children

CHILDREN WITH DISABILITIES: inclusive early literacy instruction for, 77–97

CHILDREN'S BOOKS: parent favorites, 103. *See also* Books

CHRISTINE (STUDENT): journal entry, 207, 208f

CLASSROOM: arranging, 148–151; environment for assessment, 227–229; floor plan, 150f

CLASSROOM LITERACY, 126–128

CLASSROOM LITERACY LEARNING, 126; characteristics of, 127f

COGNITION, 253–255

COLLABORATION: rules for, 154

COLLABORATIVE ACTIVITIES: organizing for, 154–155; what happens during, 155
COLLECTIONS, 157
COMMUNITY OF LEARNERS, 259
COMPETENCY BUILDING, 252
COMPUTER IMAGINATION STATION, 188–190
COMPUTER-RELATED EMERGENT LITERACY CONCEPTS: development of, 187
COMPUTER-RELATED INSTRUCTION, 182–187
COMPUTER-RELATED INTEGRATED LANGUAGE ARTS EXPERIENCES, 185–186
COMPUTER-RELATED LEARNING ENVIRONMENTS, 188–194
COMPUTER-RELATED SOCIAL INTERACTIONS, 185
COMPUTER-RELATED TECHNOLOGY: in early literacy, 180–197
COMPUTERS: forms of symbolic expression generated on, 186–187; independent explorations on, 182–183; in-school experience report written on, 48f; work-surface space, 189
CONCEPT BOOKS, 277–280
CONFERENCES, 232–235; recording forms for, 230, 231f
CONTENT AREAS: integrating literacy materials into, 152–153
CONTINUITY ISSUES, 199–200
CONVENTIONAL (TERM), 2
CONVERSATIONS, GRAND, 172–176
CO:WRITER (SOFTWARE), 90
CULTURALLY RESPONSIVE INSTRUCTION, 98–120; case example, 108–115; past practices, 105–107; study description and rationale, 107–108
CULTURALLY RESPONSIVE TEACHERS, 100–105
CULTURE, 99

D

DAILY STORYTIME, 68
DANIEL (STUDENT): writing of letters, 201, 202f
DEVELOPING PROFESSIONALS: teachers as, 251–256
DEVELOPMENT: early literacy, 121–143; professional, 250–271
DEVELOPMENTALLY APPROPRIATE PRACTICE, 20–37; considerations for, 23; description of, 22–23
DIALOGUE JOURNALS, 69
DICTATION: early-in-the-year, 68, 69f
DIFFERENCE: tolerance for, 93–94

DISABILITIES: inclusive early literacy instruction for children with, 77–97
DIVERSITY: inherent, 7–8
DON JOHNSTON DEVELOPMENTAL EQUIPMENT, 97
DRAMATIC PLAY: thematically enriched, 158–159
DRAMATIC-PLAY AREAS: literacy props for, 11; literacy-enriched, 11; materials and activities for, 153

E

EARLY ACHIEVEMENT: parents' recognition of, 139f
EARLY LITERACY: assessment of, 13–14; best practices in, 14–18; computer-related technology in, 180–197; definition, 2; developmentally appropriate practice in, 20–37; essential skills, 38–55; fostering through parent involvement, 121–143; guidelines for best practices in, 7–14; inclusive instruction, 77–97; teaching, 12. *See also* Literacy
EARLY WRITING: ORIM strand, 129
EARLY-CHILDHOOD EDUCATION: constructs from, 224–226
ECHO READING: screen and book, 189
EDUCATION: early childhood, 224–226; professional, 255–256
ELECTRONIC SYMBOL MAKING, 187
ELKONIN PROCEDURE: adaptation to, 53
EMERGENT LITERACY, 121, 182–187; computer-related concepts, 187; definition, 2
EMOTIONAL CLIMATE, 106
ENGLISH: instruction for students whose first language is not, 63–72; learning about student's facility for, 60
ENGLISH AS A SECOND LANGUAGE (ESL): instruction that supports, 66–72; students, 58; teaching literacy to children who are learning, 56–76
ENVIRONMENTAL PRINT, 149
ENVIRONMENTS: for assessment, 227–229; computer-related, 188–194; family, 106; learning, 188–194; physical, 106, 147–148; print-rich, 15; social contexts, 153–155; social learning settings, 156–159
ERRANDS: Ben's list of, 203–207, 206f
ESL. *See* English as a Second Language
EVALUATION: self-evaluation reflection charts, 240–241, 241f. *See also* Assessment
EXCLUSION: of parents, 124, 125f, 132–134

EXPLICIT SEGMENTATION ABILITY, 33–35

EXPLORATIONS: direct, 215–216; of form, 215–216; independent, 182–183; integrated with language experiences, 15–16; of student's language ability, 59–60

EXPRESSIVE SOFTWARE, 183; examples, 184*f*

F

FAMILY ENVIRONMENTS: categories, 106

FAMILY LITERACY: definition, 132

FIRST GRADERS: case example, 108–115; science journal entry, 213–215, 214*f*

FIRST LANGUAGE: learning about, 59; strategies that support, 65–66

FIRST STEPS™ PROJECT, 135

FLOOR PLANS: early childhood classroom, 150*f*

FORMS: meaning-form links, 199; of writing, 199; writing from direct exploration of, 215–216

FUNCTION OF WRITING, 199

G

GAMES: related to literacy skills, 184*f*; for young writers and readers, 294–297

GRAHAM, KAYLE (STUDENT), 109–110; defining, 111–112; relationship with mother, 111; school experiences, 113–115; teacher concerns, 108–109

GRAHAM, SHARON (PARENT), 109–110; knowledge of Kayle's school experiences, 113–115; recollections of school, 112–113; relationship with son, 111

GRAND CONVERSATIONS, 172–176; examples, 174–176

GROCERY LIST: kindergartner's, 228, 228*f*

H

HELPFUL HINTS DISPLAYS, 190

HOME LITERACY: versus classroom literacy, 126–128; linking with school literacy, 134

HOME LITERACY LEARNING, 126; characteristics of, 127*f*

HOME-FOCUSED PROGRAMS: preschool, 137–138; for school-age children, 136–137

HOMEMADE BOOKS, 47*f*

HOMEPAGES, 300

I–J

IMAGINATION STATION, 188–190

IMPLIED READERS, 167–169

INCLUSION: balancing with instruction, 86–93

INCLUSION-BASED LITERACY PROGRAMS, 10–12

INCLUSIVE LITERACY INSTRUCTION, 77–97; importance of, 95–96

INFANTS: ability to form perceptually based categories, 28–29; visual discrimination ability, 25–26

INFORMATIONAL BOOKS, 280–281

IN-SCHOOL EXPERIENCE REPORT, 48*f*

INSTRUCTION: balancing with inclusion, 86–93; children's writing and, 209–216; computer-related, 182–187; culturally responsive, 98–120; first language, 65–66; implications of Molly's reading and writing, 49–54; inclusive, 77–97; literacy, 95–96, 98–120; for students whose first language is not English, 63–72; that supports both languages, 63–66; that supports learning English, 66–72; thematic, 72. *See also* Teaching

INSTRUCTIONAL TUNING CLINICS, 261

INTEGRATED LANGUAGE ARTS EXPERIENCES: computer-related, 185–186

INTELLITOOLS, 97

INTERACTIONS: computer-related, 185; examples, 163–164, 168–169; interpersonal, 106; with literature, 170–176; modifying, 165–166; monitoring, 166–167; ORIM concept, 129; social, 8, 185

INTERACTIVE SHARING, 170–172

INTERACTIVE STORYBOOKS, 184*f*

INTERPERSONAL INTERACTIONS, 106

INTERVIEWS, 232–235; questions for developing protocols for, 233

JENNIFER (STUDENT): story, 209, 210*f*

JOURNALS, 67; Christine's journal entry, 207, 208*f*; dialogue, 69; first grader's science journal entry, 213–215, 214*f*; responses to *The Great Kapok Tree*, 70*f*–71*f*; Samuel's entry, 60, 61*f*

K

KIDWATCHING, 226

KINDERGARTNERS: grocery list, 228, 228*f*

KNOWLEDGE: literacy, 8–9; about print, 199; of speech and print match, 44; of spoken language, 40–42; of written language, 42–44

L

LANGUAGE: first, 59, 65–66; instruction that supports, 63–66; literary, 163–165; new, 60–63; oral, 129; spoken, 40–42; universalistic style, 104; written, 42–44, 139*f*; young children's sensitivity to, 29–35

LANGUAGE ABILITY: student's, 59–60

LANGUAGE EXPERIENCES: computer-related integrated, 185–186; integrated with explorations, 15–16; as strategy, 68–72; with topic of Bears, 68, 69*f*

LEARNERS: community of, 259; teachers as, 256–262

LEARNING: computer-related environments for, 188–194; elements that motivate, 146–147; English, 66–72; English as a Second Language, 56–76; to hear sounds in words, 53; literacy, 126, 182–183, 185–186; motivational contexts for, 146–147; new language, 60–63; resources for, 275–300; social, 156–159; about student's English facility, 60; about student's first language, 59

LEARNING HOW TO MEAN, 163–165

LETTERS: conventional, 202–203, 204*f*–205*f*; Daniel's writing of, 201, 202*f*; mock, 202–203, 204*f*–205*f*

LINEAR WRITING: Alonzo's, 202–203, 204*f*–205*f*

LITERACY: computer-related, 187; computer-related environments that support, 188–194; emergent, 121, 182–187; family, 132; home versus classroom, 126–128; linking home and school, 134; social interaction to foster, 8; writing from routines that include, 215. *See also* Early literacy

LITERACY CENTER, 149–151, 152*f*; materials and activities for, 153

LITERACY CLUB, 198

LITERACY INSTRUCTION: for children who are learning English as a second language, 56–76; culturally responsive, 98–120; inclusive, 95–96

LITERACY KNOWLEDGE: development of, 8–9

LITERACY LEARNING: assessing, 223–249; classroom, 126; through computer-related integrated language arts experiences, 185–186;

through computer-related social interactions, 185; home, 126; home versus school, 127*f*; through independent explorations on computer, 182–183

LITERACY MATERIALS: integrating into content areas, 152–153

LITERACY PROGRAMS: home-focused, 136–137; inclusion-based, 10–12

LITERACY PROPS: criteria for selecting, 11

LITERACY ROUTINES, 66

LITERACY SKILLS: development of, 8–9; games related to, 184*f*

LITERACY–ENRICHED DRAMATIC-PLAY AREA: designing, 11; general tips for, 11

LITERATURE: children's interactions with, 170–176; teaching to young children, 162–179; understanding, 163–165

LITERATURE CIRCLES, 158

M

MAGAZINES, 286–288

MAPS, 217

MARC (STUDENT): balancing instruction and inclusion, 86–90; beginning of school, 79–81; end of year, 93–94

MATERIALS: accessible, 147–148; for content areas, 152–153; integrating into content areas, 152–153; literacy, 152–153

MATH CENTER: materials and activities for, 153

MEANING: learning, 163–165; of writing, 199

MEANING–FORM LINKS, 199

MEANING–MAKING DEVELOPMENT, 165–169

MEDIATORS: story readers as, 165–169

MODEL, 129

MOLLY (STUDENT): alphabetic principle, 47–49; concept of word, 46; concepts about print, 46; homemade book page, 47*f*; in-school experience report written on computer, 48*f*; instructional implications, 49–54; phonemic awareness, 49; self-evaluation, 38, 39*f*; what we learn from, 45–49

MONITORING INTERACTIONS, 166–167

MOTIVATION, 144–161; arranging classroom for, 148–151; contexts for learning, 146–147; for learning, 146–147; physical contexts for, 147–148; social contexts for, 153–155; social interaction to foster, 8

MOTIVATIONAL CLIMATE, 106

MOUSE PADS, 190
MUSIC CENTER: materials and activities for, 153

N

THE NATIONAL CENTER TO IMPROVE PRACTICE, 97
NATIONAL WRITING PROJECT, 263–264
NEEDS, 10–12
NEW LANGUAGE LEARNING: requirements of, 60–63
NEWS TEAM, 191

O

OBSERVATIONS, 229–232; conclusions drawn from, 230–232; recording forms for, 230, 231f
OPPORTUNITIES: helping parents provide more, 139f; ORIM concept, 129
ORAL LANGUAGE, 129; knowledge of, 40–42
ORGANIZATION, 154–155
ORIENTATION, 26
ORIM MODEL, 128–132; applying to writing strand, 139f; concepts, 129–130; parent involvement possibilities map, 130, 131f; strands, 130

P

PAGE PUFFERS, 89
PARENT BOOK CLUBS, 103; favorite stories, 103
PARENT EXCLUSION, 124; unintended, 125f; unnecessary, 132–134
PARENT INVOLVEMENT, 12; fostering early literacy development through, 121–143; key questions, 137f; limited, 124; possibilities map, 130, 131f; from theory to practice, 132–138; what we know about, 140; what we should do, 140–141
PARENT STORIES: addressing, 115–118; improving classroom practice through, 117–118; issues surrounding them, 115–118; what teachers should do with, 116
PARENTS: definition, 122n; focus and location of work with, 126, 128f; model of using written language, 139f; participatory role for, 106; providing more opportunities, 139f; recognition of early achieve-

ment, 139*f*; supporting and extending interactions with children, 139*f*; teaching role, 128–132; working with, 137*f*

RECOGNITION, 129

RECORDS: forms for observations and conferences, 230, 231*f;* running, 235–236, 237*f;* teacher, 238–239

REFLECTION, 240–241, 241*f*

REPORTING, 242–246; in-school experience reports, 48*f*

RESOURCES: learning, 275–300; for young writers and readers, 275–300

RESPONSES: best practices, 16–17; writing samples, 239, 240*f*

ROUTINES: writing from, 215

RUNNING RECORDS, 235–236, 237*f;* simplified method, 235–236

S

SAMMY (STUDENT): response to *The Great Kapok Tree*, 71*f*

SAMUEL (STUDENT): journal entry, 60, 61*f*

SCHOOL: beginning of, 79–84; Kayle's experiences, 113–115; responsibility, 12–13; Sharon's recollections of, 112–113

SCHOOL LIFE: teacher concerns about, 108–109

SCHOOL LITERACY: linking with home literacy, 134

SCHOOL YEAR: beginning, 85–86; end of, 93–95

SCHOOL-AGE CHILDREN: home-focused programs for, 136–137

SCIENCE CENTER: materials and activities for, 153

SCIENCE JOURNALS: first grader's entry, 213–215, 214*f*

SCREEN AND BOOK ECHO READING, 189

SCREEN AND BOOK READ ALONG, 189

SEGMENTATION ABILITY, 33–35

SELF-EVALUATIONS, 38, 39*f;* reflection charts, 240–241, 241*f*

SETTINGS: social learning, 156–159. *See also* Environments

SHARING, 170–172

SKILLS: best practices, 17–18; development of, 8–9; essential, 38–55; literacy, 8–9, 184*f*

SLOAN (STUDENT): balancing instruction and inclusion, 90–92; beginning of school, 81–84; end of year, 94–95

SOCIAL COLLABORATION: rules for, 154

SOCIAL COLLABORATIVE ACTIVITIES: organizing for, 154–155; what happens during, 155

SOCIAL CONTEXTS: for motivating reading and writing, 153–155

SOCIAL INTERACTIONS, 8; computer-related, 185

SOCIAL LEARNING SETTINGS: illustrations, 156–159

SOCIAL STUDIES CENTER: materials and activities for, 153

SOCIODRAMATIC-PLAY CENTERS: incorporating technology into, 190–194

SOFTWARE: expressive, 183, 184*f*; receptive, 183, 184*f*; for young writers and readers, 288–294

SONG SUBSTITUTION (ACTIVITY), 31

SOUND-CATEGORIZATION ABILITIES, 32–33

SOUNDS: learning to hear, 53

SPEECH AND PRINT MATCH: knowledge of, 44

SPOKEN LANGUAGE, 129; knowledge of, 40–42

STABILITY, 253

STANDARDIZED ACTIVITIES, 235–242

STEVEN (STUDENT): response to *The Great Kapok Tree*, 70*f*

STORIES: Alonzo's, 202–203, 204*f*–205*f*; Jennifer's, 209, 210*f*; parent, 115–118; parent favorites, 103

STORY READERS: as mediators, 165–169

STORY RETELLINGS, 236–238, 237*f*; variations, 236–238

STORY WALLS: building, 173

STORYBOOKS, 284–286; interactive, 184*f*

STORYTIME, 68

STRATEGIES: to address specific concerns, 216–219; best practices, 17–18; language experience as, 68–72

STUDENTS: with disabilities, 85–86; English as a Second Language, 58; English facility, 60; first language, 59; whose first language is not English, 63–72; first-grade case example, 108–109; language ability, 59–60. *See also* Children; *specific students*

SURVIVAL, 252

SYMBOL MAKING, 187

SYMBOLIC EXPRESSIONS: computer-generated forms in, 186–187

SYMBOL-MAKING EXPERIENCES, 187

T–U

TALKING: providing time for, 66–68

TEACHABLE MOMENTS, 107

TEACHER NETWORKS, 263–265; features of, 265

TEACHER RECORDS, 238–239

TEACHER RESOURCES, 96–97

TEACHERS: career phases, 252–253; case example, 108–109; cognition, 253–255; concerns, 252; culturally responsive, 100–105; as developing professionals, 251–256; as learners, 256–262; past, 105–107; practicing, 250–271; professional development, 250–271; role in enriching children's interactions with literature, 170–176

TEACHING: alphabet, 27–28; diversity in, 7–8; early literacy, 12; literacy, 56–76; literature, 162–179; parent's role, 128–132. *See also* Instruction

TECHNOLOGY: computer-related, 180–197; incorporating into sociodramatic-play centers, 190–194

THEMATIC INSTRUCTION, 72

THEMATICALLY ENRICHED DRAMATIC PLAY, 158–159

TOLERANCE FOR DIFFERENCE, 93–94

TOYS, 294–297

TRIANGULATION, 247

TURNING PAGES, 89

USER–FRIENDLY MOUSE PADS, 190

V

VASQUEZ, MRS. (FIRST-GRADE TEACHER): concerns about Kayle's school life, 108–109

VIDEOS, 298–299

VISUAL DISCRIMINATION ABILITY, 25–26

VISUALLY ACCESSIBLE ENVIRONMENTAL PRINT, 149

VITAMIN PILL ACTIVITIES, 18

W

WALLS: building, 173

WEB SITES: jumping off points, 300; for young children, 299–300

WEST HEIDELBERG EARLY LITERACY PROJECT, 138

WORDS: concept of, 46; learning to hear sounds in, 53

WORK–SURFACE SPACE, 189

WRITE OUT:LOUD (SOFTWARE), 90

WRITING: active participation in, 10; Alonzo's story, 202–203, 204f–205f; applying ORIM to, 139f; for authentic purposes, 212–215; balance and continuity issues, 199–200; beginnings of, 198–199; Ben's list of errands, 203–207, 206f; buddy, 156–158; children's, 209–216; from direct exploration of form, 215–216; early, 129; forms of, 199; functions of, 199; Jennifer's story, 209, 210*f*; journal, 207, 208*f*; kindergartners grocery list, 228, 228*f*; learning resources for, 275–300; linear, 202–203, 204*f*–205*f*; meaning of, 199; motivating children toward, 144–161; National Writing Project, 263–264; opportunities for, 69; partner, 156; from play, 211–212; responsive samples, 239, 240*f*; from routines that include literacy, 215. *See also* Journals